# Keep Talking that Book!

## Booktalks to Promote Reading

## Volume II

## By Carol Littlejohn

A Publication of THE BOOK REPORT & LIBRARY TALK
Professional Growth Series

Linworth Publishing, Inc.
Worthington, Ohio

Library of Congress Cataloging-in-Publication Data

Littlejohn, Carol.
    Keep talking that book! / Carol Littlejohn.
        p. cm. — (Professional growth series)
    "Booktalks to promote reading, volume two."
    "This book is a companion to: Talk that book : booktalks to promote reading"—Introd.
    Includes indexes.
    ISBN 0-938865-92-7
        1. Book talks. 2. Best books.  I. Title. II. Series.

Z716.3 .L58 2000
028'.9—dc21

                                                                        00-023064

Published by Linworth Publishing, Inc.
480 East Wilson Bridge Road, Suite L
Worthington, Ohio 43085

Series Information:
        From The Professional Growth Series

ISBN 0-938865-92-7

5 4 3 2 1

# Table of Contents

# Table of Contents continued

# Table of Contents continued

# Table of Contents continued

# Table of Contents continued

# Table of Contents continued

# Table of Contents continued

# Introduction

This book is a companion to *Talk That Book: Booktalks to Promote Reading.* Like my first book, this book offers booktalks on classics and best sellers, for voracious readers and reluctant readers ages eight to 80.

A *booktalk* is a recommendation of a book, a snapshot of a book's appeal. A booktalk's main purpose is to introduce a reader, especially a reluctant one, to reading. Booktalks connect readers with a book of their choice. Through booktalks, readers gain freedom to select well-written, entertaining books at their reading level. By booktalking a wide variety of books, we encourage the activity of selecting a book, entering its world, and departing forever changed. For, as all voracious readers know, books take us on a mind-spinning flight to worlds outside our own.

If books take us on a journey of imagination, then booktalks are the travel guides. Like any guide, a booktalk must reflect the time, setting, and characters of the book.

> My main requirement is to select high-interest, quality books that can hook a student into developing a reading habit.

Just as important, a booktalk must indicate the reading level. These booktalks are written at the reading level of the book. If a reader can't understand the words of the booktalk, then the book is probably too advanced.

I've selected a wide range of books, from all ages and reading interests. I've tried to choose best sellers, award-winning books, and timeless classics. My main requirement is to select high-interest, quality books that can hook a student into developing a reading habit. Many have been recently published. Others are shelf-sitters, excellent books that are in most libraries, but remain on shelves, seldom enjoyed by readers. Many are favorites of voracious readers and experienced librarians, but unknown to the novice.

Most of these books are still in print. However, books go in and out of print with an illogical consistency. For those who want to search for out-of-print books, I recommend

the Web site <www.bookfinder.com> or <www.evenbetter.com>, sites that use various databases for locating unavailable books at competitive prices. Also, garage sales and used bookstores hold some literary treasures.

You can use this book in several ways. Usually, *booktalking* is an oral presentation of about 10 or 20 booktalks, lasting about 30 minutes. However, this book can also be your guide when you need a quick answer to the question "What can I read that's good?" Busy librarians can write the call numbers in this book so curious readers can locate the book in the library. You can also display books with the booktalks inside or on display. At times you might read booktalks over the intercom as a welcome message from the librarian.

I also advocate books on audiotapes as an effective way to stimulate reluctant readers, and these booktalks can be copied and placed inside the box. A booktalk could be a good introduction to a silent reading program. Some of the books make good group readings, such as a *Battle of the Books* selection. Just use these booktalks any way that gets the attention of the readers, including the reluctant readers, the readers who say they hate to read.

If the booktalk is to be photocopied, you might decide not to include the "Note." The note reveals additional information about the book or author that will help a booktalker, but not necessarily a reader. A reader must never be told the ending of the book. At times, a note may discuss a plot detail or controversy that will reveal the ending. For the most effective use, this booktalk should be photocopied without the note.

As in my last book, these booktalks are arranged by the author's last name, followed by reading level, genre, and subjects. To sup-

> ...This book can also be your guide when you need a quick answer to the question "What can I read that's good?"

plement *Talk that Book,* I selected more nonfiction, biography, and poetry books. "Related books" recommend other books similar to the book. Sometimes a book is not available after booktalking, and these suggested books can substitute as an appealing read. Also, use this section when a reader wants a book "exactly like the one I've read." Many reluctant readers need a push to read other books. Try to make that book similar to one they liked and they have a better chance of continuing to read.

As before, I've added information on book awards, if known. I've selected these books from a variety of booklists, including the *New York Times* best sellers, American Library Association, and various Web sites on reading. The American Library Association, through the Young Adult Library Science Association, has several committees that read and recommend books for young adults: Best Books for Young Adults, Top 10 Best Books for Young Adults, Alex Awards, and Quick Picks for Reluctant Young Adult Readers. The Newbery award is given annually by the American Library Association for the best children's book by an American author. The Coretta Scott King Award is awarded annually to an African-American author for an outstanding contribution to children's literature. *School Library Journal,* a useful publication for young adult and children's librarians, selects the best books annually. The ABBY Awards is an annual selection of adult and juvenile books by the American Booksellers Association. The Edgar Allan Poe Award is awarded annually by Mystery Writer's Association for the best children's and young adult mystery. The Bram Stoker Award for Horror is awarded by the Horror

Writers of America. The *Los Angeles Times* has recently established a Teen Book Award. The Christopher Award is awarded "to the producers, directors and writers of books, motion pictures and television specials which affirm the highest values of the human spirit." All of these organizations helped me select books for booktalks.

At times I found it difficult to categorize a book's reading level. Research demonstrates that individual readers differ in reading attitudes and interests. A middle school reader may be a mature reader who is not offended by complex issues or controversial topics. A reluctant reader may feel more comfortable reading elementary level books. All levels of reading should be contained in a library and in booktalking.

Still, for the most effective use, books are categorized by reading levels, according to their vocabulary and content. The elementary school titles have a G rating for all audiences, sometimes useful for a read-aloud; middle school, grades 6 and up, a PG rating, with some adult language and topics; high school, grades 9 and up, an R rating for mature audiences that may include profanity, graphic violence, and controversial issues. I recommend all these books to adults.

Unlike my previous book, this book does not separate the booktalks into separate chapters according to reading level. I would like you to give attention to all the books, hoping to inspire you to read for your own knowledge and pleasure.

I would love to hear from other booktalkers. Write or e-mail me with suggestions or ideas. We can share ideas on the best way to hook readers on books. Let's keep talking that book!

*Carol Littlejohn*
*carol_littlejohn@hotmail.com*

# About the Author

Carol Littlejohn is a library media specialist on a mission to promote reading. She has worked in public and school libraries, writing and performing booktalks to students, teachers, and parents. As a writer, she is the author of *Talk That Book! Booktalks to Promote Reading* and has contributed articles to *Library Talk, Book Report, JOYS, VOYA, the ALAN Review,* and other journals. She lives in Pittsburgh, Pennsylvania, and is a library media specialist at the Deer Lakes Middle School.

# Acknowledgments

Thanks to the Linworth staff, who are both professional and supportive: Carol Simpson, my excellent editor; Marlene Woo-Lun, the publisher; Wendy Medvetz, editorial assistant; Amy Robison, marketing assistant; Cindy Allen, former production manager; and all those anonymous reviewers who gave me helpful advice on improving the book.

Also, a big thanks to these friends and colleagues for their helpful suggestions and support: all the teachers and students at Deer Lakes Middle School, including the principal, William McClarnon; Cathy Thomas; Margie Bragg; Jeanette Gerlach; Nikki Fieser; Karen Swanson; Sarah Boggs Conaster; Connie Maxwell; the staff at Northland Library in McCandless, Pennsylvania, especially Mary Morgan Smith, Dot Phillis, and Linda Farmerie; and my mentor, Professor Magdaleen Bester.

My family always nourishes me with love and support, giving me those wings beneath my feet. Thanks, Drew, Karl, LJ, Dad!

# Why Booktalks Work

We booktalkers know that booktalks promote reading, but we may not be sure how or why. Usually librarians and teachers are too busy to keep up-to-date on reading research. But sometimes the information could be vital for a board meeting or a budget discussion. Or perhaps you just want to know the facts about booktalking. Why do booktalks work? What are the short-term and long-term effects? Do booktalks motivate reluctant readers?

Those questions also intrigued me. Recently I considered completing a doctoral dissertation on booktalking. Let me share my research with you so that you are prepared when someone asks you why booktalks work. If you want more information on the sources, go to the annotated bibliography at the end of this chapter.

## ▷ PURPOSE OF BOOKTALKS

Booktalking has no known inventor. It began spontaneously as a way to introduce books to a group of people in a library. In 1950, A. H. Munson's book *An Ample Field* described booktalking at the New York Public Library as a common practice, but credited no one with creating the technique. Later, other librarians, such as Margaret Edwards, Mary Kay Chelton, and Joni Richards Bodart wrote about booktalking.

In 1985, Bodart was the first to conduct exploratory research on the effectiveness of booktalking, concluding that booktalking affects behavior, such as increasing library circulation, but does not necessarily affect reading attitudes. Bodart has continued to promote booktalking and has written numerous books, periodicals, and videotapes on booktalking. Her workshops have inspired librarians and teachers to use booktalking to promote reading.

Two other major studies on booktalking confirmed Bodart's findings. Terence David Nollen's dissertation studied booktalking with fourth grade students. Like Bodart, he found that booktalking increased library circulation, but had no long-term effects on reading attitudes. He also discovered that booktalking affected students' choice of materials, but only for a short time. However, he believed booktalking could be an important teaching resource to develop reading interests.

In 1991, Gail Reeder wrote a dissertation on booktalking with seventh grade students. She obtained the same results as Bodart and Nollen, but also discovered males were not as positive toward reading as females. In her thesis, Pamela Dahl also supported Reeder's claim, saying 61 percent of females read one book a week compared to 21 percent of males. All these studies point to short-term changes in behavior, with the possibility of continual booktalking having long-term effects in reading attitudes.

Studying the long-term effects of booktalking is an overwhelming task. Booktalking encompasses reading attitudes, reading interests, reader response, reading development, and readership (a European-based study of reading that is separate from the American research). Its effects depend on readers' gender, temperament, and age. Unfortunately, these research fields are not integrated, but instead branch into many theories and studies, sometimes overlapping each other.

> All these studies point to short-term changes in behavior, with the possibility of continual booktalking having long-term effects in reading attitudes.

## ▷ BOOKTALKING CONCEPTS

Understanding these various terms and theories can be daunting but necessary to ensure that booktalking incorporates all of these concepts:

- **BOOKTALKS.** Short, formalized descriptions of books. They are not book reviews or reports, but brief sketches of books given with the intention of "hooking" a reader. There is one hard rule: Booktalkers must never reveal the ending because there would be no incentive to read the book.
- **READING ATTITUDE.** Encompasses reading interest and comprehension. Simply put, a reading attitude is a reader's *feeling* about reading—positive, negative or mixed.

- **READING INTEREST.** One of the main components in developing positive reading attitudes. Students need to be motivated to continue reading, and interest plays a significant role in this motivation. Also, according to a study by Van Jura, reading interest can be directly related to reading comprehension.
- **READING MOTIVATION.** Involves two ingredients: reward and effort. According to W. Schram, reading motivation can be treated as a fraction:

$$\text{motivation} \quad = \quad \frac{\text{expectation of reward to be gained}}{\text{expectation of effort to be expended}}$$

- **READER DEVELOPMENT.** Stages of reading progression, with reading maturity as the final achievement. Some scholars, such as Jeanne Chall, Gerald Maring, and Jack Thomson have identified stages of reading development. One basic requirement is an elementary understanding of reading. Thomson's model has six progressive stages of reader development from reluctant to mature reader.
- **RELUCTANT READER.** Does not read voluntarily. A reluctant reader is not always physically or mentally challenged; instead, the student may have no motivation to read. In many cases, a reluctant reader does not need reading instruction, rather motivation, opportunity, and time to read.
- **MATURE READER.** Achieves highest cognitive skills in reading. Thomson says, "A mature reader understands the textual relationship between the reader and author, bringing a sophisticated understanding of word play" (p. 23).

- **READER RESPONSE.** School of thought advocating that each reader plays an active role in determining meaning from the text. Daniels states, "Text is just ink on a page until a reader comes along and gives it life" (p. 13). Louise Rosenblatt compares reading to listening to a symphony. Each listener responds differently to a musical piece. Like music, reading brings an individual emotional response.

## ▶ WHY BOOKTALKS WORK

Based on the research, booktalking should be an effective way to promote reading.

- According to Louise Rosenblatt and other scholars, each student brings an individual response to a book. Booktalking allows readers to choose a book that fits their individualized reading level and reading interest. Those two factors can motivate more reading.

- Studies demonstrate that the more reading one does, the more skilled one becomes at reading. Booktalks can motivate even a reluctant reader to read a book. If the book is a perfect match with a reader, that reader will continue to read, increasing her reading skills.

- With reluctant readers, our aim should be to recommend a book that will appeal to their reading interests. According to educators Faber and McNeil, reading high-interest books, even comic books, can contribute to continued reading. To reach reluctant readers, booktalks should include comic books, paperbacks, high interest picture books, and, on occasion, harmless popular fiction.

- For all readers, reading development is a highly individual process. Educator

Jeanne Chall discovered that students develop reading skills faster by selecting their own books. By selecting their reading material, students can improve their reading skills at their own pace. Teachers and librarians can monitor a student's reading development by introducing high-interest books at the appropriate reading level. Booktalking plays an important role in this process.

- Booktalking can be effectively used to introduce books that are required reading. Students respond more positively to knowing something about a book before they begin reading it. Booktalking provides enough information to motivate a reader to continue the story, perhaps even provoking thoughtful discussions.

> Booktalking provides enough information to motivate a reader to continue the story, perhaps even provoking thoughtful discussions.

- According to scholars Ribovich and Erickson, life-long readers usually develop the reading habit before adulthood. Promoting reading should be a vital part of the elementary, middle, and high school curriculums, with booktalking playing a significant role. Booktalks can connect a meaningful book to a reader, possibly initiating a lifelong habit.

- As an additional benefit, librarians who give booktalks introduce themselves positively to students. They are building a continuing relationship with them. Students should also feel more comfortable about asking for advice or assistance.

- Those students who are reluctant to request a title from a librarian may also benefit from booktalks. Booktalks add an element of anonymity for the shy student.

- Booktalks endorse reading as a positive lifelong skill. Educator Charlotte Huck predicts that "if we teach a child to read, yet develop not the taste for reading, all of our teaching is for naught. We shall have produced a nation of 'illiterate literates'— those who know how to read, but do not read" (p. 53).

We bookworms agree: reading changes lives. Our next mission should be to engage the reluctant readers into our universe, this awe-inspiring, mind-bending world of reading.

## ▷ FUTURE RESEARCH

Until a longitudinal study is conducted over time, we won't know if booktalking permanently changes reading attitudes. In that study, booktalks need to be fully integrated into the curriculum. In the past, booktalks have been been scheduled only at inconsistent intervals for short periods of time.

Perhaps one of the long-term effects of consistently scheduled booktalks will be a positive reading attitude. That attitude might lead to a lifelong reading habit.

Reluctant readers should be analyzed in depth to determine how booktalks might motivate them. The reading addicts will continue to read with or without the booktalkers (although they certainly appreciate our validation), but reluctant readers need educated reading guidance.

Certainly reading attitude, especially the gender issue, needs to be explored in more depth.

These areas need more research so that booktalkers can effectively use booktalks. Until then, we will keep the faith and keep talking those books!

# ANNOTATED BIBLIOGRAPHY ON BOOKTALKING

Bodart, Joni. "Booktalks do Work! The Effects of Booktalking on Attitude and Circulation." *Illinois Libraries,* June 1986, 378-381. A synopsis of Bodart's dissertation.

Bodart, Joni. *The Effect of a Booktalk Presentation on Selected Titles on the Attitude Toward Reading of Senior High School Students and On the Circulation of These Titles in the High School Library.* Unpublished dissertation. Texas Women's University, 1985. Exploratory study that researches the effect of booktalking. Booktalking increases library circulation, but not necessarily reading attitudes.

Chall, Jeanne S., *Stages of Reading Development.* McGraw-Hill, 1983. Chall was one of the first educators to develop stages and levels of reading development.

Daniels, H., *Literature Circles: Voice and Choice in the Student-Centered Classroom.* Markham ON: Pembroke, 1994. Describes the importance of student choice in book selection.

Edmonds, Leslie, "Selling Reading: Library Service to Reluctant Adolescent Readers." *Illinois Libraries,* June 1986, pp. 374-377. Offers helpful tips on how to reach adolescent reluctant readers.

Edwards, Margaret A. and Campbell, Patty, *The Fair Garden and the Swarm of Beasts.* American Library Association, 1994. First published in 1974, this young adult work was one of the first to recommend booktalking to promote reading. Mary Chelton also recommends booktalking in her out-of-print book, *Booktalking: You Can Do It.*

Fader, Daniel N., Ph.D. and McNeil, Elton B., Ph.D., *Hooked on Books: Program and Proof.* Berkeley, 1968. Advocates using comic books and popular paperbacks in the classroom to promote reading.

Huck, Charlotte S., et al., *Children's Literature in the Elementary School.* 5th ed. Brown and Benchmark, 1993. An inspiring and helpful textbook on children's literature.

Jones, Patrick, "Booktalking Works!" *American Econo-Clad Services,* Spring 1994, 6-7. Most of the information about dissertation research comes from this well-written, concise article.

Kaebein, Paul; Bryan Luckham; and Valerie Stelmach, eds., *Studies on Research and Libraries: Approaches and Results from Several Countries.* K. G. Saur, 1991. Shram's study on reading motivation (and his mathematical equation) is contained in this book.

Krashen, Stephen, *The Power of Reading: Insights from the Research.* Libraries Unlimited, 1993. Highly readable text about research on reading. All libraries should own this gem.

Littlejohn, Carol, "Reading Levels of Development of Young Adults (Ages 11-17) at an American International School in South Africa." Unpublished paper, March 1996. Study of middle school and high school students' reading development and interests.

Lomax, Mary Elizabeth, *To Choose or Not to Choose: The Effect of Varied Influences on the Selection of Library Books by Junior High School Students.* Unpublished dissertation. University of Nebraska, 1993. Lomax discovers that more reading occurs when students choose their own books to read.

Loertscher, David V., "Objective: Achievement. Solution: School Libraries." *School Library Journal*, May 1993, 30-33. Vital article that links the school library media center to improvement of reading achievement test scores. The author recommends purchasing the complete 1993 study by Keith Curry Lance, Lynda Welborn, and Christine Hamilton-Pennell, *The Impact of School Library Media Centers on Academic Achievement,* Hi Willow Research and Publishing, P.O. Box 266, Castle Rock, CO 80104.

Maring, Gerald H., "Maturity in Reading for Seventh Graders." *Journal of Reading*, October 1980, 20-26. Helpful study on a selected group of readers: mature readers.

Olson, W., *Child Development.* Heath, 1949. Landmark study on reading as related to physical and psychological development.

Purves, Alan C., and Richard Beach, *Literature and the Reader: Research in Response to Literature, Reading Interest, and the Teaching of Literature.* University of Illinois at Urbana-Champaign, 1972. Research by leading scholars on reader response.

Reeder, Gail M., *Effect of Booktalks on Adolescent Reading Attitudes.* Unpublished dissertation. University of Nebraska, 1991. Reeder confirms Bodart's findings, that short-term effects of booktalking develop positive reading attitudes. However, it is not known if booktalking has a long-term effect.

Rosenblatt, Louise M., *Literature as Exploration.* 4th ed. The Modern Language Association, 1983. This book was originally published in 1933 and its effect is still being felt. Educator Rosenblatt, and others, inspired the school of theory of reader response.

Sanders, Barry, *A is for Ox: The Collapse of Literacy and the Rise of Violence in an Electronic Age.* Vantage, 1995. Sanders argues literacy is on the decline, due to society's fixation on electronics—TV, computer games, videos, software. Advocates book discussion groups, read-alouds, journals, but, alas, overlooks booktalking.

Thomson, Jack, *Understanding Teenagers' Reading: Reading Processes and the Teaching of Literature.* Nichols, 1987. High school teacher studies his adolescent literature classes as they climb the ladder of reading development. I used his reading model of development for my study on the American school.

U.S. Department of Education, Office of Educational Research and Improvement. National Center for Education Statistics, *NAEP 1998 Reading Report Card for the Nation*, NCES 1999-459, Washington DC, 1999. Recent report makes important points about students who read and achieve academically. With regard to booktalking, students who talked about books had higher average reading scores.

Van Jura, Sarah A., "Secondary Students at Risk: Two Giant Steps toward Independence in Reading." *Journal of Reading,* April 1980, 609-614. Study on the adolescent reluctant reader, especially in terms of reading interests.

Veatch, J, ed., *Individualizing Your Reading Program: Self-Selection in Action.* Putnam, 1959. Veatch was the first to study basal readers and self-selected books. She advocated the importance of individualizing a reading program by having students read at their own levels and interests.

# Booktalks for
# Ages 8 to 80

## Abelove, Joan. *Go and Come Back.*

DK, 1998, 177pp. Middle School & Up. An ALA Best Book for Young Adults; School Library Journal's Best Books selection; nominee for the L.A. Times Teen Book Award.

■ **REALISTIC FICTION.** *Caribbean and Latin America (Peru); ethics; sex and sexuality; trust; women's issues.*

■ **RELATED BOOKS:** *A Girl Named Disaster* by Nancy Farmer; *Shadow Spinner* by Susan Fletcher; *The Cow of No Color: Riddle Stories and Justice Tales from World Traditions* by Nina Jaffe and Steve Zeitlin.

*Based on the author's real experiences as a cultural anthropologist, the story is told by the main character, Alicia, a Peruvian teen. The anthropologists, Joanna and Margarita, learn humility and later meet some American missionaries, ironically finding them selfish. Recommended for young adult reluctant readers because of its brief length and humorous discussions of sexual customs between the cultures.*

Two old white ladies came to our village. Nonti, my mother's brother's wife's brother, said they were called anthropologists. They looked like plain old *gringos* to me. They wore no beads, no nose rings, no lip plugs, no anklets. They did nothing to make themselves beautiful.

These women are stingy. They have so much, but they do not share easily and are mad if we ask for things. They shared only half a bottle of sugarcane liquor so we only had half a party. They gave us only six batteries for music when they have a big metal box full of batteries. What is the matter with them?

They have so much to learn from us.

## Ackerman, Ned. *Spirit Horse.*

Scholastic, 1998, 168pp. Elementary School & Up.

■ **ADVENTURE.** *Animals (horses); Native Americans (Siksika & Kainaa); men's issues; peer pressure; rites of passage; rivalry; revenge; self-identity.*

■ **RELATED BOOKS:** *Call it Courage* by Armstrong Sperry; *Canyons* by Gary Paulsen; *Light in the Forest* by Conrad Richter.

*In the author's note, Ackerman gives historical background on the Blackfoot People who were comprised of three major groups: the Siksika, the Kainaa, and the Peigans. Although this is historical fiction, this is a compelling adventure of a boy's search for self-identity. Recommended as a book report choice or group read.*

Running Crane had fallen off his horse again.

"Falls Off, that should be his name." Weasel Rider laughed with the other young riders.

Running Crane gazed wistfully at the departing riders. He hated riding this nag because he knew it made him look foolish. He and his mother had just arrived in the Kainaa camp with her new husband, who was Running Crane's uncle. The tribe was slow to accept Running Crane, perhaps because he was a horse-poor Siksika.

I would like to capture the Spirit Horse, thought Running Crane. This stallion of the Snake People would bring much admiration from the tribe. Spirit Horse is huge, fast, and pale blue like the moon-of-deep-snows.

If I do ride Spirit Horse, I might fall, thought Running Crane, but I shall get back on and ride!

## Adler, C. S. *Her Blue Straw Hat.*

Harcourt Brace, 1997, 105pp. Elementary School & Up.

■ **REALISTIC FICTION.** Divorce; immigrants (Puerto Rico); pregnancy; rivalry; stepparents.

■ **RELATED BOOKS:** *The Animal, The Vegetable and J. D. Jones* by Betsy Byars; *Walk Two Moons* by Sharon Creech

*Note:* Tina also arrives with a Puerto Rican teen, Carlos, who is Tina's mother's boyfriend. He provides another set of problems. An excellent book for younger readers about the problems of blending stepfamilies.

Rachel first realized she loved her stepfather when he gave her the blue straw hat. Before then, she had been wary of anyone taking over her mother's life. Her stepfather, Ben, insisted on buying Rachel the blue straw hat because "it matches your eyes."

Now the three were off for their annual summer to the Cape. Things were different this year. Ben's daughter Tina joined them and shared Rachel's bedroom. Tina was spoiled, bossy, and demanding. She also hid Rachel's blue straw hat, refusing to return it.

Then Rachel's mother announced she was pregnant. Rachel hadn't recovered from spending the summer with her stepsister. Now she had a half-brother or sister on the way.

Rachel never dreamed her life would end up like a bad TV sitcom. Her life was turning into the Brady Bunch and she wanted to change channels!

## Aiken, Joan. *Arabel's Raven.*

Illustrated by Quentin Blake. Doubleday, 1974, 118pp. Elementary School & Up. Part of a series; **Arabel and Mortimer** follows.

■ **HUMOR.** Animals (birds); crime; family; Great Britain.

■ **RELATED BOOKS:** *Mr. Popper's Penguins* by Richard and Florence Ackerman; *The Twits, BFG* and *The Witches* by Roald Dahl.

*Note:* A great read-aloud. Read the first chapter and notice the positive results. Don't forget to show Quentin Blake's humorous drawings. All of Joan Aiken's books are recommended as entertaining reads, and would benefit elementary classroom libraries.

"Good heavens, what is that?" Mrs. Jones shrieked.

What was a bird doing in her refrigerator? Mrs. Jones didn't know Mr. Jones had brought the raven home, fed him, and accidentally locked it inside. By that time, the bird had already eaten a pound of sausages, five pints of milk, and half a pound of New Zealand cheddar cheese.

"His name is Mortimer," Arabel said, putting her arms around her new pet.

Mortimer was one strange bird. He liked to answer the phone by saying "Nevermore." His favorite pastime was eating the stairs and roller skating in parking lots. He liked Arabel to dry his feathers with a hair dryer. And he was always up to something exciting, like the time he was kidnapped and left a trail of cheese crumbs.

Have lots of laughs with *Arabel's Raven.*

## Albom, Mitch. *Tuesdays with Morrie: An Old Man, a Young Man, and Life's Great Lesson.*

Doubleday, 1997, 192pp. High School & Up.

■ **NONFICTION.** Aging; death; ethics; friendship; illness (physical); men's issues; religion; rites of passage; work.

■ **RELATED BOOKS:** *Letting Go: Morrie's Reflections While Dying* by Morrie Schwartz; *Conversations with God* series by Neal Donald Walsch.

 *The audiotape, read by the author on BrillianceAudio, is also highly recommended. This true story is told in a compelling journalistic style that avoids pathos. An excellent choice for book groups.*

Once I thought I had it all.

After college, I bought, I invested, I accomplished greatness in the material world. I might have stayed that way, had I not been flicking through the TV channels. That night I saw Professor Morrie Schwartz, my favorite college teacher. Morrie was on Ted Koppel's *Nightline* talking about his death sentence. He had been diagnosed with Lou Gehrig's disease, but, before he died, he planned to teach us all about The Meaning of Life.

I enrolled in my professor's class. Each Tuesday I flew from Detroit to meet Morrie in West Newton, Massachusetts. We met 14 Tuesdays to discuss life, love, marriage, and death. It was taught by experience. Each week Morrie gave me an oral exam. I asked many questions as well. All that was expected was to produce one long paper on what was learned. That paper is presented here.

Enroll with me in Morrie's class. Let's spend *Tuesdays with Morrie.*

## Alexander, Lloyd. *The Arkadians.*

Dutton/Penguin, 1995, 272pp. Elementary School & Up.

■ **FANTASY.** Animals, friendship; magic; supernatural.

■ **RELATED BOOKS:** *The Dragonslayers* by Bruce Coville; *The Lion, the Witch, and the Wardrobe* by C. S. Lewis; *Gypsy Rizka* and *The Cat Who Wished to Be a Man* by Lloyd Alexander.

 *This hilarious tale, told in epic style, focuses on the goddess culture and its role in both history and myth.*

This is a tale with some mighty strange characters. First, there's a talking jackass who claims to be a poet. Next, a young bean-counter enters our twisted fairy tale. Then, a girl called Joy-in-the-Dance joins the Arkadians.

The Arkadians are a cast of humorous and heroic characters weaving their way through danger, daring, and romance.

Take thee heart and join these merry folk on their celebration.

## Alexander, Lloyd. *The Cat Who Wished to be a Man.*

E. P. Dutton, 1973, 107pp. Elementary School & Up.

■ **HUMOR.** *Animals (cats); love; magic; Middle Ages.*

■ **RELATED BOOKS:** *The Arkadians* and *Time Cat* by Lloyd Alexander; *To Visit the Queen* by Diane Duane.

 *An amusing, tongue-in-cheek commentary on human foibles told by a cat. Recommended as a group read, book report choice, or read-aloud.*

"Please, master," said the cat, "will you change me into a man?"

The wizard Magister Stephanus stopped stirring the soup kettle and frowned. "Lionel, I gave you the power of speech. Don't force me to withdraw it. Humans are a feeble, sickly, lazy lot who take all my gifts and misuse them. Once I built a man in Brightford a bridge. What did he do? That villain set up a toll gate. Now that villain is Mayor of Brightford."

"Master," said Lionel. "I do so wish to be a man to see Brightford for myself."

"Stubborn cat! Very well, but I've warned you. Take this wishbone with you for protection. Should you be in distress or danger, break it in two. It will take you wherever you want to be."

With the wizard's warning in his human ears, Lionel set off for his adventure. As a man, Lionel discovered danger, adventure, and, yes, even love. Will he win the fair maiden Gillian? Will he save Brightford from the villainous Mayor and his Enforcer? Will he return to his boring life as a cat? Find out in this purr-fectly delightful tale about *The Cat Who Wishes to be a Man.*

## Alexander, Lloyd. *Gypsy Rizka.*

Dutton's Children's Books, 1999, 195pp. Elementary School & Up.

■ **FANTASY.** *Animals (cats); class conflict; Middle Ages.*

■ **RELATED BOOKS:** *The Arkadians* and *The Cat Who Wished to Be a Man* by Lloyd Alexander; *The Whipping Boy* by Sid Fleischmann; *The Wish Giver* by Bill Brittain.

 *This comic opera with a folktale flavor is a hilarious read-aloud with elementary and middle school students because of its buffoonery, farce and slapstick.*

"It's high time we run Gypsy Rizka out of our celebrated town," Mr. Podskalny blustered. "She's an eyesore, a walking ragbag. Her cat is just as bad."

"Hear, hear," murmured the members of the town council.

"I have an idea," suggested Chief Counselor Sharpnack. "Her scoundrel of a cat ate one of my chickens. I'll make a formal accusation and begin the legal procedure: an investigation, a hearing, a trial—"

A town clerk pondered the suggestion. "I suppose that's proper. After all, the law, as it's written, specifies no difference between a human or an animal."

"Quite right. I shall conduct the trial and the cat will be found guilty of murder. I shall recommend banishment and, hopefully, that gypsy will leave with the cat."

"You'll need an arrest warrant," the town clerk said.

Sharpnack flexed his fingers and rolled up his sleeves. "Fetch me my pen."

## Alger, Stephen. *All the Way to Heaven: An American Boyhood in the Himalayas.*

Henry Holt, 1998, 319pp. Middle School & Up.

- **BIOGRAPHY.** *India and Pakistan; religion; self-identity.*
- **RELATED BOOKS:** *Seven Years in Tibet* by Heinrich Harrer; *Within Reach: My Everest Story* by Mark Pfetzer and Jack Galvin.

 *Note: This entertaining book tells many stories for the adventure and nature lover, but can also be used as a biography.*

I hate answering the question, "Where are you from, originally?" You see, I was an American living in India up the Himalayas. I spoke a mixture of Hindustani and English. It seemed normal to me until I had to answer that dreaded question.

I'm Stephen Alter. My family were Presbyterian missionaries, living in India. I have amazing memories of each Fourth of July. The monsoon season had begun. We Presbyterians would congregate at the community center for our annual potluck supper. Eventually someone would shout, "Leech!" Everything would stop. Everyone would check their pants or skirts, looking for blood. "It's me, it's come off me," someone would shout. We would drown the leech with salt. Eventually, we would resume our socializing, ignoring the monsoon, ignoring the leeches.

With these experiences, can you see how much easier it became for me say I was from Boston?

## Allen, Tim. *I'm Not Really Here.*

Hyperion, 1996, 253pp. Middle School & Up.

- **HUMOR.** Men's issues; religion; science; show business.
- **RELATED BOOKS:** *Don't Stand Too Close to a Naked Man* by Tim Allen; Stephen Hawking's *Universe: The Cosmos Explained* by David Filkin.

 *Note: Tim Allen's hilarious search for a missing car ornament is perfect for the older reluctant reader.*

I'm Tim Allen. You may know me as the comic star on TV's *Home Improvement.*

I'm not really here.

You see, I've been reading all these books on the universe and quantum physics. According to scientists, it's all a matter of molecular energy, all based on what we think we see. According to Eastern philosophy, it's all an illusion. So that must mean: I'm not really here. Neither are you. We're an illusion. So don't bother turning on my television show because I won't be there. See how crazy this all gets?

Join me on my hilarious journey through all kinds of experiences I thought I had.

## Alvarez, Julie. *In the Time of Butterflies.*

Penguin, 1994, 324pp. High School & Up.

- **REALISTIC FICTION.** *Caribbean and Latin America; death; ethics; family; politics; survival; war.*
- **RELATED BOOKS:** *Animal Dreams* by Barbara Kingsolver; *Like Water for Chocolate* by Laura Esquivel; *The House of the Spirits* by Isabel Allende; *Evita: An Intimate Portrait of Eva Peron* edited by Tomas De Elia and Juan Pablo Queiroz.

 *This novel is based on a true story. Under the fascist regime of Raphael Trujillo in the Dominican Republic, the Mirabel sisters were murdered on a deserted road on November 25, 1960, their deaths officially an accident. Known as Las Mariposas (the Butterflies), they have become legends in Latin America.*

Every November for the last 34 years, Dede Mirabel prepares herself for the interviews and tributes of her three dead sisters. They were *Las Mariposas* or The Butterflies. These women sacrificed their safe, comfortable lives in the name of freedom under the Dominican dictator Trujillo.

Somehow this *gringo* interviewer is different from the other journalists. She has not read the biographies of Dede's sisters, Minerva, Maria Teresa, and Patria. It is somehow easier for Dede to tell her sisters' stories, from their secret crushes to gun running to prison torture.

Now the martyred Butterflies can live again.

## Anderson, Christopher. *Jackie After Jack: Portrait of the Lady.*

William Morrow, 1998, 472pp. High School & Up. Sequel to **Jack and Jackie**.

- **BIOGRAPHY.** *Family; love; politics.*
- **RELATED BOOKS:** *Just Jackie: Her Private Years* by Edward Klein; *Jackie* by David Heyman; *Jackie O!* by Kitty Kelley.

 *Recommended for those high school students who are looking for an interesting biography, but may be too lengthy for reluctant readers. Incidentally, Edward Klein's book about Jackie disputes many of Anderson's claims.*

Jackie Kennedy was 34 when her husband, President John Kennedy, was killed. She lived another 30 years without him. With each decade, the legend of Jackie Kennedy Onassis grew. By 1994, the year she died, she had become an icon.

Who was the private Jackie? According to the author, she was quite different from the public one. For instance, her three-pack-a-day nicotine habit was never exposed in photographs. She had other addictions that she kept private. She kept her romances with Marlon Brando, Frank Sinatra, and Robert Kennedy secret as well. In spite of her difficulties, she continued to live a productive life until the end. Her children were her greatest legacy.

Read this fascinating account of *Jackie after Jack.*

## Anderson, Rachel. *The Bus People.*

Henry Holt, 1989, 102 pp. Elementary School & Up.

- **SHORT STORIES.** *Abuse; adoption; disability; self-identity; trust.*
- **RELATED BOOKS:** *The Summer of the Swans* by Betsy Byars; *My Louisiana Sky* by Kimberly Willis Holt.

*Note:* This unforgettable book contains short stories about physically challenged children. Useful as a read-aloud for group discussions.

The Bus People ride the "fruitcake bus" to school. Betrum is the bus driver. He loves the Bus People, explaining, "I love these kids. Wouldn't swap my fruitcakes for the world."

There's Rebecca—a girl with 47 chromosomes instead of 46. She's a girl with Down's Syndrome who is to be a bridesmaid at her sister's wedding until relatives interfere. There's Jonathan who feels useless until the Dinner Lady lets him help at church. There's silent Fleur, who finally finds a family who doesn't care if she's silent or tears holes in curtains. There's Thoby, whose brain injury doesn't keep him from enjoying his sister's music.

Join *The Bus People* for a journey straight to your heart.

## Arnoldi, Katherine. *The Amazing "True" Story of a Teenage Single Mom.*

Hyperion, 1998, unnumbered pages. High School & Up. Top 10 Best Books for Young Adults; Top 10 Quick Picks for Reluctant Young Adult Readers.

- **BIOGRAPHY.** *Abuse; homelessness; single parents; sex and sexuality; sexual abuse; women's issues; work.*
- **RELATED BOOKS:** *The Hip Mama Survival Guide* by Ariel Gore; *Dear Nobody* by Berlie Doherty; *Annie's Baby: The Diary of Anonymous, a Pregnant Teenager* by Beatrice Sparks.

*Note:* An inspirational memoir, pictorially drawn by the author as a comic book fable. Highly recommended, especially for older reluctant readers, aspiring writers, and, of course, pregnant teens and teen mothers.

At 17, I became a single mother.

Although I loved being a mother, I kept my dreams. One day I plan to graduate from college. Of course, that takes money. Money was one thing I haven't been able to keep.

Although I hated leaving my daughter, I had to work to earn money. Once I was a stripper. I stripped surgical gloves off the ceramic forms at a factory. (Gotcha!)

Now I want to be a person becoming something, not a person without a job. I want to be treated like someone becoming someone, not like someone to be kept in her place. One day I want to publish my story so I can inspire other single moms to fight for their rights for an education.

## Avi. *Perloo the Bold.*

Scholastic, 1998, 225pp. Elementary School & Up.

■ **FANTASY.** *Animals; rivalry.*

■ **RELATED BOOKS:** *Redwall series by Brian Jacques; Poppy series by Avi; The Rats of NIMH by Robert C. O'Brien.*

 *An excellent read-aloud for younger students, a recommended book report selection, and a good group read for older students.*

"Perloo!" Lucabara banged on a small wooden door at the top of the mound. "If you're there, let me in. It's important!"

Just like Lucabara, Perloo was three hops high and 12 years new. Like all Montmers, Perloo wore loose-fitting smocks to cover his short, curly fur. He peered in the peephole, making certain it was not a dangerous Felbart. He released the safety peg and let the door drop.

"Perloo, come quickly. Granter Jolaine is very ill, perhaps fatally. She's been asking for you. She says it's a matter between life and death. I think she means for the entire Montmer tribe."

Perloo was astonished. "Why should our leader want to see me? I've only talked to her about Montmer history. I don't think her son would want me to see his mother at a time like this."

Perloo was right. Berwig the Big did not want Perloo to see his mother. His mother was dying, and Jolaine didn't want her war-mongering son to succeed her. Instead, she has placed her faith in Perloo.

Can Perloo the reader become *Perloo the Bold?*

## Avi. *Poppy.*

Illustrated by Brian Floca. Orchard, 1995, 147pp. Elementary School & Up. First in a series: **Poppy and Rye** follows; **Ragweed**, the prequel.

■ **FANTASY.** *Animals (mice, owl, porcupine); death; responsibility; survival.*

■ **RELATED BOOKS:** *Mrs. Frisby and the Rats of NIMH by Robert O'Brien; Redwall by Brian Jacques.*

 *In the animal world, the book's violence is, of course, realistic. However, a sensitive reader might be happier reading the lighter **Mrs. Frisby and the Rats of NIMH.***

"Ah, Poppy," Langwort announced. "You're late for our special mouse meeting. Where's your friend Ragweed?"

Poppy stammered to her father, "May I tell you after the meeting?"

"Very well. Fellow mice, our family is expanding at a rapid rate. We have almost 200 family members and it's vital that we find space. I suggest that we go to the New House, on the northern side of Dimwood Forest. That means we must ask permission of Mr. Ocax. You and I will go together, Poppy, to see Mr. Ocax."

Poppy shuddered. She was sickened by the thought of asking permission of Mr. Ocax, a cruel, arrogant owl who dominated the forest. Poppy had just returned from Bannock Hill. Alone. She and her boyfriend Ragweed had sneaked away to the forbidden area. Without warning, the owl swooped down on them and ate Ragweed! Mr. Ocax had left his mark on Poppy's nose, a long white claw streak.

Will Poppy have the courage to face the cruel Mr. Ocax? Of course. That's when the adventure begins. Read the *Poppy* series.

## Avi. *What Do Fish Have to Do with Anything? And Other Stories.*

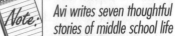

Illustrated by Tracy Mitchell. Candlewick , 1997, 203pp. Middle School & Up.

- ■ **SHORT STORIES.** *Animals (cats); divorce; homelessness; runaways; substance abuse (alcohol); suicide; supernatural.*
- ■ **RELATED BOOKS:** *The Bus People* by Rachel Anderson; *Stay True: Short Stories for Strong Girls* by Marilyn Singer.

*Note:* Avi writes seven thoughtful stories of middle school life that are varied in tone and narrative voice. Recommended for reluctant readers.

What happens when a troublemaker is mistaken for an angel? Who keeps calling and hanging up on Maria? How did Gregory get his name "Teacher Tamer"? Can animals become ghosts?

These short stories answer all these questions, especially one perplexing query: *What Do Fish Have to Do with Anything?*

## Avi. *Windcatcher.*

(Pbk.) Avon Camelot, 1991, 120pp. Elementary School & Up. An Accelerated Reader selection.

- ■ **ADVENTURE.** *Crime; hobbies (sailing); sports (sailing); survival.*
- ■ **RELATED BOOKS:** *The Pirates' Mixed-Up Voyage* by Margaret Mahy; *The Treasure of Alpheus Winterborn* by John Bellairs; *The Pink Motel* by Carol Ryrie Brink.

*Note:* Recommended for students who like the **Hardy Boys** or **Nancy Drew** series.

"Did you notice those folks in the speedboat? They're looking for the Swallows Bay treasure." Chris stopped her sailing lesson to explain. "It's only a legend, but this pirate, Captain Littlejohn, supposedly buried his treasure around one of the Thimbles Islands."

Tony was fascinated. This summer was turning out better than he planned. He didn't think several weeks with his grandma would be much fun. But he had his own sailboat and was learning to sail. Now, a buried treasure. Cool.

On his first solo sail, Tony spotted the same people in the speedboat. Being curious, he followed the man and woman around the Thimbles Islands. It's obvious that they are up to something.

If those people can look for the treasure, then so can I, thought Tony. I'll keep my eye on them. I have to be careful. If they catch me, they might make me walk the plank!

## Bach, Richard. *One: A Novel.*

London: Pan Books, 1988, 284pp. High School & Up.

- ■ **FANTASY.** Ethics; love; men's issues; supernatural; time travel; work; women's issues.
- ■ **RELATED BOOKS:** All books by Richard Bach, including *Jonathan Livingston Seagull.*

 *This book is hard to categorize because it's a mixture of biography, fantasy, and New Age philosophy. However, it's a compelling read for all types of older readers.*

What if we could meet ourselves as we'll be 20 years from now? What if we lived parallel lives in two worlds? What choices would we make?

The author Richard Bach and his wife Leslie take a fantasy flight into their past. They learn what might have happened if they had not met. Like Ebenezer Scrooge, they meet the Ghost of the Past.

They also meet the Ghost of the Future. Richard discovers what might have happened if he had dropped the bomb he was carrying as a pilot during the Berlin Crisis of 1961. Leslie discovers what might have happened if she had remained in Hollywood as the actress Leslie Parrish.

Did they make the right choices?

## Bacon, Katharine Jay. *Finn.*

Margaret K. McElderry Books, 1998, 171pp. Middle School & Up. Nominee for the Edgar Allen Poe Award for the Best Young Adult Mystery.

- ■ **MYSTERIES, THRILLERS.** Animals (coyotes and horses); crime; death; disability (physical and mental); substance abuse (cocaine).
- ■ **RELATED BOOKS:** *The Silent Storm* by Sherry Garland; *Harper and Moon* by Ramon Royal Ross; *Rimwalkers* by Vicki Grove; *Hero of Lesser Causes* by Julie Johnston.

 *Because of Finn's disability, this mystery is realistic. Can be used as a group read.*

Finn hadn't talked since the airplane crash that killed his parents and sister. The doctor told him how important it was to remember the crash if Finn ever wanted to talk again.

Staying with Gram was supposed to help Finn recover, but it brought only painful memories. Gram's young friend, Julia, was also little help. Finn thought Julia should just stick to taking care of Gram's horses and leave him alone.

Others lurked on Gram's property for more sinister purposes. Unknown to Gram, the farm was used as a local drop for drug dealers. Once, the dealers saw Finn and Julia on the path to the hidden drugs. Once was enough.

No doubt about it. Finn and Julia were in danger. How could they protect themselves if Finn refused to talk?

B

## Ball, Edward. *Slaves in the Family.*

Farrar, Straus and Giroux, 1998, 503pp. High School & Up. Winner of the National Book Award.

- **NONFICTION.** *African Americans; American Revolutionary War; Civil War; interracial relations.*
- **RELATED BOOKS:** *To be a Slave* by Julius Lester; *Roots* by Alex Haley.

 *The book's length of over 500 pages will turn away the reluctant readers.*
*Recommend this one to the mature reader who enjoys a lengthy, engrossing read of our tainted American history.*

When I was 12, before my father died, he gave me a copy of the published history of the family. "One day you'll want to know about your ancestors," he told me.

I know he had mixed feelings about his heritage. So do I.

Since 1698 until 1865, my family was in the slave business. Close to 4,000 slaves were born or bought into slavery. My family's plantations were the oldest in the South. Our crop was rice, and we stayed in business as sharecrop farmers until about 1900.

The more I learned, the more fascinated I became. An important part of my heritage had been lost. I hoped to reclaim it. To complete the legacy, I would try to find the descendants of the slaves.

I began by interviewing relatives, black and white. Some of my relatives were tentative about my project. No matter. I was on a quest. This quest was part history, part discovery.

This is my family's story, black and white, who lived side by side for 300 years. We are forever linked.

## Bauer, Joan. *Rules of the Road.*

Putnam's Sons, 1998, 210pp. Middle School & Up. An ALA Best Book for Young Adults; Top 10 Best Books for Young Adults; SLJ's Best Books; winner of the L.A. Times Teen Book Award.

- **REALISTIC FICTION.** *Aging; death; illness (physical); problem parents; responsibility; substance abuse (alcohol); women's issues; work.*

- **RELATED BOOKS:** *Checking on the Moon* by Jenny Davis; *Shoot for the Moon* by Norma Howe.

 *Joan Bauer has won awards for her humorous romances,* **Squashed** *and* **Thwonk.**
*In this book, her humorous style covers serious issues, such as learning to be responsible in spite of an alcoholic father and dysfunctional family. Recommended for book reports or for group reads.*

"Jenna Boller, you may be my driver."

I shook my head. "Mrs. Gladstone, I'd rather keep on selling shoes after school. Besides, I'm 16. I've only had my driver's license for a couple of months."

You could tell Mrs. Gladstone wasn't used to hearing the word "no." "Nonsense, young woman. I need a driver for the summer to drive me through Texas, Kansas, Missouri, and Arkansas. I will pay you well." I opened the passenger door, and Mrs. Gladstone stepped grandly out of the Cadillac.

Hmmm, I thought. Driving for Dollars. Maybe this could solve all my problems. Or would I be running away from them? Can my younger sister Faith and Mom manage without me? What about Dad, whom I never see except when he's drunk? (Once he had the nerve to stumble into the Gladstone's shoe store, calling my name. That's enough to drive anyone away.) What about Grandma? She's got Alzheimer's and needs me to go through her scrapbooks of memories.

Later, I discovered that, like Dorothy of Oz, you have to leave home to find it. Join me on my ride through Life while I explain the *Rules of the Road.*

## Bawden, Nina. *The Real Plato Jones.*

Clarion Books, 1993. Middle School & Up.

- **REALISTIC FICTION.** *Great Britain; immigrants; Middle East (Greece); problem parents; self-identity; World War II.*
- **RELATED BOOKS:** *The Outside Child* by Nina Bawden; *The Eclipse of Moonbeam Dawson* by Jean Davies Okimato; *The Window* by Michael Dorris.

 *Note:* There is an implied lesbian relationship with the guardians of Jane, Plato's best friend. Jane's story (with an appearance by Plato) is in Bawden's **The Outside Child.**

Will the real Plato Jones please stand?

I am the real Plato Jones. Plato Constantine Jones, to be exact. Plato because my mother is Greek, and Jones because my father is Welsh, and Constantine after his father, my grandfather.

Got all that? Neither have I and I've been living with this problem for 13 years. Just who is the real Plato Jones? Am I Greek like my mother, Welsh like my father, or English like my grandfather? Am I heroic like my English grandfather, who was an English spy in Greece? Am I a traitor like my Greek grandfather, who tried to turn my grandfather over to the Nazis? Confusing, isn't it? Well, try living it!

Come on my journey with me to find the real Plato Jones.

## Bellairs, John *The Treasure of Alpheus Winterborn.*

Illustrated by Judith Gwyn Brown. (Pbk.) Bantam Skylark, 1980, 180pp. Elementary School & Up. First in the **Anthony Monday series; The Dark Side of Weatherend** and **The Lamp From Warlock's Tomb** follow.

- **MYSTERIES, THRILLERS.** *Crime; revenge; secrets.*
- **RELATED BOOKS:** *The Pink Motel* by Carol Ryrie Brink; *The Dark Stairs* by Betsy Byars; *Help, I'm a Prisoner in the Library!* by Eth Clifford.

 *Note:* Light, entertaining mystery books are always requested by elementary and middle school students. Recommend this series.

"Miss Eells, do you think the man who built this library hid a treasure in here?"

Miss Eells sighed. She wished her young friend Anthony Monday would stop worrying about money. "Who knows if it's true? Alpheus Winterborn was known as a odd millionaire. After all this time, it's not likely you'll find any treasure. Would it help if I offered you a job at the library?"

Anthony's face brightened. "Wow! That's great. Thanks, Miss Eells." That will give me time to look for the treasure, thought Anthony.

One day, while dusting the library's bookshelves, Anthony discovers a gold coin and a strange message from Alpheus Winterborn. Now it's up to Anthony to find the rest of the treasure.

Unfortunately, Mr. Winterborn's nephew, Hugh Philpotts, is after the treasure, too. Hugh Philpotts is willing to lie, cheat, and even murder to get it!

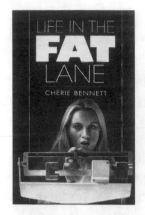

## Bennett, Cherie. *Life in the Fat Lane.*

Delacorte, 1998, 260pp. Middle School & Up. An ALA Best Book for Young Adults.

■ **REALISTIC FICTION.** *Eating disorders; peer pressure; problem parents; self-identity; suicide; women's issues.*

■ **RELATED BOOKS:** *Wake Up, I'm Fat!* by Camryn Manheim; *Beyond Beauty* by Jane Pratt; *Real Girl, Real World: Tools for Finding Your True Self* by Heather M. Gray and Samantha Phillips; *The Tribes of Palos Verdes* by Joy Nicholson.

Once I had it all. At 16, I was a pageant queen, honor student, and on top of the high school world. If I wasn't such a nice person, I'd hate myself. :-)

 *Note:* The narrator, Lara Ardeche, eventually discovers she may have Axell-Crowne Syndrome, a rare metabolic disorder with no known cure. Meanwhile, Lara's self-image goes into a tailspin. Lara's angst about weight gain and appearance will be familiar to many readers, and, hopefully, Lara's insight about appreciating her inner beauty may help other anxious readers. School counselors should read this one.

Then, one horrible day, things began to change. I got hives and became bloated from my medication. No matter how I dieted, I kept gaining. Eventually I gained over 80 pounds! I now weigh over 200 pounds! :-(

I don't know who I am any more. My parents are horrified at my appearance. Dad stopped calling me his Princess long ago. Most of my so-called friends gloat about my weight gain. I'm so ashamed. I've become a sexless, ageless, faceless blob.

Must I spend the rest of my life wearing this fat suit?

*Life in the Fat Lane by Cherie Bennett, © 1998, Delacorte.*

## Bennett, James W. *Blue Star Rapture.*

Simon and Schuster Books for Young Readers, 1998, 134pp. Middle School & Up.

**RELATED BOOKS:** *On the Devil's Court* by Carl Deuker; *The Squared Circle* by James. W. Bennett; *The Last Shot: City Streets, Basketball Dreams* by Darcy Frey.

**SPORTS.** *African Americans; diaries; disability (mental); ethics; interracial relations; religion; sports (basketball); suicide.*

*Note: This thin book is recommended as a book report for reluctant readers. However, be aware of the profanity throughout the book.*

"Look at that. Strong hands. He catches the basketball with one hand while holding his position. That's what a college scout looks for."

*College scout?* thought T.J., astonished. He decided to be frank with Gaines, a sportswriter he barely knew. "Do you think Tyron has a chance to win a basketball scholarship?"

"Look, kid, your friend's only a Junior. Who knows? He has to look and play sharp at the Full Court basketball camp. For now, that's the main thing. Now I've got something to ask you. While you're at the camp, I would like you to take a few notes. Maybe we can get a story out of it."

T.J. shook his head. "I can't promise anything, but I'll keep my ears open."

Once the camp began, T.J. frequently recalled their conversation. He began to observe illegal practices between the coaches, street agents, and players. He thought about writing his observations in his diary. True, this had nothing to do with Tyron, but, on the other hand, this sounded exactly like the kind of thing the sportswriter Gaines would want to hear about.

T.J. had to smile in spite of himself: Was this basketball or espionage?

## Berendt, John. *Midnight in the Garden of Good and Evil: A Savannah Story.*

Random House, 1994, 388pp.; (Pbk.) Random House, 1995, 388pp. High School & Up.

■ **NONFICTION.** *Class conflict; crime; death; homosexuality; sex and sexuality.*

■ **RELATED BOOKS:** *In Cold Blood* by Truman Capote; books by Joe McGinnis: *Fatal Vision; Cruel Doubt; Blind Faith.*

*Note: This booktalk, as well as 10 others, were contained in my first book,* **Talk That Book!** *However, the booktalks were integrated within a chapter and not easily reproduced. Some are slightly changed. This best seller is an entertaining read for older reluctant readers.*

I'm John Berendt, a Yankee reporter from New York.

The first time I heard about Savannah, Georgia, was in the book *Treasure Island*. The bloodthirsty pirate Captain John Flint lived there. Savannah is also mentioned in *Gone with the Wind* as a quiet, genteel Southern town.

Savannah is quiet on the surface and bloodthirsty underneath. I would find myself involved in an adventure that included a wide mixture of characters. They include a drag queen, a Southern belle, a voodoo priestess, and an antiques dealer. All were somehow involved in a horrific murder.

The tragedy of this story is that it is true.

## Bernstein, Jonathan. *Pretty in Pink: The Golden Age of Teenage Movies.*

(Pbk.) St. Martin's Griffin, 1997, 230pp. Middle School & Up.

■ **NONFICTION.** *Music; show business; self-identity.*

■ **RELATED BOOKS:** *Before They were Famous: In Their Own Words* by Karen Hardy Bystedt; *Hollywood: The New Generation* by James Cameron-Wilson.

*Many adolescent reluctant readers will enjoy this well-researched look at teen movies from the past.*

Young film celebrities have existed since Dorothy and Lillian Gish during the silent screen days. However, in the 1980s, teen celebrities were at their peak in popularity. Tom Cruise, Sean Penn, Demi Moore, and many others were known as the *Brat Pack*, youthful actors who became overnight stars.

Also, in the 1980s, teen movies were original and fresh. *Risky Business, The Breakfast Club, Fast Times at Ridgemont High,* and *Heathers* were beacons for other teen flicks that followed.

Read this, then rent the videos. See why the 1980s were a period when the parents left for an entire decade, leaving the kids to run the movie industry. Suckers.

## Bernstein, Sara Tuvel. *The Seamstress: A Memoir of Survival.*

Introduction by Edgar M. Bronfman; contributions by Marlene Bernstein Samuels. G. P. Putnam's Sons, 1997, 353pp. (Pbk.) Berkley Publishing Group, 1999, 384pp. Middle School & Up. An ALA Best Young Adult Book of the Year.

■ **BIOGRAPHY. ABUSE;** death; Europe (Romania and Hungary); Holocaust; Jews; religious prejudice; women's issues; work; World War II.

■ **RELATED BOOKS:** I Lived a Thousand Years by Livia Bitton Jackson; No Pretty Pictures by Anita Lobel; Shattered! 50 Years of Silence: History and Voices of the Tragedy in Romania and Transnistria by Felicia Carmelly.

*Note:* *Published posthumously, this book is considered one of the best Holocaust memoirs. Sara (Seren) ended up in Ravensbruck, a women's concentration camp in Germany. Nineteen out of every 20 women died there, but Sara survived. Also, because of Sara's independent spirit, the book could be presented as feminist literature.*

On April 25, 1918, my mother delivered me by herself. My father was gone, the midwife could be reached only by horse and wagon, and the closest neighbor lived miles away. I was named Seren. Even from birth, I was a survivor.

I was considered the smartest girl in my Rumanian mountain village. I was also Jewish. I say this because I was reminded of this constantly by my teachers, classmates, and priests. Once, at school, when hearing a priest degrade Jews, I threw an inkwell at him.

That rash action led to my expulsion from school and to my career as a seamstress. I lived a satisfying, middle-class life with many friends. In 1935, this changed when Hitler became Chancellor. Even though we were in another European country, we could feel the negative effects of Nazism. Gradually we Rumanian Jews lost all rights and privileges. Jews could not work, marry, or even sit with Gentiles. One by one, all my friends disappeared, never to be seen again.

One early morning in October of 1941, there was a loud knocking on the door. My father shouted up the stairs, "Seren! Come downstairs!" I ran down the steps to find a bayonet pointed at my throat. My father and I were led off to an unknown destiny. As I was walking away, I wondered, is this what happened to my friends? Did they leave their lives without a chance to say goodbye?

## Blackwood, Gary. *The Shakespeare Stealer.*

Dutton Children's Books, 1998, 216pp. Middle School & Up. SLJ's Best Books.

- **HISTORICAL FICTION.** *Great Britain; class conflict; Middle Ages; orphans; rivalry; self-identity.*
- **RELATED BOOKS:** *Shakespeare Stories* by Geraldine McCaughrean; *The Princess Bride* by William Goldman; *In a Dark Wood* by Michael Cadnum; *I Am Modred* by Nancy Springer.

 *Note: The plot is similar to the movie **Shakespeare in Love,** with dueling, mixed identities, and gender switches. There's even a brief appearance by Queen Elizabeth. Recommended for middle and high school English classes, especially those studying Shakespeare.*

During the Middle Ages, England was a paradise for women, a prison for servants, and a hell for horses. As for myself, I was too lowly to mention. I was an orphan apprentice. That was like a slave with a master.

My master ordered me to steal the new play *The Tragedy of Hamlet, Prince of Denmark.* This author Shakespeare was unknown to me, but considered a master at his craft. Since my master owned a rival theatrical company, he commanded that I obtain the script. Alas, I discovered that the Bard guarded his words closely to his vest. Although I had never seen a play, I pretended to be an actor. I met Mr. Shakespeare as well as other actors who became my first friends. The stage world was filled with kindness and generosity, something I had never experienced.

During one performance, the actors placed me behind the stage and handed me the play. I was to prompt actors who forgot their lines. At last I had the play. All I had to do was run out of the theater.

Why was I hesitating?

## Block, Francesca Lia. *I was a Teenage Fairy.*

HarperCollins, 1998, 185pp. High School & Up. An ALA Best Book for Young Adults; Quick Pick for Reluctant Young Adult Readers.

■ **REALISTIC FICTION.** *Ethics; homosexuality; love; problem parents; sex and sexuality; sexual abuse; substance abuse; women's issues; work.*

■ **RELATED BOOKS:** *Am I Blue?* edited by Marion Bauer; *Weetzie Bat* series by Francesca Lia Block.

 *Block's unique language and characters add to this modern fairy tale. Due to the profanity and sexual content, this is recommended for mature reluctant readers.*

"Hey, watch it!"

Griffin heard a high, metallic buzz of a voice, and, weirdest of all, it was coming from under the blanket. He lifted the blanket to find a pinkie-sized, magenta-haired girl with transparent wings. Her face was so small that he couldn't see her angry, twisted mouth. Griffin couldn't believe he was talking to an insect: "Just what are you, anyway? Or am I having a bad trip and hallucinating?"

Mab would usually find this question offensive, but this guy was a definite biscuit. "I'm a fairy. Brownie. Pixie. Sprite. Nymph. Take your pick. Just don't think I'm a mosquito again and bash me."

The fairy tried to help unhappy teens like Griffin and Barbie. They had been child models who were abused by uncaring adults. They needed someone like Mab to help them cease their self-destructive behavior. Of course, everyone thought Griffin and Barbie were crazy since they appeared to talk to empty air.

Maybe Mab was real. Maybe this fairy was the fury, the courage, the inspiration. Maybe she was a feisty Tinkerbell who persuaded them to abandon their childhood abuses and to live happily ever after.

## Blos, Joan W. *A Gathering of Days: A New England Girl's Journal, 1830-32.*

Atheneum Books for Young Readers, 144pp. Elementary School & Up. Winner of the Newbery Medal. An Accelerated Reader selection.

■ **HISTORICAL FICTION.** African Americans; diaries; death; pioneer life; runaways; stepparents.

■ **RELATED BOOKS:** *Dear America* series by different authors, especially *So Far from Home: The Diary of Mary Driscoll, an Irish Mill Girl* and *A Picture of Freedom: The Diary of Clotee, a Slave Girl* by Patricia C. McKissack; *Sarah Plain and Tall* and *Skylark* by Pam Conrad; *Caddie Woodlawn* by Carol Ryrie Brink.

*Note: Like the **Dear America** series, the author uses a fictional diary format to reflect life in the 1830s. This style is controversial because it reads like a primary source. Booktalk this one, but don't use it as required reading. The plot and style are slow-paced, and might be boring to reluctant readers.*

Providence, Rhode Island
December 9, 1899
My very dear Catherine,

I'm so pleased that you found my journal entertaining and enlightening. Those two years, 1830-1832, were the most important time of my now 83 years. During that time, I first learned about the phantom that appeared and disappeared. Later I learned just who this mysterious phantom really was.

Also, my best friend Cassie Shipman faced a lingering illness that I hoped would not claim her short life. My dear father, who was a widower for many years, remarried. I had to learn to live with a new mother and brother. At first it was difficult, but I learned that life is like a pudding: It takes both salt and sugar to make it a good one.

Your loving great-grandmother,
Catherine Onesti

# Blume, Judy. *Summer Sisters.*

Delacorte, 1998, 400pp. (Pbk.) Mass Market Paperback, 1999, 400 pp. High School & Up.

■ **REALISTIC FICTION.** *Friendship; love; rites of passage; rivalry; sex and sexuality; stepparents; women's issues.*

■ **RELATED BOOKS:** *Wifey* and *Smart Women* by Judy Blume; *The Divine Secrets of the Ya-Ya Sisterhood* by Rebecca Wells; *Bridget Jones's Diary* by Helen Fielding.

When Vix answered the phone, she was surprised to hear from Caitlin. They hadn't talked in months and, with Cait's wanderlust, they hadn't seen each other in years.

 *Note: Blume, writer of the popular **Fudge** series, is one of the few children's writers who has written adult best sellers. Recommended as an entertaining summer read for mature readers.*

"Vix, you have to come. I'm getting married at Lamb's house on the Vineyard. You're to be my Maid of Honor. It's only appropriate, don't you think?"

"Depends on whom you're marrying. Who's the guy?"

"Bru," Caitlyn replied. "I'm marrying Bru. I thought you knew."

Victoria caught her breath and swallowed. Her thoughts tossed her into a whirlwind of emotions. What was Cait thinking? Only Cait would find such a request appropriate. How could two childhood friends share so much and be so different? She would have to refuse Cait's request, of course.

"Vix, are you still there? Will you come?"

Victoria gave a quick shake to her head to dissolve her thoughtful trance. How like Cait to be so nonchalant about their past, their many summers of heated adolescent experiences. Still, in spite of their tangled past, they were and would remain *Summer Sisters* forever.

"Yes, Cait. I'll be there."

*Summer Sister by Judy Blume, copyright © 1998, Delacorte.*

## Bolton, Carole. *Never Jam Today.*

Atheneum, 1971, 241pp. Middle School and Up.

■ **HISTORICAL FICTION.** *Love; politics; problem parents; rites of passage; women's issues.*

■ **RELATED BOOKS:** *Stay True: Short Stories for Strong Girls* by Marilyn Springer; *Cool Women: The Thinking Girl's Guide to the Hippest Women in History* edited by Pam Nelson, written by Dawn Chipman, Mari Florence, Naomi Wax.

 *Note: This book is currently out of print, but still available in used book sales and online bookstores. This romantic novel has a feminist twist. Highly recommended.*

The rule was *jam yesterday, jam tomorrow, but never jam today.* Lewis Carroll wrote this nonsensical verse in *Alice in Wonderland.* Somehow that verse seemed to express the frustrations of the women's movement in the United States.

In 1917 the United States was about to experience the beginning of the Roaring '20s, the Jazz Age, and a new era for women. Maddy Franklin wanted to do something more than marry. She was considering going to college or even getting a job. That's what the suffragists were saying, lead by the outspoken Susan Anthony.

Maddy's aunt had been a suffragist for years. She persuaded Maddy to join the picket lines, and when Maddy witnessed the brutal treatment of women, she became actively involved.

Maddy and her aunt were tired of hearing *"Never Jam Today"* for women's rights. They wanted their rights now!

## Bond, Adrienne. *Sugarcane House and Other Stories About Mr. Fat.*

Illustrated by Leuyen Pham. Harcourt Bruce, 1997, 86pp. Elementary School & Up.

■ **HUMOROUS SHORT STORIES.** *African Americans; animals (mules); pioneer life; work.*

■ **RELATED BOOKS:** *The Tales of Uncle Remus; Further Tales of Uncle Remus; The Last Tales of Uncle Remus,* all adapted by Julius Lester; *The Celebrated Jumping Frog of Calaveras County and Other Sketches* by Mark Twain; *Squids Will be Squids* by Jon Scieszka and Lane Smith.

 *Continue the booktalk by reading a favorite from the six stories, like "Fortune Store at Your Door." Mr. Fat, an escaped slave, is a trickster like Brer Rabbit, a character rooted in African-American folklore. A few "dams" and one "ass-over-whangdoodle" are intended in the exaggerated storytelling tradition. Adults will also enjoy this one.*

"Ma Minnie," DeWayne said to his great-grandmother. "I sure would enjoy to hear about that old mule, Mr. Fat. How come some folks call Mr. Fat 'John'?"

"White folks always calls Mr. Fat 'John'," said Ma Minnie. "Anyhow, that ain't no never mind. Do you want to hear a story about Mr. Fat or don't you?"

"Sure I do. Mr. Fat's always up to something. I liked the time he tricked Mr. Boar Hog to take the blame for some sugarcane that was missing. Or the time he met a book and waited for it to talk to him. Or the time ..."

"Do you want a story about Mr. Fat or not? Otherwise, I'll just take me a nap."

"No, no," DeWayne said. "I want to hear a Mr. Fat story."

Ma Minnie tipped her head back, closed her eyes, and began a story:

**B**

## Bonner, Cindy. *Lily: A Love Story.*

Algonquin Books of Chapel Hill, 1992, 336pp. High School & Up. **Looking After Lily** follows.

■ **HISTORICAL FICTION.** *Crime; ethics; love; pioneer life; pregnancy; runaways; sex and sexuality.*

■ **RELATED BOOKS:** *Buffalo Woman* by Bill Wallace; *Sunshine Rider: The First Vegetarian Western* by Ric Lynden Hardman.

 *Although this is based on real people, this love story and its sequel read like a tall tale. Lots of fun for romance lovers.*

Folks around McDade, Texas, say the Beatty boys are just plain wild and never up to no good. I thought so myself 'til I seen Marion outside Billingsley's store with that sunset red hair looking me up and down. I thought about him for days after that while I was scrubbin' Pa's shirts or feedin' the chickens.

Next, I spot Marion at the church fair. Somehow I end up going off with Marion. Couldn't help myself.

Wasn't long 'fore Marion and me was in love. His three outlaw brothers didn't like it one bit. My Pa whipped me over it. We don't care. We're in love.

Guess we're just like those two lovers I heard tell of, that Romeo and Juliet, 'cept it's 1883 and I'm packin' a pistol in my shirt pocket!

## Bono, Chastity and Billie Fitzgerald. *Family Outing.*

Little, Brown, 1998, 259pp. High School & Up.

■ **NONFICTION.** *Homosexuality; self-identity.*

■ **RELATED BOOKS:** *Am I Blue? Coming Out of the Silence* edited by Marion Dane Bauer; *Peter* by Kate Walker; *Open Secret: Gay Hollywood 1928-1998* by David Ehrenstein.

 *Bono combines her memoirs with other narratives drawn from interviews with members of Parents and Friends of Lesbians and Gays (PFLAG).*

When I told my mother I was a lesbian, she went ballistic. My mother is Cher.

Actually, my mother's reaction was pretty typical of most parents. She had to throw away her dreams of what she thought her daughter should be. She wanted me to "grow up, get married, have children, get divorced, and live happily ever after." My revelation made her face the truth.

I also had trouble facing the truth. For many years, I struggled with myself. Sometimes I thought I had a handle on it, but something would occur, like the tabloids outing me, and I would withdraw, ashamed and bewildered.

This is not only my story, but the story of others as well. Maybe this book can help others who want to risk a *Family Outing*.

## Bradbury, Ray. *Fahrenheit 451.*

Ballatine Books, 1991, 179pp. First published in 1958. Middle School & Up. An Accelerated Reader selection.

■ **SCIENCE FICTION.** *Class conflict; ethics; politics; responsibility; secrets.*

■ **RELATED BOOKS:** *Childhood's End* by Arthur C. Clarke; *Brave New World* by Aldous Huxley; *1984* by George Orwell.

*This classic still packs a punch with its look at a futuristic fascist government. Bradbury advocates reading and literacy as watchdogs against a totalitarian society. Recommended for adults, odlerl students, and book groups.*

"Fahrenheit 451 is the temperature that burns paper," Guy Montag explained to the inquisitive young girl. He tapped the numerals 451 stitched on his sleeve. "We never read the books we burn. That's against the law. We burn the books, then we burn the ashes."

Later that week something bizarre occurred during a routine burning. A woman insisted on being burned alive with her books. Guy was so shaken by this suicide that he took drastic action. He confiscated a book to read!

## Brennan, Christine. *Edge of Glory: The Inside Story of the Quest for Figure Skating's Olympic Gold Medals.*

Scribner, 1998, 416pp. Middle School & Up.

■ **SPORTS.** *Asian Americans; Hispanic Americans; rivalry; show business; sports (ice skating); work.*

■ **RELATED BOOKS:** *Inside Edge: A Revealing Journey into the Secret World of Figure Skating* by Christine Brennan; *The Passion to Skate* by Sandra Bezic and David Hayes.

*This book can be booktalked for many different ages, interests, and subjects: sports, the Olympics, Asian Americans, Hispanic Americans, and adolescent celebrities.*

The world's best figure skaters train in cold, dark rinks, year after year, pursuing one single dream: to win the Olympic gold medal. That one, brief shining moment can bring instant fame and wealth. If they stumble, they lose the Gold. Some wonder if the sacrifices are too great for these young athletes.

Michelle Kwan was expected to win the 1998 Olympics in Nagano, but, prior to the event, she had suffered many falls. Later it was discovered she had a hairline fracture in her foot, probably as a result of skating in commercially endorsed skating boots. Michelle's mishap turned into Tara Lipinski's brief, shining moment. At 13, Tara won the Gold, and became the newest idol.

In the figure-skating world, many skaters, from Rudy Galindo to Nancy Kerrigan, experienced defeat, only to rise again in victory. Here is the behind-the-scenes story of the sacrifices endured by these skaters, some of them teenagers who have never lived a typical life.

Are their sacrifices worth the Gold? You decide.

## Brittain, Bill. *Shape-Changer.*

HarperCollins, 1994, 108pp. Elementary School & Up. A Newbery Honor Book.

■ **SCIENCE FICTION.** *End of the world; rivalry; school; secrets.*

■ **RELATED BOOKS:** *Black Suits from Outer Space* by Gene DeWeese; *Stinker from Space* by Pamela F. Service.

Note: *This humorous science fiction can be enjoyed by all ages and genders. The book is reminiscent of the movie* **Men in Black.** *Also, recommended as an elementary school read-aloud.*

I couldn't believe my eyes or ears. Whoever heard a fire hydrant talk?

This hydrants says forcefully, "My name is Zymel. I am one of the Shilad from the planet Rodinam." Then, to my astonishment, the fire hydrant changes into a book. "I need your help. Take me to your house!"

What could I do? I took the book home. This book, Zymel, tells me he's an alien shape-changer. A Shape-Changer changes shapes by transforming into objects.

Zymel has a huge problem and needs help. Zymel is a policeman who was transporting a criminal when his spaceship crashed. Zymel's prisoner, Fek, is a criminal shape-changer who's insane. Fek could change his shape into anybody, like any world leader, and destroy our Earth!

Now my friends and I are on a mission to help good overcome evil. See if we destroy Fek, the evil *Shape-Changer.*

## Brittain, Bill. *The Wish Giver: Three Tales of Coven Tree.*

Illustrated by Andrew Glass. (Pbk.) HarperCollins Juvenile, 1990, 181pp. Part of **The Coven Tree series: Devil's Donkey** precedes; **Dr. Dredd's Wagon of Wonders; Professor Popkin's Prodigious Polish** follow. Elementary school & Up. An Accelerated Reader selection.

■ **FANTASY.** *Magic; Middle Ages; responsibility.*

■ **RELATED BOOKS:** *Bunnicula series* by James and Deborah Howe; *Sugarcane House and Other Stories About Mr. Fat* by Adrienne Bond; *Frindle* by Andrew Clements.

*This one is a hilarious read-aloud or group read.*

At the church social, Thaddeus Blinn set up a tent in Coven Tree and placed a sign that said, "I can give you whatever you want for only 50 cents."

Some people were curious and entered the tent. Thaddeus gave each of them a card with a red dot. "When you are ready, put your thumb on the red dot and wish wisely. That wish will come true."

They made their wishes. That's when the trouble began. For example, Rowena Jervis wished that Henry Piper would put down roots and move to Coven Tree. Guess what happened to Henry? He became a tree! The other results were just as outrageous.

Make it your wish to read *The Wish Giver* by Bill Brittain.

## Brooks, Walter R. *Freddy the Detective.*

Illustrated by Kurt Wiese. Overlook Press, 1998, 264pp. First published in 1932. Part of the *Freddy* series that includes **Freddy and the Flying Saucer Plans; Freddy and the Men from Mars; Freddy Goes to Florida.** Elementary School & Up.

■ **FANTASY, MYSTERY, THRILLER.** *Animals; crime.*

■ **RELATED BOOKS:** *Charlotte's Web* and *Stuart Little* by E. B. White.

> *Note:* From 1927 to 1958, Brooks wrote 28 **Freddy** books, all featuring a resourceful pig involved in various adventures. Now the books are back in print. Great as an amusing read-aloud to younger children.

"Freddy, just what were you doing, staring at Alice behind a clump of bushes? Now this poor duck has fainted and you're responsible." To protect Alice, Jinx had jumped in the bushes and landed on Freddy's back. The cat cuffed the pig soundly on the head.

"I'm sorry, Alice." The pig, Freddy, shook himself free of the cat. "I was just shadowing you."

"Shadowing," Jinx repeated. "What's that?"

"Oh, it's a term used by detectives. It means following someone. I'm going to be a detective and I was practicing. I got the idea from a book I found in the barn, *The Adventures of Sherlock Holmes.* Sherlock Holmes solved all crimes by finding criminals."

"Really? Look here, Freddy, there's a job for a detective on this farm. The children are missing a train of cars. When Everett went to sleep last night, the train was beside him on the bed. When he woke up, it was gone. Something's wrong."

"Of course, Jinx, I'll get on the case right away. I'll bet there are lots of mysteries to be solved on a farm like this, and I'll solve them all. Maybe I can put them in a book."

"Good idea, Freddy. Why don't you call the book *Freddy the Detective*?"

## Bryson, Bill. *A Walk in the Woods: Rediscovering America on the Appalachian Trial.*

Broadway Books, 1998, 276pp. (Pbk.) Broadway Books, 1999, 276pp. Middle School & Up.

■ **RELATED BOOKS:** Books by Bill Bryson: *The Lost Continent: Travels in Small Town America; Notes from a Small Island; Neither Here Nor There: Travels in Europe.*

■ **NONFICTION ADVENTURE.** *Animals (bears, other wildlife); ecology; friendship; hobbies (hiking); men's issues; survival.*

 *Bryson's breezy, self-mocking tone is reminiscent of Dave Barry's humor. Recommended for all types of readers, especially reluctant readers.*

Behind my house in New Hampshire is a path that vanishes into the woods. This path is part of the Appalachian Trail, running over 2,100 miles along America's eastern seaboard. From Georgia to Maine, it stretches over 14 states. The mighty AT is the granddaddy of long hikes.

A little voice in my head said, "That's neat. Take that long hike." So I decided to do it. Later, I learned about the dangers of wild animals, infectious diseases, crazy killers, and bad weather. Maybe I would have done it anyway.

I'm Bill Bryson, author of several international hiking books. Join my friend, Stephen Katz, and me on our *Walk in the Woods.*

## Buck, Rinker. *Flight of Passage: A True Story.*

Hyperion, 1997, 351pp. Middle School & Up. An ALA Best Book for Young Adults.

■ **NONFICTION ADVENTURE.** *Family; hobbies (aviation); men's issues; responsibility; rites of passage; rivalry; science.*

■ **RELATED BOOKS:** *The Spirit of St. Louis* by Charles Lindbergh; *Flight of the Gin Fizz: Midlife at 4,5000 Feet* by Henry Kisor; *Going Solo* by Roald Dahl; *A Pirate Looks at Fifty* by Jimmy Buffet; *Yeager* by Chuck Yeager.

 *Later, journalist Rinker Buck discovered that someone else had broken the aviation record, but the media had already found their story. If you present this as a booktalk, show some of the reprinted newspaper articles contained in the book. Also, this adventurous memoir is a timeless ode to fathers and sons. In spite of its length, this is recommended for older reluctant readers.*

My brother and I were the youngest aviators to fly America coast to coast. I was 15; my brother Kern was 17. In 1965, we restored a Piper Cub, a two-seat, hand-crank, tail-wheel airplane. By the summer of 1966, we were ready to fly to our adventure. Our intentions were not to make aviator history. We did it for our father.

In his youth, my father was a barnstormer as an airshow performer and ferry pilot.

My father even lost his left leg in an airplane crash, a constant reminder of his barnstorming days. His stories of perilous Appalachian ice storms and desperate landings captured our dreams.

Now we were ready to merge our dreams with his and go on the adventure of our lives. We were ready to enter our *Flight of Passage.*

## Buffet, Jimmy. *A Pirate Looks at Fifty.*

Random House, 1998, 458pp. High School & Up.

■ **BIOGRAPHY.** Caribbean and Latin America; music; rites of passage.

■ **RELATED BOOKS:** *Flight of Passage: A True Story* by Rinker Buck; *Losing My Virginity: How I've Survived, Had Fun, and Make a Fortune Doing Business My Way* by Richard Branson; *The Jimmy Buffet Scrapbook: Update* by Mark Humphrey and Harris Lewine.

*Note:* Recommend this one to a reluctant reader who enjoys music and adventure.

I'm Jimmy Buffet: musician, songwriter, pilot, world traveler, philosopher. My philosophy? Follow your instincts and keep a sense of humor.

Sometimes it's hard to laugh. Once I flipped over my seaplane in the Atlantic Ocean. That wasn't funny. Neither were the stitches in my skull from surfing in the Gulf during a hurricane. I'm known to take a risk or two.

I'll admit it. I'm a pirate. By nature, I am a creature of the swamps and the sea. I enjoy the adventure of life on the sea.

I hope you'll enjoy the ride.

## Bunting, Eve. *Jumping the Nail.*

Harcourt Brace, 1991, 172pp. Middle School & Up.

■ **REALISTIC FICTION.** Death; peer pressure; responsibility; supernatural.

■ **RELATED BOOKS:** *A Separate Peace* by John Knowles; *Killing Mr. Griffin* and *I Know What You Did Last Summer* by Lois Duncan.

*Note:* These disaster adventures are popular among teens. This is one of the better ones, even containing supernatural elements.

"Do you think Scooter and Elisa will do it? Will they really jump the Nail?" Dru asked her boyfriend Mike. "No one could be that crazy."

But Scooter and Elisa *are* that crazy and foolish. They plan to jump from the Nail. The Nail is 90 feet high from the top of the cliff to the water below. The ocean is said to be bottomless.

No one has dared to jump since that terrible accident 10 years ago when a girl was paralyzed. People say her ghost still haunts the Nail.

See what happens when Scooter and Elisa try *Jumping the Nail.*

## Byars, Betsy. **McMummy.**

Viking, 1993, 149pp. Elementary School & Up.

■ **HORROR.** *Magic; secrets; supernatural.*

■ **RELATED BOOKS:** *Shape-Changer* by Bill Brittain; *The Plant that Ate Dirty Socks* series by Nancy McArthur; *The Boggart* series by Susan Cooper.

 *Note:* *A harmless, humorous horror story for younger readers*

"Batty Batson, go to your room. No more lying!"

"It's true, Mom. Mozie can't go alone to Professor Orloff's greenhouse because of this McMummy. Mozie saw a plant that is a pod shaped like a mummy. We call it McMummy. He's scared to go there alone. He said the pod turned in his direction, like radar. I promised to go in the greenhouse with him."

My mom just didn't get it. She just wouldn't let me explain. Even as we were speaking, that plant was turning into a little shop of horrors. First, McMummy started to hummmm-mm, sounding like the purr of a tiger. Somehow McMummy shed its roots and decided to explore the area, even entering a beauty contest. I don't think the plant won first prize. As a matter of fact, McMummy broke up the place.

For the full hilarious story about this Abominable Lettuce, read *McMummy*.

## Bystedt, Karen Hardy. **Before They were Famous: In Their Own Words.**

Design by Fredrik Bystedt. (Pbk.) Oslo, 1996, 160pp. Middle School & Up.

■ **NONFICTION.** *Show business; self-identity.*

■ **RELATED BOOKS:** *Hollywood and Whine* by Boze Hadleigh; *Pretty in Pink: The Golden Age of Teenage Movies* by Jonathan Bernstein.

*Note:* *The author's photographs are revealing as well. Recommended book for a young adult reluctant reader.*

Who were Brad Pitt, Sandra Bullock, Melanie Griffith, and David Duchovny before they were famous? What were their dreams and aspirations?

The author shows you with photographs and interviews. She was fortunate enough to meet them all before they became celebrities. Here they are, in their own words.

Now you can know these icons *Before They were Famous.*

# Cadnum, Michael. *In a Dark Wood.*

Orchard, 1998, 246pp. Middle School & Up. An ALA Best Book for Young Adults; nominee for the L.A. Times Teen Book Award.

■ **FOLKLORE.** *Abuse; class conflict; Great Britain; Middle Ages; revenge; rivalry.*

■ **RELATED BOOKS:** *The Merry Adventures of Robin Hood* by Howard Pyle; *The Outlaws of Sherwood* by Robin McGinley; *The Pirate's Son* by Geraldine McCaughrean.

 *Note:* This ageless story is told from the viewpoint of the Sheriff of Nottingham. The author does not shirk from descriptions of filth, violence, and sexual desire. Useful for writing classes as a comparison of viewpoints.

"Sherriff Nottingham, the king is displeased with you. He is concerned about an outlaw in Sherwood Forest named Robin Hood. Never forget that there are dozens who could replace you."

Geoffrey, the Sheriff of Nottingham, understood the threat implied by the king's squire. Yet finding Robin Hood was a difficult task. Perhaps an archery contest would lure Robin Hood from the dark wood.

Alas, Robin Hood did not appear, only a strange potter who could draw a fine bow given to him by Robin Hood. However, the potter promises to take Geoffrey to Robin Hood. Of course, the potter is Robin Hood in disguise. To Geoffrey's humiliation, instead of being honorably killed, he is entertained, given a gift, and sent on his way. Geoffrey can never forgive this act of generosity. He orders his men to search the dark wood and to murder this merry group of outlaws!

# Campbell, Lady Colin. *The Real Diana.*

St. Martin's, 1998, 308pp.; (Pbk.) Mass Market Paperback, 1998, 352pp. Middle School & Up.

■ **BIOGRAPHY.** *Death; eating disorders; Great Britain; love; politics; women's issues.*

■ **RELATED BOOKS:** *The Day Diana Died* by Christopher Anderson; *Diana: Her True Story* by Andrew Morton; *Diana in Search of Herself* by Sally Bedell Smith.

 *Note:* Probably the best of all the Diana books, this is recommended for reluctant readers fascinated by royalty.

Who was the real Princess Diana? Was she Shy Di or a Plastic Princess? A naive young girl or a manipulative media teaser? Diana was all these things and more. Diana was more complex and complicated than her public ever suspected.

The author knew both Diana and Charles before and after their marriage. Their romance and divorce had been reported by many outsiders, but the author was a constant participant and observer of the social and royal scene.

Here is Princess Diana: clever, childlike, cunning and canny.

Here is *The Real Diana.*

## Canfield, Jack; Mark Victor Hansen; Kimberly Kirberger, editors. *Chicken Soup for the Teenage Soul II: 101 More Stories of Life, Love and Learning.*

(Pbk.) Health Communications, 1998, 351pp. Middle School & Up.

- ■ **SHORT STORIES, ESSAYS.** *Ethics; divorce; friendship; peer pressure; religion; self-identity; school.*
- ■ **RELATED BOOKS:** *Chicken Soup for the Teenage Soul* edited by Jack Canfield, et al; *Wisdom of the Ages* by Wayne Dyer.

*Note:* This collection of teens' personal stories covers relationships, friendship, love, family and peer pressure. Select a poem or short essay to read aloud. My favorites are "Practical Application" (relationships), "McDonald's" (on love and kindness), "The Cheerleader" (family), and "Remember Me?" (learning lessons).

## Capote, Truman. *In Cold Blood: A True Account of a Multiple Murder and Its Consequences.*

(Pbk.) Vintage, 1994, 343pp. First published in 1965. High School & Up.

- ■ **NONFICTION.** *Crime; death; politics.*
- ■ **RELATED BOOKS:** Books by Ann Rule; *The Executioner's Song* by Norman Mailer; *Who Killed My Daughter?* by Lois Duncan; *Another City, Not My Own* by Dominic Dunne.

*Note:* Truman Capote was one of the first to write the nonfiction novel, and his journalistic style is still being imitated by true-crime writers. This book is required reading in some high schools, and students rate this one highly. Surprisingly, despite its content, this has little graphic violence.

One morning on November 15, 1959, in Holcomb, Kansas, four shotgun blasts ended six lives. Those sounds changed the innocence of midwestern America forever. A family was killed. *In cold blood.*

The Clutters were respected and liked in their community. Two of the victims, Nancy and Kenyon, were young adults. It took months for the four murders to be solved. The murderers, Perry Smith and Dick Hickock, were former convicts who murdered the family for money. They didn't know that the Clutters kept all their money in the bank. The murderers escaped with only $40.

On October 25, 1962, Perry Smith and Dick Hickock were executed by the state of Kansas by hanging. *In cold blood.*

The author, Truman Capote, interviewed the killers as well as people who knew the family. Here is the true account of a multiple murder and its consequences.

# Carter, Alden R. **Bull Catcher.**

Scholastic, 1997, 279pp. Middle School & Up. A Best Book for Young Adults.

■ **SPORTS.** *Abuse; Asian Americans; men's issues; peer pressure; school; single parents; sports (baseball).*

■ **RELATED BOOKS:** *Staying Fat for Sarah Byrnes* and *Athletic Shorts* by Chris Crutcher.

 *This book has some profanity. Phuong is pronounced Fong.*

Jeff and I have different ideas, but throughout it all, we've remained best friends. That's because we agree on one thing: God created the world in six days, and, on day seven, he created baseball.

Running down the line between third base and home, you'll find the Bull. That's me. In my catcher's gear, I look like a bull. One time a guy ran into the Bull, and he broke his nose. The Bull is fearless.

Through my catcher's mask, I've observed many players on the field of life. There's Phuong, whom Jeff and I developed into a magnificent pitcher. There's Billy, whose dad uses Billy's arm for a punching bag. There's Billy's girlfriend Sandi, a girl I'd love to catch. As always, there's Jeff, who has stuck by me all four years. We might not have always hit home runs, but we kept on swinging.

Join me, *Bull Catcher,* in our game. Watch me hit that ball out of the ball park.

# Chambers, Aidan. **Now I Know.**

(Pbk.) Random House Children's Books/Red Fox, 1987, 237pp. Middle School & Up.

■ **REALISTIC FICTION.** *Ethics; Great Britain; love; religion; secrets.*

■ **RELATED BOOKS:** *Jacob Have I Loved* by Katherine Paterson; *Memoirs of a Bookbat* by Kathryn Lasky.

 *This book has a cult following among children's literature advocates because various religious philosophies are woven into a surrealistic mystery. Recommended for a mature reader who enjoys psychological mysteries.*

A bizarre murder has occurred.

A young man has been found crucified on a rusty metal cross. The cross was dangling from a crane in a scrap yard. Now the body has disappeared.

A police investigator sets out to solve the mystery of the missing hanging corpse. Nik, a teenage boy, is also doing an investigation; he's researching a film about the contemporary life of Jesus. During his investigation Nik meets Julie, a believer in Christianity and Jesus.

The three investigate the mystery of the disappearing body so they can say with conviction, *"Now I know."*

## Chang, Pan-Mei Natasha. *Bound Feet and Western Dress.*

Doubleday, 1996, 215pp. (Pbk.) Anchor Books, 1997, 215pp. Middle School & Up. An ALA Best Book for Young Adults.

■ Biography. *Asia (China); Asian Americans; aging; death; divorce; ethics; immigrants; women's issues.*

■ Related books: *Red Scarf Girl: A Memoir of the Cultural Revolution* by Ji Li Jiang; *The Joy Luck Club* by Amy Tan; *Women of the Silk* by Gail Tsukiyama; *Red China Blues: My Long March from Mao to Now* by Jan Wong.

*Note:* The author, a first-generation Chinese-American, tells the story of her great-aunt's remarkable life. In altering voices, Chang juxtaposes her own life experiences as a Chinese-American to her great aunt's life in China and Europe. Recommended for book reports, group readings, feminist studies, and any study of China from 1900-1950.

In China, a woman is nothing. Please remember this as I tell you my story. I was born Chang Yu-i in 1900 near Shanghai. My family thinks I was born tough, like a man. I think life made me hard.

I was brought up to honor and respect my family. However, I was born into changing times and had two faces; one listened to the old, the other listened for the new. When I was four years, my mother bound my feet. I screamed for three days. My Second Brother insisted that my mother untie my bound feet. Early on, my family learned that I could not be bound by certain ancient Chinese customs.

However, at 15, I obeyed my family and married the man they selected for me. At 22, I divorced him without asking their permission, causing shame to my family. I ended up being a successful businesswoman, on the bridge between two cultures, the East and the West, *Bound Feet and Western Dress.*

I'm not so sure we can escape our fate. With the many twists and turns of my life, I have learned to bend with the curves. My entire life, I have tried to fulfill my duty. I hope I have made my family proud.

## Clarke, Arthur C. **Childhood's End.**

(Pbk.) Ballantine Books, 1953, 218pp. Middle School & Up.

■ **SCIENCE FICTION.** *End of the world; ethics; survival; war.*

■ **RELATED BOOKS:** *Strangers in a Strange Land* by Robert Heinlein; *Fahrenheit 451* by Ray Bradbury; *Songs of Distant Earth, The Hammer of God,* and *Rendezvous with Rama* by Arthur C. Clarke.

*Note:* Many will recognize that the movie **Independence Day** borrowed many elements from this book, but this book contains more chilling depth. The ending still provides a jolt. Highly recommended for all types of readers.

Without warning, spaceships appear over major cities of the world. These *Overlords* remain overhead for 50 years, silently observing the Earthlings. During those years, disease, poverty, and war are abolished. Somehow the threatening presence of these aliens helps bring stability to Mankind.

Without warning, life begins to change for Earthlings. Now the *Overlords* have another agenda. The aliens plan to abolish one more problem. They plan to eliminate humans!

## Clements, Andrew. *Frindle.*

Pictures by Brian Selznick. Simon and Schuster for Young People, 1996, 105pp. Elementary School & Up. Winner of the Christopher Award.

■ **REALISTIC FICTION.** *Responsibility; school.*

■ **RELATED BOOKS:** *Nothing But the Truth* by Avi; *Aldo Applesauce* and *Class Clown* by Johanna Hurwitz; *Freckle Juice* by Judy Blume; *Holes* and *There's a Boy in the Girl's Bathroom* by Louis Sachar.

 *Note:* A humorous yet in-depth look at the power of language with the two sides eventually coming to a meeting of the minds. Highly recommended read-aloud or group read.

Everything Nick heard about his teacher was true: Don't mess with the Lone Granger.

Mrs. Granger loved the dictionary. Her frequent remark to her fifth grade class was "Look it up. That's why we have the dictionary."

Nick had no particular use for the dictionary, but he loved words. That's why he thought up the word *frindle,* another word for pen. During class, Nick had his friends ask for a *frindle,* driving his teacher crazy. In response, Mrs. Granger posted this notice on the main bulletin board by the office:

*Anyone who is heard using the word* **frindle** *instead of the word* **pen** *will stay after school and write this sentence one hundred times:* ***I am writing this punishment with a pen.***

*Mrs. Granger*

Who will win this *Frindle* war, Nick or his teacher?

## Colman, Penny. *Corpses, Coffins, and Crypts: A History of Burial.*

With bibliography, glossary, index and 130 photographs. Henry Holt, 1997, 212pp. Middle School & Up. Top 10 Best Books for Young Adults.

■ **NONFICTION.** *Death; science.*

■ **RELATED BOOKS:** *Grave Matters: A Lively History of Death Around the World* by Nigel Barley; *The Celebration of Death* edited by Peter Metcalf and Richard Huntington; *The Definitive Guide to Underground Humor* edited by Edward Bergin.

 *Note:* The chapters analyze these topics: understanding death; decomposition, transplants, autopsies and embalming; cremation and other ways to dispose of corpses; urns, coffins, crypts, and mausoleums; cemeteries; burial customs; and images of art. Colman is also open about her personal experiences with death, saying this book is for all ages. However, the topic might be disturbing to some students. Recommended for research and for some students who have experienced a personal loss.

Throughout history, people have been declared dead when they really weren't.

In England, in the 1500s, Matthew Wall was revived when the pallbearers dropped his coffin.

In Scotland, in the 1600s, Marjorie Elphinstone rose from her grave when grave robbers disturbed her newly buried coffin. Marjorie ended up walking home, giving her grieving family quite a shock.

Once a doctor cut into a supposedly dead person who jumped up and grabbed the doctor's throat. The "dead person" survived, but the doctor died of a stroke.

Those true stories are contained in this book, *Corpses, Coffins and Crypts.* This book is about death. The author, Penny Colman, talks openly about this forbidden subject. Death is a fascinating topic. Why not discuss it?

## Conford, Ellen. *Crush.*

HarperCollins, 1998, 138pp. Middle School & Up. An ALA Best Book for Young Adults; Quick Pick for Reluctant Young Adult Readers.

■ **SHORT STORIES.** *Love; peer pressure; school.*

■ **RELATED BOOKS:** *The Girl Who Invented Romance* by Caroline D. Cooney; *A Royal Pain* and *Genie with the Light Blue Hair* by Ellen Conford.

 *Ellen Conford's breezy, light-hearted books are recommended for the romance lover.*

The students at Cutter's Forge High School are buzzing about the Sweetheart Stomp, the Valentine's dance. Who will go as a couple? Who will stay home?

Amy and Batso are in love. If only Amy would cut her fingernails ... If only Batso would cut his hair ... On the night of the dance ... Well, all I can say is be careful what you wish. It might come true!

B. J. wants a date for the dance. She makes a wish for a date and throws a penny in the fountain of Cupid. Again, be careful what you wish. It might come true!

Enjoy these nine stories of romance in *Crush.*

## Conly, Jane Leslie. *While No One Was Watching.*

Henry Holt, 1998, 233pp. Middle School & Up. Fiction Honors winner of the Boston Globe-Horn Book Awards.

■ **REALISTIC FICTION.** *Adoption; crime; physical disability; ethics; friendship; problem parents; runaways; secrets; single parents.*

■ **RELATED BOOKS:** *Crazy Lady!* by Jane Leslie Conly; *Homecoming* by Cynthia Voight; *A Place to Call Home* by Jackie French Koller.

 *Jane Leslie Conly is the daughter of Newbery winner Robert C. O'Brien and has continued his* **The Rats of NIMH** *series. This realistic drama presents five character viewpoints: mentally-challenged Frankie; his sister, Angela, an imaginative liar; his 11-year-old brother, Earl, a petty thief; Addie, confident and secure; and Maynard, an adopted Indian son with a single parent. Recommended especially for aspiring writers.*

While no one was watching, the robbery occurred. Three neglected, troubled children left their poverty-stricken neighborhood to steal bicycles. No one cared that they ran away. No one noticed. Seven-year-old Frankie went along because he was afraid to stay home alone.

When Frankie saw the caged rabbit, he insisted on taking it home. Frankie hid the rabbit under his bed, bringing it food whenever he could.

Flag was Addie's beloved pet. She was devastated and furious that the police wouldn't help her find her rabbit. Addie and her neighbor Maynard were determined to find Flag. For the first time, while no one was watching, they entered Frankie's part of town. Nothing was safe in Frankie's part of town.

In Frankie's world, grownups disappeared and dads stayed gone. Children were never protected. In this world, anything could happen and often did. And it usually happened while *No One was Watching.*

# Cooney, Caroline B. *Burning Up.*

Delacorte, 1999, 230pp. Middle School & Up.

■ **REALISTIC FICTION.** *Abuse; African Americans; ethics; interracial relations; problem parents; racism.*

■ **RELATED BOOKS:** *Spite Fences* by Trudy Krisher; *To Kill a Mockingbird* by Harper Lee; *Black Like Me* by John Howard Griffin; *Bat 6* by Virginia Wolff.

**Note:** *Teens will be caught up in the mystery and inspired by Cooney's message that people should not remain apathetic about racism. Highly recommended.*

"Fire!" Macey screamed. "Get out! Everybody out!"

As Macey and Venita ran into the next Sunday school room, Macey's hair was blazing. Austin pulled off his T-shirt and yanked it over Macey's head, suffocating the fire and Macey. Macey yelled, but Austin pinned Macey to the wall so he could put out the fire.

"You okay, girl? There's an arsonist going after African-American churches. Guy probably looked in, saw us painting—whatever." Venita shuddered.

"Yeah, I'm fine, I guess." Macey's head was literally smoking.

*Arson.* Macey's mind went all the way back to 1959, to the past when another building burned. Inside the barn, on the very street where she lived, was an African-American science teacher. Macey was going to write a report on this for a local history project, but everyone kept telling her to forget about it. Now, 40 years later, the same thing was happening. *Arson.*

Looks like things haven't changed, Macey thought. Austin and I wouldn't even be in this section of town if we weren't volunteering. Life is still racially segregated in Connecticut with Austin and I attending the white school with all the privileges. Venita and her friends attend a school that has no computers or textbooks. And now arson!

You know what? Maddie continued her thoughts. I'll bet these two fires are connected, even though they didn't start from the same match. I'm burning up to make the connection between the past and the present. Someday I will.

*Burning Up by Caroline B. Cooney, copyright © 1999, Delacorte.*

**C**

## Cooney, Caroline B. **Flash Fire.**

(Pbk.) Scholastic, 1995, 198pp. Middle School & Up. An ALA Best Book for Young Adults.

■ **ADVENTURE.** *Adoption; class conflict; death; disability (mental); Hispanic Americans; problem parents; responsibility; self-identity; survival.*

■ **RELATED BOOKS:** *Flight Number 116 is Down* by Caroline B. Cooney; *Alive! The Story of the Andes Survivors* by Piers Paul Read; *SOS Titanic* by Eve Bunting.

 *Thanks to the **Titanic** phenomenon, disaster novels have become popular teen picks. This quick-read with its facts on fires, mud slides, and California lifestyles might be entertaining to reluctant readers.*

Why, Danna wanted to know, can't I be a terrorist or date one? But no, she whined to herself. What am I doing? Vocabulary.

Danna was clueless that only five miles away, firemen were trying to contain an ordinary brush fire. Quickly the fire spread and began to surround the wealthy neighborhood on Pinch Mountain. As Danna and her neighbors learned, fire had no boundaries, no division by social classes. Instead, this flash fire could consume and change their lives forever.

## Cooney, Caroline B. **Twins.**

(Pbk.) Scholastic, 1994, 183pp. Middle School & Up.

■ **HORROR.** *Crime; death; peer pressure; revenge; rivalry; secrets; survival.*

■ **RELATED BOOKS:** *Singularity* by William Sleator; *Fear Street* series by R. L. Stine.

 *This is a harmless thriller on the order of Christopher Pike, but other books by Caroline B. Cooney are spellbinding: **The Face on the Milk Carton; Driver's Ed.** Give the horror fans this book, and then lead them to some of Cooney's realistic fiction.*

Identical twins Mary Lee and Madrigal look alike and talk alike. No one can tell the twins apart, not even their parents.

When Madrigal is killed in a car accident, Mary Lee assumes Madrigal's identity. Mary Lee always admired her sister and now she had her chance to go to Madrigal's boarding school to meet all Madrigal's friends. Little did Mary Lee know just how evil her identical twin really was!

## Corbett, Sara. *Venus to the Hoop: A Gold Medal Year in Women's Basketball.*

Doubleday, 1997, 342pp. Middle School & Up. An ALA Best Book for Young Adults.

■ **NONFICTION SPORTS.** *African Americans; sports (basketball); women's issues.*

■ **RELATED BOOKS:** *Shooting from the Outside: How a Coach and Her Olympic Team Transformed Women's Basketball* by Tara Vanderveer; *Full Court Press: A Season in the Life of a Winning Basketball Team and the Women Who Made It Happen* by Lauren Kessler.

 *Corbett tells their story in a narrative style that is engaging. Recommended for all types of readers.*

They played for the gold. They played for the glory. They played for the future of women athletes everywhere.

In the spring of 1995, twelve extraordinary women were selected to represent the United States in the yearlong march to the 1996 Olympics. These basketball players included a "female Michael Jordan," a runway model, and a forward who barely survived a car accident that left her in a coma. In spite of their differences, these women combined their talents to win all 51 games they played, eventually winning the Olympic gold medal.

The author, Sara Corbett, was given exclusive access to the team for the duration. She tells their amazing story, how they came together, both on and off the court. Learn how this other Dream Team won the gold and the hearts of millions of fans.

## Cormier, Robert. *Heroes: A Novel.*

Delacorte, 1998, 135pp. Middle School & Up. An ALA Best Book for Young Adults; Quick Pick for Reluctant Young Adult Readers.

■ **REALISTIC FICTION.** *Physical disability; ethics; Europe (France); revenge; sexual abuse; suicide; war; World War II.*

■ **RELATED BOOKS:** *Soldier's Heart* by Gary Paulsen; *A Farewell to Arms* by Ernest Hemingway; *The Red Badge of Courage* by Stephen Crane.

 *Note: Cormier raises many ethical questions about heroism, guilt, and forgiveness. Like the movie **Saving Private Ryan,** this story confirms that war is hell and leaves many shattered lives.*

My name is Francis Joseph Casavant. I've just returned from fighting the war. I have no face.

I do have eyes, but no ears or nose. I wear a scarf that covers my face. I'm a horror to everyone, especially myself.

People call me a hero. How can I be a hero if I plan to kill Larry LaSalle?

People call Larrry LaSalle a hero. How can he be a hero after what he did to Nicole Renard?

I guess the writer F. Scott Fitzgerald said it best: "Show me a hero and I will write you a tragedy."

## Cormier, Robert. *Tenderness.*

(Pbk.) Bantam Doubleday Dell Books for Young Readers, 1997, 229pp. Middle School & Up. An ALA Best Book for Young Adults.

■ **REALISTIC FICTION.** *Crime; death; ethics; mental illness; love; runaways; sex and sexuality; sexual abuse.*

■ **RELATED BOOKS:** *Loves Music, Loves to Dance* by Mary Higgins Clark; *In Cold Blood* by Truman Capote.

*Note:* Cormier's journalistic style always packs a wallop. This one explores the mind of a serial killer and of the woman who loves him. Also, try Cormier's **The Chocolate War** for another jolt.

It had been so easy to lure the girl away from the mall. With his fake limp, Eric got her attention at the bus stop. Then he turned on The Charm. Usually The Charm worked. It didn't work on his stepfather Harvey. That's why Eric had to kill him.

Eric thought of his murdered mother and stepfather as his victim lay in his arms, limp and still. He laid her carefully in the bushes, brushed away her long dark hair, and gave her a kiss. Bliss filled him. He had never known such tenderness before.

He knew he must find *Tenderness* again.

## Creech, Sharon. *Bloomability.*

Joanna Cotler Books, 1998, 273pp. (Pbk.) HarperCollins Children's, 1999, 288pp. Middle School & Up. An ALA Best Book for Young Adults.

■ **REALISTIC FICTION.** *Europe (Switzerland); friendship; problem parents; school; sports (skiing).*

■ **RELATED BOOKS:** *Chasing Redbird* and *Walk Two Moons* by Sharon Creech; *Real Friends* by Susan Sharpe; *The Tulip Touch* by Anne Fine.

*Note:* The main character, Dinnie Doone, misses her parents who are living in Bybanks, Kentucky. Creech's **Chasing Redbird** and Newbery winner **Walk Two Moons** have characters from Bybanks, but these are not a series, only a detail that adds intriguing depth.

I put a sign in my bedroom window that said, KIDNAPPED! HELD AGAINST MY WILL!

Aunt Sandy said, "People may not be able to read that sign in English. Here, take this English-Italian dictionary."

That night I looked up the Italian word for *kidnapped*. I picked one of several choices for my new sign, *portare via a forza.* Aunt Sandy said, "I think that phrase translates as being held by force. It implies that your Uncle Max and I are forcing you to live in Switzerland. Some people would think it a great opportunity to live in a beautiful country. I know you miss your parents, Dinnie, but you'll make friends at the American School."

I thought about what Aunt Sandy said. Maybe I'm just bothered about my parents always dumping me, like I'm a package they don't want. That's a reality that's just too painful to face. So I give my aunt and uncle grief.

Slowly, I removed the sign from my bedroom window.

## Crompton, Anne Eliot. *Gawain and Lady Green.*

Donald I. Fine Books, 1997, 201pp. Middle School & Up. An ALA Best Book for Young Adults.

■ **FOLKLORE.** *Class conflict; ethics; Great Britain; love; magic; Middle Ages; revenge; supernatural.*

■ **RELATED BOOKS:** *I am Mordred* by Nancy Springer; *Merlin's Harp* by Anne Eliot Crompton; Mary Stewart's *Merlin Trilogy: The Crystal Cave; The Hollow Hills; The Last Enchantment.*

 *Note:* Inspired by the medieval Middle English poem, **Sir Gawain and the Green Knight**, this retelling of an Arthurian tale explores themes of hypocrisy, betrayal, romantic love, and female power. Highly recommended, especially for older literature classes and mature readers who enjoy folklore and Arthurian legends.

Long ago, storytellers sang the tale of Gawain, a knight in King Arthur's court at Camelot. One ballad claimed Gawain arrived in an infidel land of goddess-worshipping Druids, was crowned May King and destined to marry the May Queen. To his horror, Gawain discovered that, at Sumersend, he would lose his head. With only a knife and a horse, Gawain escaped certain death and returned to Camelot.

Many full moons later, a grotesque Green Knight arrived in Camelot, carrying an ax and challenging any knight to cut off his head. Gawain reluctantly accepted the challenge and chopped off the Green Knight's head. The Green Knight calmly picked up his severed head and spoke: "Meet your fate on New Year's Day at the Green Chapel."

Within a year, once again, Gawain must face certain death. Unknown to Gawain, he will also face Lady Green. Lady Green and he shared a secret past, a past of bittersweet memories.

Discover what next transpires between the doomed knight and the mysterious sorceress, *Gawain and Lady Green.*

## Crowe, Carole. *Sharp Horns on the Moon.*

Boyds Mills, 1998, 112pp. Elementary School & Up.

■ Horror. *Death; family; rivalry; supernatural.*

■ Related books: *Wait Till Helen Comes* by Mary Downing Hahn; *Stonewords* by Pam Conrad.

 Note: A better-than-average horror read with a surprise ending. Recommended for those who like the **Goosebumps** series.

While snorkeling off Boneyard Reef, I breathed in my loneliness, the bubbles of water surrounding my mask. Would I always live in the only house at the far end of Mystic Island? Would I never go to school or have a friend?

Suddenly, through my diver's mask, I saw the shimmering image of a girl's face. Just as suddenly, she disappeared. I felt a warmth and pressure on my hand. Inside my fist was a Spanish gold coin.

That ghost, Eleanor Moneypenny, became my first friend. She's strange, though. She keeps calling me by my dead mother's name, Rose. Once I overheard my father and Aunt Ethel talking and they think some kind of spirit killed my mother.

What danger lies in becoming friends with a ghost? Am I doomed to the same fate as my mother?

## Davis, Jenny. *Checking On the Moon.*

Orchard, 1991, 208pp. Middle School & Up. An Accelerated Reader selection.

■ **REALISTIC FICTION.** *Aging; crime; family; politics; responsibility; work.*

■ **RELATED BOOKS:** *The Sabbath Garden* by Patricia Greene; *Bambi and the Bel-Air Mall Rats* by Richard Peck; *Western Wind* by Paula Fox.

*Note:* Jenny Davis writes with a realism that doesn't date. Recommended for book reports and group reads.

My name is Cab Jones. That's right. Cab. My mom gave me that name because I was born in a taxi. I was born in Pittsburgh, but I've lived in Blue Cloud, Texas, all my 12 years.

Then, *on the last day of school,* my mom informed me that my brother and I were going to spend the summer with my grandmother. Now, first of all, I've never met my grandmother. I have no interest in living in my mom's hometown outside Pittsburgh. I don't want to work at my grandmother's restaurant *EATS.*

Then, when I arrived, I found out Washco was a *slum.* Crime was rampant. At least two crimes were committed a week. Something had to be done, and the only way to do it was to involve the whole neighborhood. Strangely enough, that was when things became interesting. The more people I met, the more attached I became to the neighborhood.

Are you ready for this? I ended up having the most exciting summer of my life! Find out why. Read the book Jenny Davis wrote about me: *Checking on the Moon.*

---

## Deuker, Carl. *On the Devil's Court.*

(Pbk.) Avon Flare, 1988, 252pp. Middle School & Up. An ALA Best Book for Young Adults. An Accelerated Reader selection.

■ **SPORTS.** *Ethics; men's issues; peer pressure; problem parents; school; sports (basketball); substance abuse (alcohol).*

■ **RELATED BOOKS:** *Danger Zone* by David Klass; *The Heart of a Champion* by Carl Deuker; *Dr. Faustus* by Christopher Marlowe.

*Note:* Carl Deuker's books combine action-packed sports with intriguing ethical issues. Recommended for sports fans as well as students who have studied Christopher Marlowe's **Dr. Faustus.**

Not long ago, my father gave me a book to read: *Dr. Faustus* by Christopher Marlowe. This book was written hundreds of years ago, but the story is so cool. This doctor had a great life, but he wanted unlimited power. So this Faustus sells his soul to the devil for 24 years of power.

What's so weird is that I am Joseph Faust. It's so strange to be named after someone who made a pact with the devil. There aren't many people with our last name. If Dr. Faustus were a person who really lived, and the book said he did, then it was possible he was an ancestor of mine. I don't know whether to be proud or ashamed.

All I know is that somehow, like Dr. Faustus, I must have made a pact with the devil.

Odd things are happening. Due to another player's injury, I am suddenly promoted to play varsity basketball. At the first game, I scored 30 points! I became a hero overnight. I'm even getting more respect from my father, the great Professor Joseph Faust, Sr.

What kind of bargain did I make *On the Devil's Court?*

## Deuker, Carl. *Painting the Black.*

Houghton Mifflin, 1997, 248pp. (Pbk.) Mass Market Paperback, 1999, 248pp. Middle School & Up.

■ **SPORTS.** *Ethics; physical disability; friendship; peer pressure; sexual abuse; sports (baseball, football).*

■ **RELATED BOOKS:** *Bull Catcher* by Alden Carter; *Tangerine* by Edward Bloor; *Peeling the Onion* by Wendy Orr.

*Note:* This high-interest novel uses the competition and drama of sports as a metaphor for the angst of adolescence. Recommended for all types of readers.

Josh Daniels was a genius at *Painting the Black.* When he was on the pitcher's mound, he could send that ball over the edge of the plate, right there on the borderline. Experts call that kind of pitching *Painting the Black* and Josh lived on that borderline. I know because I was his catcher. I was also his best friend.

In real life, too, Josh lived on that borderline. He seemed to straddle the line between what was right and wrong. He made excuses for his decisions, but I questioned his choices. Why did he sit in the cafeteria, center stage, and hoot and holler at the girls? Once, for a joke, in front of everybody in the cafeteria, he yanked up Celeste's halter top! For days, he joked about her pink underwear.

Josh's latest joke wasn't so humorous. He and his cronies tried to assault Monica Roy, a student who was vocal about Josh's pranks. Luckily, I was able to stop the assault. To my horror, I recognized Josh behind his wolf mask. Josh begged me not to tell, and so far I've been lying to the police, my parents, and my teachers.

Now I feel like I'm the one painting the black, straddling the line between right and wrong behavior. Should I report Josh? Should I snitch on my best friend? What would you do?

## Dillard, Annie. *An American Childhood.*

HarperCollins, 1987, 255pp. High School & Up. An Accelerated Reader selection.

■ **BIOGRAPHY.** *Ethics; family; hobbies; interracial relations; rites of passage.*

■ **RELATED BOOKS:** *A Gift from the Sea* by Anne Morrow Lindbergh; *A Tree Grows in Brooklyn* by Betty Smith.

*Note:* The author reflects on all turns of life, even the ordinary, and does it in a style that encourages all of us to write our biographies. Recommend this to aspiring writers.

I grew up in Pittsburgh during the 1950s. I had many favorite places, but I can still vividly recall the Homewood Library. This was in the Negro section of town and was our nearest library. On the library was graven *Free to the People.*

My favorite book was *The Field Book of Ponds and Streams.* I so longed to write the author Ann Haven Morgan—who had to be a man, surely—and tell "him" I discovered this jewel in the dark near the marble floor at the Homewood Library.

I loved reading the book pocket to see who had checked out this book. All kinds of names were scrawled on the checkout card. Apparently there were many Negro adults who also shared my enthusiasm for dragonfly larvae and single-celled plants.

Who were these people? Might I contact them someday? How very odd is this connection between the reader and author. Don't you agree?

## Duane, Diane. *To Visit the Queen.*

(Pbk.) Warner Books, 1999, 354pp. With glossary and epilogue. Second in a series; **The Book of Night with Wind** precedes. Middle School & Up.

■ **FANTASY.** *Animals (cats); end of the world; Great Britain; supernatural; time travel.*

■ **RELATED BOOKS:** *The Book of Night with Wind* by Diane Duane; *Howl's Moving Castle* by Diane Wynne Jones; *The Cat Who Wished to be a Man* by Lloyd Alexander; *To Say Nothing of the Dog ...* by Connie Willis.

 *Note:* A satisfying blend of humor and horror makes this one a winner with fantasy and cat lovers. Also has its own cat language, such as ehhif for human beings.

"I never get to have any fun with wizardry," Arhu complained. "It's all work and dull stuff."

"Oh, really?" Urruah angrily shook his feline paw at his apprentice. "Perhaps you will consider this crisis something to purr about. The evil Lone Power has induced a time gate to malfunction, allowing unsuspecting humans to slide from the past or into the past. One man has left a scientific encyclopedia in the timeslipping gate, changing history forever. The past will be altered and that will change our future."

"Which precisely means, my dear colleagues, that we must act quickly," said Rhiow, swishing her townhouse cat tail. "We must stabilize the timeline. We feline wizards must return to Victorian England in 1816. Like Dick Whittington's cat, we must go to London *To Visit the Queen.*"

# Duncan, Lois. *Gallows Hill.*

(Pbk.) Bantam Doubleday Dell Books for Young Readers, 1997, 229pp. Middle School & Up.

■ **HORROR.** *Peer pressure; rivalry; school; single parents; stepparents; supernatural; women's issues.*

■ **RELATED BOOKS:** *Summer of Fear* and *Stranger with My Face* by Lois Duncan; *The Witch of Blackbird Pond* by Elizabeth George Speare; *A Break with Charity (A Stitch in Time)* by Ann Rinaldi.

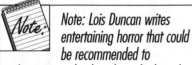

*Note: Lois Duncan writes entertaining horror that could be recommended to elementary school readers who love the* **Goosebumps** *series, or to any reluctant reader. Includes a bibliography about the Salem witch trials.*

It was a dirty job, but someone had to do it.

Someone had to be the gypsy fortune-teller at the senior class carnival in Pine Crest, Massachusetts. That perfect someone was Sarah Zoltanne. She was the new girl with the exotic name. Since Sarah wouldn't know any of her classmates, if she provided accurate information, she would bring in a high financial return.

What the students didn't know was that Eric Garrett, the president of the senior class, had rigged a hidden microphone in Sarah's ear. Kyra, her soon-to-be stepsister, told Sarah the relevant details. Sarah improvised her gypsy dialogue. It was all a scam. Or so they thought.

However, Sarah's predictions began to come true. As predicted, Charlie Goodman fell down a flight of stairs. Likewise, Debbie Rice's sister ran away with Debbie's boyfriend, the bodybuilder. Cindy learned what really happened to Dorcas, her childhood doll. Apparently, when Sarah gazed into the crystal paperweight, she saw images that represented both the future and the past.

Is Sarah a witch? That's what everyone in Pine Crest is saying. Hundreds of years ago, witches were hanged on *Gallows Hill.* Of course, today they don't hang witches. Or do they?

## Duncan, Lois. *I Know What You Did Last Summer.*

(Pbk.) Pocket Books, 1973, 198pp. Middle School & Up. An Accelerated Reader selection.

■ **MYSTERIES, THRILLERS.** *Crime; death; ethics; movie novels; peer pressure; responsibility; revenge; secrets; substance abuse.*

■ **RELATED BOOKS:** other books by Lois Duncan, including *Don't Look Behind You.*

 *Note:* This book is now a horror movie. Unlike the movie, this book has no graphic violence and can also be recommended to younger mystery lovers.

*I KNOW WHAT YOU DID LAST SUMMER*

Julie found this unsigned note waiting for her at the breakfast table. Her heart skipped a beat.

Helen received her message taped on her apartment door. It was a picture of a bicycle.

Their friend Ray received a letter at the college he was attending. Inside was an old newspaper clipping that stated:

*A 10-year-old boy was killed last night in a hit-and-run accident. Dead is David Gregg who was riding his bicycle when he was struck by an unidentified automobile. Police are looking for the car that struck David Gregg.*

Barry received an anonymous phone call at the college dormitory: "I know what you did last summer."

"How do you know?" Barry demanded.

"I was there. I have proof. Meet me on the athletic field in 10 minutes."

Barry was carried back from the athletic field, shot and seriously injured.

It looks as if someone knows the terrible secret that all four friends have been hiding for almost a year. They were involved in a hit-and-run accident that killed a young boy. It looks as if that person plans revenge.

What should they do?

## Duffey, Betsy. *Alien for Rent.*

Delacorte, 1999, 71pp. Elementary School & Up.

■ **SCIENCE FICTION.** *Abuse; school; supernatural.*

■ **RELATED FICTION:** *Stinker from Space* by Pamela Service; *Black Suits from Outer Space* by Gene DeWeese; *My Teacher Is an Alien* series by Bruce Coville.

"There's no such thing as aliens," J.P. said.
"I don't know about that," said Lexie. "Look at this sign."
On the school bulletin board, the sign said ALIEN FOR RENT.

> *Note:* A humorous sci-fi for younger readers that also deals with the serious issue of abuse by a bully.

J.P. rubbed his eyes and looked again. "This has to be a joke. There are no aliens, so how can you rent one? Uh-oh. Here comes trouble."

A large boy walked down the hall toward them. His T-shirt said BE AFRAID. Bruce was a fifth-grader. He was mean to anyone smaller. "Hey, babies. It's school and I need to teach you a lesson." He swung his fist toward J.P.'s stomach.

The fist stopped in midswing. Bruce froze like a statue. That bully seemed to glow a ghastly green.

"What happened?" J.P. said. "One minute I was going to get a knuckle sandwich. The next minute Bruce turned green."

"That's not all." Lexie pointed to her lunch box at her feet. Her lunch box was glowing a ghastly green.

Burrrp! A noise came from the lunch box. Lexie gently kicked the lunch box with her foot. "J.P., you might change your mind about aliens. I think we've just rented one."

*Alien for Rent by Betsy Duffey, copyright © 1999, Delacorte.*

## Dyer, Wayne W. *Wisdom of the Ages: A Modern Master Brings Eternal Truths into Everyday Life.*

HarperCollins, 1998, 268pp. (Pbk.) HarperCollins, 1999, 268pp. High School & Up.

■ **POETRY.** *Ethics; love; politics; religion; responsibility; work.*

■ **RELATED BOOKS:** *Best Loved Poems to Read Again and Again* compiled by Mary Sanford Laurence; *Making Your Own Days: The Pleasure of Reading and Writing Poetry* by Kenneth Koch; *Improve Your Life Using the Wisdom of the Ages* by Wayne W. Dyer.

 *Dyer's selections also include brief biographies of Buddha, Michelangelo, St. Francis of Assisi, Rumi, Shakespeare, Whitman, Jesus, Emily Dickinson, George Bernard Shaw, Einstein, and Emerson. Useful book for language arts classes and adult book groups.*

I'm Wayne Dyer, best-selling author of self-help books. Join me on my journey to philosophers and poets of the past. These men were our profound teachers who sometimes risked their lives by revealing their wisdom. I have chosen 60 ancestral teachers who represent ancient, medieval, Renaissance, early modern, and modern times. I will also explain how these noble masters' work will directly benefit you.

Be prepared to let go, to let your life be guided by greatness.

## Dygard, Thomas J. *River Danger.*

Morrow Junior Books, 1998, 151pp. Middle School & Up. A Quick Pick for a Reluctant Reader.

■ **ADVENTURE.** *Crime; family; hobbies and sports (camping); responsibility; survival.*

■ **RELATED BOOKS:** *Deathwatch* by Robb White; *Hatchet* by Gary Paulsen.

 *The plot is similar to the movie **The River Wild** but not nearly as sinister. A reluctant reader will enjoy this fast-paced adventure.*

"I think we should have some kind of secret code worked out, in case we run into trouble. Two quick taps, then a pause, then another tap mean 'Get help fast.'"

I rolled my eyes. I'm 18, so I don't listen to my 11-year-old brother. Robbie was really getting on my nerves. I'm not thrilled about taking him canoeing and camping for seven endless days and nights.

Still, Robbie was the first to spot those three men with a rowboat. That was weird because who'd take a rowboat onto the Buffalo River? Canoes, kayaks, rafts, maybe, but a rowboat?

Later, to my amazement, Robbie's code would come in handy. Those men were up to something illegal, and I had unknowingly stumbled onto their secret. Now I needed Robbie's help. The sooner the better!

## Engdahl, Sylvia Louise. *Enchantress from the Stars.*

Atheneum, 1973, 222pp. Elementary School & Up. A Newbery Honor book. First in a series; **The Dark Side of Evil** follows.

■ **SCIENCE FICTION.** *End of the world; ethics; responsibility; science; secrets; war.*

■ **RELATED BOOKS:** *Children of the Star* trilogy: *This Star Shall Abide (a.k.a. Heritage of the Star), Beyond the Tomorrow Mountains, The Doors of the Universe* by Sylvia Louise Engdahl; *Invitation to the Game* by Monica Hughes.

*Note:* This booktalk is different from my booktalk in **Talk That Book.** Recommend this to readers who like romance and think they don't like science fiction.

The Enchantress in no way resembled any woman I had ever seen before. She was tall, dressed in green with dark shining hair, and had a radiance that I knew without question conveyed a good magic.

I am Georyn, a woodcutter's son from the planet Andrecia. I know this Enchantress will help me slay the dragon that is destroying our land.

I had no way of knowing that she was just a student at school. This school was called the Federation's Anthropological Center. This Enchantress was studying planet life. She came from another star, far away. I wish I had known those things. Maybe I would have asked this young and beautiful Enchantress for assistance!

## Enzensberger, Hans Magnus. *The Number Devil: A Mathematical Adventure.*

Illustrated by Rotraut Susanne Berner; translated by Michael Henry Heim. Henry Holt, 1997, 262pp. Elementary School & Up.

■ **NONFICTION AND FANTASY.** *School; science.*

■ **RELATED BOOKS:** *Math Curse* by Jon Scieszka and Lane Smith; *Math for Kids: And Other People Too!* By Theoni Pappas; *Once Upon a Number: The Hidden Mathematical Logic of Stories* by John Allen Paulos; *G is for Googool: A Math Alphabet Book* by David Schwartz, et al.

*Note:* The book brings the surreal logic of **Alice in Wonderland** to 12 simply explained lessons on numbers. During Robert's dreams, the Number Devil explains different mathematical mysteries. Recommended for all math teachers and all libraries.

"Who are you?" Robert asked the elderly man who was the size of a grasshopper.

"I am the number devil!" shouted the small man with a surprisingly loud voice.

Robert retorted, "I'm dreaming. If you give me homework in my dream, I'll scream bloody murder. That's child abuse!"

"Calm down, I just wanted to perk you up a little. We need numbers. That's why I invented them."

"You invented numbers? You expect me to believe that?"

"Me or a few others. It doesn't matter. Come on, I'll show you the amazing world of numbers: infinite numbers, prime numbers, numbers that magically appear in triangles, and numbers that expand without end. For 12 nights, I'll appear in your dreams and we'll learn it all. Just close your eyes ..."

"All right. I'll give it a try." Robert closed his eyes ...

**E**

## Esquivel, Laura. *Like Water for Chocolate: A Novel in Monthly Installments with Recipes, Romances, and Home Remedies.*

Doubleday, 1989, 246pp. High School & Up.

■ **ROMANCE.** *Caribbean and Latin America; death; family; love; movie novels; rivalry; secrets; sex and sexuality; work.*

■ **RELATED BOOKS:** *The Law of Love* by Laura Esquivel; *In the Time of Butterflies* by Julie Alvarez; *The Bridges of Madison County* by Robert James Waller.

*Note:* Recommended for all romance lovers and for groups of mature readers.

Your mouth will water over the delectable recipes in each chapter. Your eyes will water over this bittersweet romance between two star-crossed lovers: the narrator's Great Aunt Tita and her brother-in-law Pedro.

Tita is from a wealthy Mexican family. She is the youngest of three daughters born to Mama Elena, the tyrannical owner of the De la Garza ranch. In well-born Mexican families, tradition dictates that the youngest daughter remain single to take care of her mother. Even though Tita loves Pedro, Mama Elena arranges for Tita's older sister to marry Pedro. Tita is ordered to bake the wedding cake and her tears in the butter produce a remarkable reaction among the guests.

Feast on this unforgettable and compelling love story. Mmmm.

## Estes, Clarissa Pinkola. *Women Who Run with the Wolves: Myths and Stories of the Wild Woman Archetype.*

Ballantine Books, 1992, 520pp. High School & Up.

■ **FOLKLORE.** *Aging; animals (wolves); ethics; rites of passage; supernatural; women's issues.*

■ **RELATED BOOKS:** *The Divine Secrets of the Ya-Ya Sisterhood* by Rebecca Wells; *Cool Women: The Thinking Girl's Guide to the Hippest Women in History* edited by Pam Nelson.

*Note:* A recommended mother-daughter read. All high school and public libraries should own this one.

Who are these women who run with the wolves?

These Wild Women are fearless, strong, loyal, and wise. They embrace both life and death. Aging brings experience and, with experience comes wisdom.

These Wild Women appear through our folklore and myths. These stories are moral lessons to all females.

Join these Wild Women on their journey to self-identity. However, be warned. These Wild Women are an endangered species.

## Feinberg, Barbara Silberdick. *American's First Ladies: Changing Expectations.*

Franklin Watts, 1998, 144pp. Includes notes, index and glossary. For all libraries.

■ **BIOGRAPHY.** *Politics; women's issues.*

■ **RELATED BOOKS:** *America's First Ladies* by Betty Boyd Coroli; *America's Most Influential First Ladies (Profiles)* by Carl Sferrazza; *Lives of the ... (Writers, Musicians, Artists, Athletes)* series by Kathleen Krull.

 *At last, a reference book that is both entertaining and informative for reluctant readers. Recommended for all libraries and social studies classrooms.*

All right, here's a quick quiz about the wives of Presidents, the First Ladies. You don't need a pencil for this, but I'll throw out some questions and see how you score.

Who was the first president's wife to be called First Lady? (Dolly Madison, at her funeral in 1849.)

What First Lady said the term *First Lady* sounded like a racehorse? (Jacqueline Kennedy.)

What First Lady expected women to curtsy when introduced? (Martha Washington.)

Who entertained the first African American in the White House? (First Lady Lou Hoover in 1930.)

Most of us don't know these answers because we don't know much about First Ladies. This book changes all that. Find out all the facts, including some fascinating gossip, about *America's First Ladies*.

## Fenner, Carol. *The King of Dragons.*

Margaret K. McElderry Books, 1998, 216pp. Elementary School & Up.

■ **REALISTIC FICTION.** *Homeless; mental illness; survival; Vietnam.*

■ **RELATED BOOKS:** *Slate's Limbo* by Felice Holman; *Darnell Rock Reporting* by Walter Dean Myers; *Plain City* by Virginia Hamilton.

 *Fenner's book also depicts a mentally ill father who has flashbacks of Vietnam and suffers from memory loss.*

"Dad?" Ian whispered in the darkness. Where was his dad? He'd been gone for days, looking for food and discarded clothing.

When Ian was small, he thought being homeless was fun. What better way to get out of attending school? As the years passed, it became hard not talking to people and being hungry. Ian's father taught Ian how to take up space with leaving a trace. These skills came in handy when Ian, now 11, had to learn to survive without his father.

Currently, Ian and his father were living in the Hall of Justice. Living there was much better than the railroad station because this building was heated, with showering facilities. The Hall was being renovated into a museum, so there was a lot of activity. That made it perfect for two tired, homeless people.

The museum fascinated Ian. There was a kite exhibit that contained masterpieces from around the world. His favorite kite was called the *King of Dragons,* a brilliantly colored Chinese kite. His fascination with the exhibit probably kept Ian from being as cautious as he should.

One day he overheard a conversation that made his heart drop. "I knew it! Someone's hiding in this building. Who is it and where is he hiding?"

**F**

## Ferris, Jean. *Love Among the Walnuts.*

Harcourt Brace, 1998, 216pp. Middle School & Up. Top 10 Best Books for Young Adults.

■ **HUMOR.** *Crime; love; mental illness.*

■ **RELATED BOOKS:** *The Pirates' Mixed-Up Adventure* by Margaret Mahy; *I Want to Buy a Vowel* by John Welter; *Sunshine Rider: The First Vegetarian Western* by Ric Lynden Hardman.

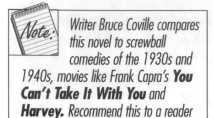
*Note:* Writer Bruce Coville compares this novel to screwball comedies of the 1930s and 1940s, movies like Frank Capra's **You Can't Take It With You** and **Harvey.** Recommend this to a reader who appreciates satire.

Once upon a time there was a poison birthday cake.

A very wealthy man, Horatio Alger Huntington-Ackerman—whose initials spelled HAHA—ate the cake. His wife and pet chicken also ate the cake. Shortly afterwards, all three went into a mysterious coma.

Now, Horatio's son, Alexander Huntington-Ackerman—whose initials spell AHA—wants to catch the villains who baked the cake. Those varmints are his conniving, lazy uncles, Bart Huntington and Bernie Ackerman.

Alexander's family lives next to Walnut Manor, an insane asylum. Sometimes it's hard to know where the property begins and ends. Luckily, that's when the fun begins. Plunge into insanity with *Love Among the Walnuts.*

---

## Filipovic, Zlata. *Zlata's Diary: A Child's Life in Sarajevo.*

With an introduction by Janine Di Giovanni; translated with notes by Christina Pribichevich-Zoric. Viking, 1994, 184pp. For all libraries.

■ **BIOGRAPHY.** *Diaries; Europe (Yugoslavia, Bosnia); politics; religious prejudice; war.*

■ **RELATED BOOKS:** *The Diary of a Young Girl: The Definitive Edition* by Anne Frank; *I Have Lived a Thousand Years* by Livia Bitton Jackson; *The Seamstress: A Memoir of Survival* by Sara Tuvel Bernstein.

*Note:* This may be a stretch for some elementary students, but recommend this to the more developed readers. Also useful for social science and language arts teachers.

Dear Mimmy,

My idol Anne Frank named her diary Kitty. I will name my diary Mimmy and tell her all my secrets and fears.

It's strange. I began this diary in 1991 as a ordinary student from Yugoslavia. I spent my days watching MTV, eating pizza, and calling friends from school. Two years later, I live in Bosnia and experience the daily rigors of war.

I have learned much in my 13 years, some things that no human being should experience: death, injuries, shells, sadness, and sorrow. Maybe this diary can remind people that, no matter what, human beings must avoid war. I keep asking myself, why war? We're innocent. But helpless!

Zlata

## Filkin, David. *Stephen Hawking's Universe: The Cosmos Explained.*

Foreword by Stephen Hawking. The Authorized Companion to the Television Series. BasicBooks, 1997, 288pp. For all libraries.

- **NONFICTION SCIENCE.** *Ecology; end of the world; science; time travel; survival.*
- **RELATED BOOKS:** *A Brief History of Time* by Stephen Hawking; *Black Holes and Time Warps: Einstein's Outrageous Legacy* by Kip S. Thorne with introduction by Stephen Hawking; *I'm Not All Here* by Tim Allen.

*Note:* This book is an authorized companion to the television series **Stephen Hawking's Universe,** produced by David Filkin. Hawking's scientific model is described in everyday language, juxtaposed against some spectacular stellar photography. Stephen Hawking is physically challenged with the genetic motor neuron disease. With the help of a computer and a voice synthesizer strapped to his wheelchair, he is able to communicate his brilliant theories in lay language. This book is a must for all libraries and, if affordable, homes. Also recommended for group reads.

What happened that formed the universe? In the universe, was there a beginning? According to scientist Stephen Hawking, yes, there was a beginning to the universe. At the Big Bang, the universe and time itself came into existence. Stephen Hawking's universe reconciled Einstein's General Theory of Relativity with the Quantum Theory. This true-life mystery began with the Big Bang, might end with the Big Crunch, and will include numerous *black holes, white dwarfs,* and *worm holes.*

Stephen Hawking's universe is determined by the laws of science, even its very creation. By knowing these laws of physics, Hawking believes that we can become Masters of our Universe.

## Fitzgerald, F. Scott. *The Great Gatsby.*

The Authorized Text, with notes and preface by Matthew J. Bruccoli. Colliers, 1992, 216pp. First published in 1925. High School & Up. An Accelerated Reader selection.

- **REALISTIC FICTION.** *Class conflict; crime; ethics; love; secrets; self-identity.*
- **RELATED BOOKS:** *The Last Tycoon* by F. Scott Fitzgerald; *The Sun Also Rises* by Ernest Hemingway; *Main Street* by Sinclair Lewis.

*Note:* Unfortunately, many students dislike this cautionary tale of the American dream because it is required reading, and Fitzgerald's poetic prose may be too difficult for reluctant readers. Recommend this masterpiece only to mature readers.

"Do you come to Gatsby's parties often?" I inquired of the young woman beside me, during a brief lull in the party conversation.

"Oh yes, often," she replied, grandly waving her cigarette holder in my direction. "Of course, no one knows anything about Gatsby. Someone told me he once killed a man."

"I've heard he was a German spy," answered another.

"I've heard he was a bootlegger, selling illegal alcohol to desperate souls, " I said.

Everyone laughed as we sipped our champagne. The truth is, even though we attended his lavish parties, no one knew the rich, elusive Jay Gatsby. I was to discover that Gatsby knew himself least of all. He had invented himself to possess the love of a heartless beauty. He had changed his name, his background, and his identity. In the process, he lost himself.

Who was *The Great Gatsby?* Who lived behind Gatsby's mask?

## Flagg, Fannie. *Fried Green Tomatoes at the Whistle Stop Cafe.*

Vintage, 1987, 395pp. With recipes. High School & Up. An Accelerated Reader selection.

■ **REALISTIC FICTION.** *Aging; crime; friendship; homosexuality; movie novels; secrets; sexual abuse; work; women's issues.*

■ **RELATED BOOKS:** *Welcome to the World, Baby Girl!* by Fannie Flagg; *Cold Sassy Tree* by Olive Ann Burns; *Steel Magnolias* by Robert Harling.

*Note:* The book is just as unforgettable as the movie. Recommended as an older group read.

Set down a spell and I'll tell you a story that happened long ago. Every word is true. I may be 86, but I still got my senses intact.

I'm Mrs. Cleo Threadgood. Cleo told me once, "Ninny— my name is Virginia but folks call me Ninny—he said, 'Ninnie, all I hear is Idgie said this and Idgie did that.'"

It's true. Idgie was Cleo's baby sister and a real cutup. She and Ruth once owned the Whistle Stop Cafe.

Idgie used to do crazy harebrained things like putting poker chips in the church collection. She was a character all right, but how anybody thought she could have killed that man is beyond me.

You didn't hear tell of the murder? It made all the papers. That's right, that's right. It was a long time ago.

Well, get comfortable and I'll tell you the story of Idgie, Ruth, and *Fried Green Tomatoes at the Whistle Stop Cafe.*

## Flake, Sharon G. *The Skin I'm In.*

Hyperion Books for Children, 1998, 169pp. Middle School and Up. An ALA Best Book for Young Adults; Quick Pick for Reluctant Young Adult Readers.

■ **REALISTIC FICTION.** *Abuse; African Americans; interracial relations; peer pressure; racism; responsibility; self-identity; school.*

■ **RELATED BOOKS:** *A White Romance* by Virginia Hamilton; *Yolanda's Genius* by Carol Fenner; *Jazmin's Notebook* by Nikki Grimes.

*Note:* In Sharon Flake's first novel, she tells the story through Maleeka Madison's eyes, as Maleeka is victimized by bullies. There is realistic dialogue between the characters, including an eccentric, strong-willed teacher who encourages Maleeka to develop her writing skills. Highly recommended for book reports, group reads, and reading aloud.

Seems like people been teasing me all my life. I'm too black, I'm the worst-dressed, I'm too tall, I'm too skinny.

Then, last week, something happened. Enough is enough. I deserve better than for people to treat me any old way they want. Lately I been not doing Char's homework and been giving her some lip. I been writing in a journal for Miss Saunder's class. I even entered a writing contest. I been doing things like I never have before.

I'm learning to live in my skin.

## Fleischman, Paul. *Whirligig.*

Henry Holt, 1998, 133pp. Middle School & Up. An ALA Best Book for Young Adults; School Library Journal's Best Books selection.

■ Realistic fiction. *Death; hobbies; responsibility.*

■ Related books: *Missing May* by Cynthia Rylant; *Holes* by Louis Sachar; *Walk Two Moons* by Sharon Creech.

Note: In reverse chronology and alternating chapters, the reader learns of the effects Brent's whirligigs have on individuals whose paths they cross. Like the movie *It's a Wonderful Life*, Brent learns that small deeds can have large consequences.

"This is my only request. That you make four whirligigs of a girl that looks like Lea. Put her name on them. Set them up in the corners of the United States—Washington, California, Florida, and Maine. Then she will live again."

Brent Bishop pondered Mrs. Zamora's proposal. He could hear his parents protesting, but he ignored their complaints. At least the trip would get him away from Chicago, his parents, and his past.

Brent was on his second life. His first life ended at the car crash. The crash occurred because he was trying to kill himself. Now it seemed so ludicrous. By trying to kill himself, he had killed someone else, some teenager named Lea Zamora. She didn't deserve to die, thought Brent, and, if I have to, I will do penance for the rest of my life. Maybe by building these whirligigs in Lea's memory, I can forgive myself.

Brent spoke up over his parents' complaints. "I'll do it."

## Fletcher, Susan. *Shadow Spinner.*

Atheneum Books for Young Readers, 1998, 219pp. Middle School & Up. An ALA Best Book for Young Adults; School Library Journal's Best Books selection.

■ **FOLKLORE.** *Class conflict; Middle ages; Middle East; physical disability.*

■ **RELATED BOOKS:** *The Book of a Thousand Nights and a Night* translated by Richard F. Burton; *Shabanu, Daughter of the Wind* and *Haveli* by Suzanne Fishers Staples; *Sirena* by Donna Napoli.

This powerful story can be used as a class read-aloud. The story delves into many themes through storytelling and ancient folklore. Don't miss this one.

Shahrazad is my hero. She tells stories to the Sultan night after night. In the past, the Sultan would marry and then behead his wife the next morning.

Until Shahrazad.

Shahrazad keeps the Sultan so entertained with stories that the killing of young girls stopped. As long as Shahrazad tells a compelling story, she will continue to save her life as well as others'.

What happens when Shahrazad runs out of stories? That's where I come in. I'm Marjan, a humble orphan with a maimed foot. One thing I do possess is stories, lots of them. By destiny I am led to Shahrazad.

Often, in stories, the humblest creatures turn out to be powerful. The tortoise and the mouse are two examples. This is not just a storyteller's trick. Sometimes it really happens.

## Forman, James. **Becca's Story.**

Atheneum, 1992, 180pp. Middle School & Up.

■ **HISTORICAL FICTION.** *Aging; Civil War; death; love; pioneer life; rivalry.*

■ **RELATED BOOKS:** *The Last Silk Dress* by Ann Rinaldi; *The Witch of Blackbird Pond* by Elizabeth George Speare.

 The flaw in this book is that the author, James Forman, is writing about his great-great-grandparents. Alexander Forman is one of the main characters, so, of course, it becomes fairly obvious which beau Becca chooses. However, the letters are authentic primary sources and are skillfully woven into the plot.

Becca Case has two admirers. Alex offers Becca a stable future. Charlie offers adventure and laughter. Becca is content with both of them. She's sure that one day she'll know who holds the key to her heart.

Suddenly the War Between the States erupts. One beau enlists, the other disappears.

Which one will Becca choose?

## Forster, E. M. **A Passage to India.**

(Pbk.) Harcourt Brace, 1984, 362pp. First published in 1924. High School & Up. An Accelerated Reader selection.

■ **REALISTIC FICTION.** *Ethics; India and Pakistan; movie novels; racism; religious prejudice; sexual abuse.*

■ **RELATED BOOKS:** *The God of Small Things* by Arundhati Roy; *The City of Joy* by Dominique Lapierre.

 Set against the backdrop of colonial India during the end of the nineteenth century, this masterpiece remains relevant because it examines prejudice and psychological delusion. Especially recommended for advanced language arts classes, along with E. M. Forster's **Aspects of the Novel.**

What really happened in the mystic Marabar caves in India? Did the Indian doctor, Dr. Aziz, sexually assault the English lady, Miss Adela Quested? The only eyewitness was Adela's future mother-in-law, Mrs. Moore. Although Mrs. Moore saw and heard nothing, she sided with Adela. The doctor's prestigious reputation was destroyed as he was brought to trial for a crime he swore he didn't commit.

The only person who supported Dr. Aziz was the distinguished English scholar, Professor Fielding. He believed Adela had a hysterical reaction to the dark, dank atmosphere of the mysterious caves.

What is the truth? Is Dr. Aziz innocent? To find out, book *A Passage to India.*

## Freedman, Russell. *Martha Graham: A Dancer's Life.*

Houghton Mifflin, 1998, 175pp. For all libraries. An ALA Best Book for Young Adults; Nonfiction Winner of the Boston Globe-Horn Book Awards.

■ **BIOGRAPHY.** *Show business; women's issues; work.*

■ **RELATED BOOKS:** *Martha Graham: Founder of Modern Dance (Book Report Biography)* by Gerald Newman and Eleanor Layfield Neman.

*Russell Freedman's award-winning biographies are always written in an entertaining style accompanied by revealing photographs. Check out his books on Eleanor Roosevelt, the Wright Brothers, and Abraham Lincoln.*

Martha Graham called her dancers "acrobats of God" because she saw dance as a celebration of life. She recognized that dance was a choreographed movement of emotions. For 70 years, Martha Graham danced, choreographed, and taught. Her techniques are still being taught today.

What's amazing is that Graham overcame many difficulties. She was considered too old, too short, too heavy, and too homely.

This book celebrates her life in dance. "I did not choose to be a dancer," Martha Graham often said. "I was chosen."

## Frey, Darcy. *The Last Shot: City Streets, Basketball Dreams.*

Houghton Mifflin, 1994, 230pp. Middle School & Up.

■ **SPORTS.** *African Americans; class conflict; men's issues; responsibility; sports.*

■ **RELATED BOOKS:** *Sacred Hoops: Spiritual Lessons of a Hardwood Warrior* by Phil Jackson and Hugh Delehanty; *Danger Zone* by David Klass; *The Moves Make the Man* by Bruce Brooks.

*Give this to a reluctant reader who loves sports. A page-turner.*

In Coney Island, New York, basketball is a religion.

Basketball has "saved" Russell, Corey, and Tchaka. Their prayer is for a scholarship to college and a one-way ticket out of the ghetto. They are just three kids of the hundreds who study basketball like the Bible. They meditate, they study, they practice the rituals.

Will basketball bring them salvation?

## Gauthier, Gail. *A Year with Butch and Spike.*

G. P. Putnam's Sons, 1998, 216pp. Elementary School & Up.

■ **HUMOR.** *Abuse; school.*

■ **RELATED BOOKS:** *The Best Christmas Pageant Ever* and *The Best School Year Ever* by Barbara Robinson; *Nasty, Stinky Sneakers* by Eve Bunting.

*Note:* Spike and Butch are hilarious cut-ups under a teacher who uses unfair methods to gain control. Elementary readers will relate to either the teacher's pet or the cut-ups.

"Oops! My mistake! I see I've been placed next to a girl!"

At this remark, I'm thinking, *Excuse me? A girl?*

Don't get me wrong. Girls are fine people. That is, if you happen to be a girl. I try to be friendly to this jerk. "I don't believe we've been introduced. I'm Jasper Gordon. Welcome to the sixth grade."

"Yeah, yeah, I know you. Teacher's pet. Everyone knows I'm Spike Couture. Tell me, am I being punished? Where are the cool guys sitting?"

*Spike Couture! I'm sitting next to Spike Couture!* I'm screaming this in my head and then I look to the other side of my desk. *Butch Couture! I'm sitting next to the Coutures, better known as the Cootches, the biggest troublemakers in the school.*

Looks like I'm headed for big trouble. How do I get out of this mess?

## Gee, Maurice. *The Champion.*

Simon & Schuster, 1989, 212pp. Elementary School & Up.

■ **HISTORICAL FICTION.** *African Americans; ethics; interracial relations; New Zealand; racism; runaways; World War II.*

■ **RELATED BOOKS:** *The Cay* by Theodore Taylor; *A Cageful of Butterflies* by Lesley Beake.

*Note:* The author also deals with white racism of the Maoris and Dalmationas, two New Zealand tribes. Like Theodore Taylor's **The Cay,** this book has a predictable ending, but the characters are well-developed and realistic.

Yawn. Things were so boring in Kettle Creek, New Zealand. It was 1943 and a World War was happening everywhere else. Life was a drag for 12-year-old Rex Pascoe.

Then Rex learned that a wounded American soldier would stay with his family. Rex wanted to ask the soldier all sorts of questions about war. After all, a solider was a champion just like his favorite comic book, *Champion.* A champion was a rough and tough man ready for fighting and war.

Surprisingly, Private Jackson Coop didn't look or act like a champion. He was a courteous, kind African-American soldier who didn't like to fight. Yet Jack was strong in his convictions, a defender of causes. Eventually, Rex realized that heroes aren't always what you expect and that courage shows itself in unique ways.

Jack was everything a hero should be. Jack was a champion.

## Glassman, Miriam. *Box Top Dreams.*

Delacorte Press, 1998, 184pp. Elementary School & Up.

■ **REALISTIC FICTION.** *Hobbies; peer pressure; rites of passage; school.*

■ **RELATED BOOKS:** *A Girl Named Al* by Constance Greene; *Nasty, Stinky Sneakers* by Eve Bunting; *The Egypt Game* by Zilpha Keatley Snyder.

 *Note:* This novel is a well-written portrait of a girl facing many changes in her life, including a bully. Recommended for others facing the same adolescent changes.

"Why don't you two grow up?" Lydia snatched the comic book from her 11-year-old sister. "You and Danny spend a small fortune on comic books, supermarket tabloids, and gossip magazines. That's pitiful and totally irrelevant."

Ari wasn't sure what *irrelevant* meant, but she knew it was an insult. What was the big deal? Sure, she and Danny lived in their own world of magic kits, movies, musicals, and amazing games. One day they would hit the jackpot.

When Danny moved away, Ari was left to face Martina Wallhoffer, Queen of the Fifth Grade. Martina was a sneaky bully who fooled adults into thinking she wouldn't hurt a fly. Then, when the adults left, she would yank off the fly's wings. Martina insisted that Ari end her friendship with Danny, throw away her childish games, and become part of Martina's group.

Ari was uncertain what to do. Should she give up her *Box Top Dreams*?

## Glenn, Mel. *The Taking of Room 114: A Hostage Drama in Poems.*

Dutton, 1997, 182pp. Middle School & Up. An ALA Best Book for Young Adults; Quick Pick for Young Adult Readers.

■ **POETRY.** *Crime; death; mental illness; school.*

■ **RELATED BOOKS:** *Who Killed Mr. Chippendale? A Mystery in Poems* by Mel Glenn; *Making Up Megaboy* by Virginia Walter and Katrina Roeckelin; *Heroes* by Robert Cormier; *Killing Mr. Griffin* by Lois Duncan; *Monster* by Walter Dean Myers.

 *Note:* An insightful book about school violence, written in free verse, narrated by the captured students. Can be used as Reader's Theater with each student reading a poem.

... We interrupt our regular TV broadcast to bring you this late-breaking story. Police have been called to Tower High School to investigate a possible hostage situation. Here is what we know: A senior history class has been taken over by the teacher, Mr. Wiedermeyer. He has a gun and is dangerous. As soon as we can, we will be bringing you a live update. Now back to our regularly scheduled program ...

**G**

## Godden, Rumer. *Pippa Passes.*

Macmillan, 1994, 172pp. High School & Up.

■ **ROMANCE.** *Europe (Italy); homosexuality; love; rites of passage; sex and sexuality; work; women's issues.*

■ **RELATED BOOKS:** *For the Love of Venice* by Donna Jo Napoli; *The Music of Summer* by Rosa Guy; *Snowfall* by K. M. Peyton; *Daddy Long Legs* by Jean Webster.

*A perfect romance by a masterful writer. Contains some discreet sexual scenes.*

If you had the choice, would you choose to be a solo ballerina or a singer in a pop band? Pippa is equally good at both, but she knows she must make a career choice.

Pippa must also face her deep feelings for a handsome boy she met in the romantic city of Venice, Italy—where streets become rivers and *gondoliers* become lovers.

Pippa passes through the rites of passage from naïve, innocent girl to mature, determined woman. Journey with Pippa in Venice as *Pippa Passes.*

## Golden, Arthur. *Memoirs of a Geisha.*

Alfred A. Knopf, 1997, 434pp; (Pbk.) Random House, 1999, 458pp. High School & Up.

■ **REALISTIC FICTION.** *Abuse; Asia (Japan); class conflict; love; sex and sexuality; women's issues.*

■ **RELATED BOOKS:** *Sayonara* by James Mitchner; *Women of the Silk* by Gail Tsukiyama; *Bound Feet and Western Dress* by Pang-Mei Natasha Chang.

*This compelling best seller reads like an autobiography, but is actually fiction. Great for older reading groups.*

I'm Nitta Sayuri. Writers have called me one of the greatest geisha of Kyoto. I assure you that I was never the greatest geisha. Yet my story twists and turns like the Sea of Japan, beginning in the fishing village of Yoroido.

My sign is water. Water never waits. Water changes shape and flows around things and finds secret paths. When Mr. Tanaka persuaded my father to live with him in Senzuru, I began my journey. My destiny was changed forever.

Mr. Tanaka took me to an *okiya,* a place where geisha live, and sold me. I began as a servant and was subject to beatings and abuse.

The head geisha, Hatsumomo, was particularly cruel. She accused me of stealing money and of pouring ink on her rival's kimono. Luckily, her rival Mameha knew I had not damaged her kimono and began training me as her apprentice.

Like water, I began to adapt to my surroundings. I learned the dances, music, makeup; I learned the art of making my customers satisfied. I became what dreams are made of.

My dream is about only one man, the Chairman. He was the only person kind to me during my years of torment. Can the Chairman rescue me from the life I never chose, the life of a geisha?

# Gordon, Sheila. *Waiting for the Rain.*

Orchard, 1987, 214pp. Elementary School & Up. An Accelerated Reader selection.

■ **HISTORICAL FICTION.** *Africa (South Africa); apartheid; friendship; interracial relations; racism.*

■ **RELATED BOOKS:** *A Long Walk to Freedom* (abridged) by Nelson Mandela; books by Beverly Naidoo: *Journey to Jo'burg;* its sequel, *Chain of Fire; No Turning Back.*

 *Apartheid (pronounced apar-thide) is an Afrikaner word meaning separateness. During apartheid, all races were to be separated in all areas. Since 1991, apartheid no longer exists in South Africa. Useful as multicultural historical fiction.*

Two friends lived in South Africa under the segregationist policy called *apartheid.* Frikkie was a white Afrikaner who visited his uncle and aunt each year. Frikkie met Tengo, a black South African whose family lived and worked on the farm. Frikkie and Tengo developed a friendship that lasted throughout childhood.

Tengo longed for a better life and education, so he went to Johannesburg to study. For the first time, Tengo confronted his anger about *apartheid.*

Frikkie joined the army and was assigned to preventing the race riots in Jo'burg. When a riot occurred, Frikkie entered the township, armed and ready. Now the childhood friends will face each other. Now two friends are enemies.

# Greenberg, Joanne, a.k.a. Hannah Green. *I Never Promised You a Rose Garden.*

(Pbk.) Signet/Penguin, 1964, 252pp. High School & Up. An Accelerated Reader selection.

■ **REALISTIC FICTION.** *Mental illness; responsibility; trust.*

■ **RELATED BOOKS:** *Ordinary People* by Judith Guest; *Lisa Bright and Dark* by John Neufield; *One Flew Over the Cuckoo's Nest* by Ken Kesey.

 *Joanne Greenberg was writing of her personal battle with schizophrenia and used the pen name, Hannah Green, to disguise her identity. Her autobiography, disguised as fiction, is a classic, appearing on many high school lists.*

Deborah lives in two different worlds—one, a mental hospital; the other, the Kingdom of Yr.

Lately the two worlds are colliding. It's difficult to move from the intricacies of Yr's Kingdom, from the Collect of Others, the Censor, and the Yr Gods. Now Deborah has fallen into the Pit, where everything is gray and words have no meaning.

Dr. Fried tries to help Deborah gain control of her schizophrenia. Can Deborah leave the safety of her fantasy and live in the real world?

**G**

## Grimes, Nikki. *Jazmin's Notebook.*

Dial Books, 1998, 102pp. Middle School & Up. Coretta Scott King Author Honors.

- ■ **REALISTIC FICTION.** *African Americans; diaries; racism; single parents; substance abuse (alcohol).*
- ■ **RELATED BOOKS:** *Spite Fences* by Trudy Krisher; *Leon's Story* by Leon Walter Tillage; *The Skin I'm In* by Sharon Flake.

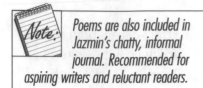 *Poems are also included in Jazmin's chatty, informal journal. Recommended for aspiring writers and reluctant readers.*

I'm Jazmin with a z. My dad named me in homage of jazz. No one gets the spelling right, but I know folks will figure out how to spell it after I'm famous (smile). I plan to write a best seller. Maybe this notebook will bring me fame.

I certainly can't be famous with my looks. A pair of contacts would help. It's the 1960s and no one wears coke-bottle glasses but me.

Meanwhile, I sit on my stoop in Harlem and write. I don't know what God's got planned for me. Or why Dad had to die. Or why Mom can't stop drinking. Or why my older sister CeCe got stuck with raising me. All I've got is my dreams. Now I just have to make them come true.

## Guest, Judith. *Ordinary People.*

Viking, 1976, 214pp. High School & Up. An Accelerated Reader selection.

- ■ **REALISTIC FICTION.** *Death; movie novels; problem parents; sex and sexuality; suicide.*
- ■ **RELATED BOOKS:** *I Never Promised You a Rose Garden* by Joanne Greenberg, a.k.a. Hannah Green; *One Flew Over the Cuckoo's Nest* by Ken Kesey.

 *This classic is on many high school reading lists. Recommended for older reluctant readers.*

Conrad Jarrett needs his own bumper sticker to keep on living. Maybe the sticker should say *Danger! Severe Risk of Suicide!* He has the thin, vertical scar on his wrist to prove it.

Conrad's mother will never forgive him for the bloody mess he left on the floor. The tile had to be replaced; the rug had to be destroyed. She believed he was sending some sort of hostile signal to her.

Maybe he was subconsciously punishing his mother. She had never forgiven him for the boating accident and the death of his brother. Conrad thought Buck had been hanging on to the other side of the boat during the violent storm, but then ...

Circles and more circles. When does it end? How will it end?

## Hamill, Pete. *Snow in August.*

Little, Brown, 1997, 327pp. High School & Up. An ALA Best Book for Young Adults; Alex Award; Accelerated Reader.

■ **HISTORICAL FICTION.** *Crime; death; friendship; Holocaust; immigrants; Jews; men's issues; religion (Kabbala); religious prejudice; racism; sports (baseball); supernatural.*

■ **RELATED BOOKS:** *The Chosen* by Chaim Potok; *A Tree Grows in Brooklyn* by Betty Smith; *A Drinking Life* by Pete Hamill.

 *This book begins as believable historical fiction in 1946 Brooklyn and gradually switches to fantasy with the appearance of the Golem. Brilliantly conceived and written, this book is written for the mature reader of all ages.*

Michael Devlin is only 11, but he's confused. He knows he supposed to hate Jews, but that's what confuses him. He's just an Irish Catholic boy from Brooklyn who loves *Captain Marvel* comic books. He doesn't hate anyone.

How can Michael hate the Rabbi down the block? In many ways, Rabbi Hirsch is the wisest man Michael has ever known. They've become friends. In fact, Michael took the Rabbi to his first baseball game with Jackie Robinson playing for the Brooklyn Dodgers.

Rabbi Hirsch told Michael about another superhero, the Golem, a monster who destroys evil. Michael wonders why the Golem and Captain Marvel aren't real. What's the point of heroes if they can't protect the victims from bullies like Frankie McCarthy? Frankie and his gang, the Falcons, terrorize Michael at every opportunity. However, when Frankie attacks the Rabbi and a Jewish store owner, Michael wants revenge.

How can innocent people fight evil?

## Hamilton, Virginia. *Second Cousins.*

Blue Sky/Scholastic, 1998, 168pp. Middle School & Up. Second book in series; **Cousins** precedes.

■ **REALISTIC FICTION.** *African Americans; computers; family; single parents.*

■ **RELATED BOOKS:** *The Watsons go to Birmingham* by Christopher Paul Curtis; *Cousins* and *The House of Dies Drear* series by Virginia Hamilton.

 *Virginia Hamilton never writes a dull book, but this one integrates the computer into an African-American family saga. Recommended for all middle and some high school libraries.*

Cammy Colman had so many cousins—first cousins, second cousins, third cousins. She had so many cousins that she called them all *Second Cousins.* She looked forward to seeing all her second cousins at the family reunion.

Then Cammy met her second cousins GiGi and Jahnina. They were tough-talking, street-wise mamas from New York. Jahnina was the strongest and strangest of the pair. She insisted on being called Fracal because of her computer skills. Through this cousin, Cammy would learn a family secret that would change things forever.

How can a cousin whom Cammy has never met become the most important person in Cammy's past?

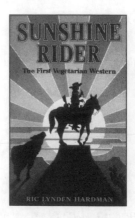

## Hardman, Ric Lynden. *Sunshine Rider: The First Vegetarian Western.*

Delacorte, 1998, 343pp. Middle School & Up. An ALA Best Book for Young Adults.

- **HUMOR.** *Ecology; men's issues; pioneer life; responsibility.*
- **RELATED BOOKS:** *Buffalo Woman* by Bill Wallace; *Lily: A Love Story* and *Looking After Lily* by Cindy Bonner; *Sugarcane House and Other Stories About Mr. Fat* by Adrienne Bond.

Howdy, folks. I'm Sunshine Rider. I'm also Wylie Jackson, Dr. Axel Beane, and any other name I can think up.

 *Note.* *In a humorous style, this book subtly suggests a vegetarian, New Age philosophy. Even the old-time recipes between the chapters add to the flavor of this entertaining page-turner.*

I'm on the lam, escaping from a cattle drive. All I got is Roselle and Alice's drawers. Roselle is Alice's pet *cattalo*: part buffalo, part-longhorn cow. Alice is my childhood friend and enemy. She insisted on giving me her underpants to keep Roselle close to me. It's a sorry thing when a cowboy brings a woman's drawers to a cattle drive, but there it is.

I'm also a vegetarian. That's mighty odd in 1881, but there it is. Truth is, I've become mighty attached to Roselle and other four-legged critters.

Saddle up and gallop with me, Sunshine Rider, on our hilarious ride through the American West. Happy trails!

*Sunshine Rider by Ric Lynden Hardman, copyright © 1998, Delacorte.*

## Harrah, Madge. *My Brother, My Enemy.*

Simon and Schuster Books for Young Readers, 1997, 137pp. With author's note, glossary, and bibliography. Elementary School & Up.

- **HISTORICAL FICTION.** *American Revolutionary war; Native Americans (Susquehanna); revenge.*
- **RELATED BOOKS:** *Cast Two Shadows* by Ann Rinaldi; *The Fighting Ground* by Avi; *My Brother Sam is Dead* by James Lincoln Collier and Christopher Collier.

*Note.* *Bacon's Rebellion in 1676 was known as "the dress rehearsal of the American Revolution." This thoughtful and well-written novel provides information about a little-known event in American history.*

I'm 14 and sentenced to hang. In the morning. At dawn.

A guard brought me a pen, paper, and pot of ink. "You might want to write farewell notes to your friends and family," he said.

I have no family. They were killed by the Susquehanna. At first I believed my blood brother, Naokan, took part in the raid. I vowed revenge and joined Nathaniel Bacon's rebel army, which is bent on killing every Indian in Virginia. Later, I found out I was wrong about Naokan, but it was too late. Sir William Berkeley, governor of the colony and a loyal supporter of Charles II, shows us rebels no mercy and has condemned us to death.

Now I have six hours until dawn. Six hours to tell my story about Naokan, my brother, my enemy. Naokan, this is for you.

Signed, respectfully,
Robert Bradford
October 1676, Jamestown, Virginia

## Harrer, Heinrich. *Seven Years in Tibet*, with a new epilogue by the author.

Translated from the German by Richard Graves with an introduction by Peter Fleming. London: Flamingo, 1997, 298pp. Middle School & Up.

■ **BIOGRAPHY.** *Asia (Tibet); China; movie novels; politics; religion; religious prejudice; sports (mountain climbing); war; World War II.*

■ **RELATED BOOKS:** *The Art of Happiness* by Dalai Lama, et al; *Into Thin Air* by Jon Krakauer; *Within Reach : My Everest Story* by Mark Pfetzer and Jack Galvin; *All the Way to Heaven: An American Boyhood in the Himalayas* by Stephen Alger.

*Note:* *The book is controversial because after it's publication, the press discovered the author was once a Nazi. However, since Harrer undergoes a spiritual metamorphosis, this might be a good choice for an older group read.*

I knew somehow, some way I would escape the prison-of-war camp. I was captured by the British while I was climbing the Himalayas during World War II. Being Austrian, I was interned in India. I escaped twice unsuccessfully. My third attempt was successful and led me to the country of Tibet.

I'm Heinrich Harrer, a mountaineer and Olympic ski champion. My companion Hans Kopp and I were the first Westerners to enter the forbidden city of Lhasa in Tibet. I stayed for seven years and even became a friend and tutor to the young Dalai Lama. The Dalai Lama was only 14, but he was considered to be an incarnated God to the Tibetans.

Climb aboard for my story of a lost paradise that I discovered during my *Seven Years in Tibet.*

## Harrison, Michael. *It's My Life.*

Holiday House, 1997, 132pp. First published in Great Britain in 1997 by the Oxford University Press. Middle School & Up. An ALA Best Book for Young Adults.

■ **REALISTIC FICTION.** *Crime; divorce; Great Britain; single parents.*

■ **RELATED BOOKS:** *Killing Mr. Griffin* and *Don't Look Behind You* by Lois Duncan; *You'll Never Guess the End* by Barbara Wersba; *Skinhead* by Jay Bennett.

*Note:* *An entertaining mystery for reluctant readers.*

*Dear Mum,*

*I have been kidnapped. So far, I'm okay. Wait for further instructions.*

*Marvin*

Marvin wrote the message that the kidnapper demanded. Marvin was taken to a boat and told to call his dad. Apparently the kidnapper wanted half of Dad's win of the lottery. All Marvin could do was wait and hope his Mum wouldn't worry. Since their divorce, his Mum worked hard to make ends meet.

"Everything go all right?" Marvin heard a familiar voice some distance away.

Marvin shuddered. He knew that voice. It was his Mum's voice and that had to be her boyfriend who kidnapped him.

What kind of parent would kidnap her own child?

H

**H**

## Hemingway, Ernest. *A Farewell to Arms.*

Macmillan, 1957, 332pp. First published in 1929. High School & Up. An Accelerated Reader selection.

■ **ROMANCE.** *Death; Europe (Italy); love; men's issues; movie novels; pregnancy; sex and sexuality; substance abuse (alcohol); World War I.*

■ **RELATED BOOKS:** *For Whom Bells Toll* and *The Sun Also Rises* by Ernest Hemingway.

*Note:* This classic romantic war story still packs a punch. Contains mild profanity and understated sexual scenes. Recommended for older reluctant readers.

At first I knew her as Catherine Barkley, an English nurse trying to save Italian soldiers on the battlefield. My friend Rinaldi even thought he was in love with her.

Next, I knew her as Miss Barkley, a companion I would visit from time to time. She liked to pretend I was her fiancee who was killed during the war. I thought she was a little crazy. I did not love Catherine Barkley, nor had I any idea of loving her. This was a game, like bridge, in which you said things instead of playing cards.

Then I was wounded and while I lay in the hospital bed, Catherine came to visit. Everything turned over inside of me. God knows I had not wanted to fall in love with her or with anyone. But God knows I had.

Now I just call her Cat. Strange. I have this eerie feeling that this war will do its best to break us apart. Why do I sense death in the misty rain?

## Hesser, Terry Spencer. *Kissing Doorknobs.*

Delacorte, 1998, 149pp. Middle School & Up. Top 10 Best Books for Young Adults; Top 10 Quick Picks for Reluctant Young Adult Readers.

**REALISTIC FICTION.** *Mental illness; sex and sexuality; women's issues.*

**RELATED BOOKS:** *The Luckiest Girl in the World* and *The Best Girl in the World* by Steven Levenkron; *Gone from Home* by Angela Johnson; *Funny, You Don't Look Crazy* by Constance H. Foster; *Tormenting Thoughts and Secret Rituals* by Ian Osborn.

*Note:* The main character, Tara Sullivan, has an obsessive-compulsive disorder (OCD). The author admits to the same disorder. Hesser also addresses anorexia, shoplifting, drug use, and unsafe sex, reinforcing the idea these behaviors are different from OCD because OCD offers no reward or enjoyment. Highly recommended, even for reluctant readers.

*Step on a crack, break your mother's back!*

I heard that stupid rhyme when I was 11 and, for three years, that rhyme has hit the Replay button in my brain. Over and over. Again and again.

Next, I began counting cracks in the sidewalk. On the way to school there were exactly 495 opportunities to break my mother's back.

I guess I have a lot of fears. Before I leave home I need to touch the doorknob and kiss my fingers 33 times. At confession, I tell every sin, every sinful thought. That can take hours or 120 minutes.

I have been driving my family and friends nuts. Myself, I'm miserable. I know I need help. I must stop *Kissing Doorknobs.*

## Hickam, Homer H., Jr. *October Sky: A Memoir.*

Originally published as *Rocket Boys.* (Pbk.) Island Books, 1998, 428pp. Middle School & Up.

■ **HISTORICAL FICTION.** *Hobbies (rocketry); science; movie novels; problem parents; rivalry.*

■ **RELATED BOOKS:** *Apollo 13* by Jim Lovell and Jeffrey Kluger; *Back to the Moon* by Homer H. Hickam; *Handbook of Model Rocketry* by G. Harry Stine.

Hickam, who eventually became a respected NASA engineer, calls his memoir fiction; he changes names and uses composite characters. Recommended for reluctant readers who enjoy science.

On October 25, 1957, my life changed forever. That day the Russian space satellite *Sputnik* was launched. We Americans were jealous that the Russians beat us to the punch.

At first it wasn't a topic in Coalwood, West Virginia. Football was the main topic. Only coal mining was more important. But when the papers printed that *Sputnik* was going to fly over our town, I decided to see for myself. That night I saw a bright little ball moving across a narrow star field. I couldn't believe it. In less than a minute, it was gone.

On November 3, the Russians launched *Sputnik II.* That day I gathered Roy Lee, O'Dell, and Sherman in my room. "Listen, guys, we may only be 14, but we're gonna make history. From now on, we're gonna be rocket boys. We're going to build a rocket and launch it. Look out, world, here we come!"

## Hinton, S. E. *Rumble Fish.*

HarperCollins, 1975, 123pp. An ALA Best Book for Young Adults. Middle School & Up. An Accelerated Reader selection.

■ **REALISTIC FICTION.** *Class conflict; crime; family; friendship; men's issues; movie novels; rivalry; single parents.*

■ **RELATED BOOKS:** *The Outsiders* and *Tex* by S. E. Hinton.

All of S. E. Hinton's books are young adult classics: **The Outsiders; That Was Then (This is Now); Tex;** and **Taming Star Runner.** She began publishing at 16 and was first thought to be male. Her books do deal with men's issues. Recommend her books to reluctant male readers and watch the positive results.

Motorcycle Boy is the coolest person in the world. Even if he wasn't my brother, he is still cool, so cool. I plan to be like Motorcycle Boy one day.

At least I thought so. Then my best friend Steve and me seen what could happen to some guy who was once leader of a rumble fish. *Rumble Fish* was what we called a gang who would kill just for fun.

Maybe I better think this whole thing over.

## Hobbs, Will. *The Maze.*

Morrow Junior Books, 1998, 198pp. With author's note and map. Middle School & Up. An ALA Best Book for Young Adults; nominee for Edgar Allen Poe award for Best Young Adult Mystery; Quick Pick for Reluctant Young Adult Readers.

■ **ADVENTURE.** *Animals (birds); ecology; orphans; responsibility; runaways; science; self-identity.*

■ **RELATED BOOKS:** *Canyons* by Gary Paulsen; *River Danger* by Thomas J. Dygard; other books by Will Hobbs: *Downriver; Bearstone; Far North;* and *Ghost Canoe.*

*The author's notes gives the background and details of his research on the Pelregrine Fund, a project to release condors into the wild. He also gives a Web site for further information about the condors.*

The maze. A maze was nothing new to Rick Walker. He'd been trapped in one for almost all of his 14 years.

Orphaned and alone, Rick ran away from a juvenile detention home. He entered the Maze, a network of canyons in Utah at the Canyonlands National Park. He met Lon Peregrino, a bird biologist who was trying to release captured condors into the wild. Together they try to stop the pothunters from pillaging Native American sites on public land.

Can they save the Maze? Just as important, can Rick escape his lifelong maze and save himself?

## Holt, Kimberly Willis. *My Louisiana Sky.*

Henry Holt, 1998, 200pp. Elementary School & Up. Winner of Fiction Honors of the Boston Globe-Horn Book Award; Top 10 Best Books for Young Adults.

■ **REALISTIC FICTION.** *Disability (mental); death; peer pressure; problem parents; secrets.*

■ **RELATED BOOKS:** *The Bus People* by Rachel Anderson; *Summer of the Swans* by Betsy Byars.

*The main character, Tiger Ann Parker, lives in 1950s rural Louisiana and, without sentimentality, discusses her mixed emotions about her mentally challenged parents. Highly recommended for all types of readers, also as a group read or read-aloud.*

Some people in my town say Momma and Daddy should never have married. Folks call them "retarded." I think "slow" sounds better. As for me, I'm not slow at all. I make straight A's and have won the spelling bee five times.

I love my parents but they can embarrass me. At 12, I act older than they do. Like, Momma's favorite show is *Howdy Doody*, a stupid puppet show for kids. Sometimes I wish Momma wasn't my momma. I just want to fit in, and my parents are part of the reason I will never be accepted.

My Aunt Dorie Kay wants me to live in Baton Rouge with her. At least I would have a normal life. Should I leave my family behind to find myself?

## Howe, Norma. *Shoot for the Moon.*

Crown, 1992, 224pp. Middle School & Up.

■ **ROMANCE.** *Aging; Europe (Italy); family; love; secrets.*

■ **RELATED BOOKS:** *Relative Strangers* by Jean Ferris; *For the Love of Venice* by Donna Napoli; *Pippa Passes* by Rumer Godden; *Snowfall* by K. M. Peyton.

*Note:* The international background will appeal to romance readers.

Congratulations, Gina Gari! You've won first prize! A round-trip ticket to Italy!

Gina is just an average girl, but she can do one great thing—yo-yo tricks. Her grandfather taught her a particularly difficult trick, *shoot for the moon.* This feat led to Gina's trip to her ancestors' homeland, Italy.

Before Gina left for Italy, Gina's dying grandmother made a mysterious last request. While in Italy, Gina discovered a shocking family secret. She also discovered love with a handsome Dutchman, Stefan.

*Shoot for the Moon.* Read this exotic romance by Norma Howe.

## Hughes, Monica. *Invitation to the Game.*

(Pbk.) Aladdin Paperbacks, 1993, 183pp. Middle School & Up.

■ **SCIENCE FICTION.** *Computers; end of the world; friendship; survival.*

■ **RELATED BOOKS:** The *Tripod* series by John Christopher; *New World* by Gillian Cross.

*Note:* You could put the booktalk on stationery for the appearance of an invitation to be read during a presentation or put on display.

*You are cordially invited to participate in the Game. Date: 17.06.2154 Time: 14:30 Place: Barton Oaks*

The invitation has arrived.

At last, Lisse and her seven friends have been invited to participate in the Game. Finally, the highly robotic government will have some use for these unemployed teens.

At first, it's exciting playing the Game. Each Game transports the group to a computer-accessed world that is an unexplored wilderness. One Game takes them to the planet Prize where they decide to settle permanently.

Is this world a dream? A computer simulation? A mind-game designed to keep the unemployed busy? To find out, you'll have to accept the *Invitation to the Game.*

## Hunt, Irene. *Up a Road Slowly.*

Grosset, 1966, 186pp.; (Pbk.) Tempo, 1966, 186pp. Elementary School & Up. Winner of the Newbery Award. An Accelerated Reader selection.

■ **REALISTIC FICTION.** *Death; family; love; responsibility; rites of passage; stepparents.*

■ **RELATED BOOKS:** *A Tree Grows in Brooklyn* by Betty Smith; *Anne of Green Gables* series by L. M. Montgomery; *Rebecca of Sunnybrook Farm* by Kate Douglas Wiggin.

 *This book may seem archaic with its slow-paced recounting of a young girl's rites of passage, but its compelling story, vivid characters, and universal themes are timeless. Younger readers may benefit from a read-aloud.*

Life is a journey with many roads to travel. With each crisis, we approach a crossroad of choices. With each choice, we are led to a journey of new experiences.

Julie's journey begins with her mother's death when she is five. Leaving behind her sister, brother, and father, Julie is sent to live with her Aunt Cordelia. This road leads to a kaleidoscope of unforgettable people.

There's Danny Trevort, who received a black eye for attempting to kiss Julie. There's Aggie Kilpin, a scorned classmate until she contracts an unfortunate illness. There's Aunt Cordelia's first love, Dr. Jonathan Eltwing, who returns 20 years later with his mentally unstable wife. There's Julie's first love, Brett Kingsman, who insists that Julie do his homework.

Travel with Julie as she confronts the crossroads of her life, step by step, *Up a Road Slowly.*

## Ibbotson, Eva. *The Secret of Platform 13.*

Illustrated by Sue Porter. Dutton Children's Books, 1994, 231pp. Elementary School & Up. School Library Journal's Best Books selection.

■ **FANTASY.** *Great Britain; secrets; supernatural.*

■ **RELATED BOOKS:** *Alice in Wonderland* by Lewis Carroll; *Harry Potter and the Sorcerer's Stone* by J. K. Rowling; *To Say Nothing of the Dog* by Connie Willis.

 *A hilarious fantasy in the best English tradition, this novel is recommended for the young and young at heart.*

There's a secret under Platform 13.

In London, in an abandoned railway station, under Platform 13, is an old, poster-peeling door that door leads to an island so beautiful it takes the breath away. On the island are the usual creatures: dragons, ogres, giants, and mermaids. Also on the island live the King, Queen, and their three-month-old baby.

One disastrous day the triplet nurses take the baby for a quick trip to London, through the magical door, under Platform 13, where the prince is kidnapped by Mrs. Trottle! Sadly, nothing can be done since the magical door opens only every nine years.

Nine years later, the rescue for the kidnapped prince begins. An ancient wizard, an invisible giant, a fey, and a very young hag are the unlikely team of rescuers. Can these creatures troop around London unnoticed? What chance do they have against the wealthy and resourceful Mrs. Trottle, whose favorite perfume is called *Maneater*? What if the prince doesn't want to go back?

These answers, and more, are revealed in *The Secret of Platform 13.*

# Jackson, Phil and Hugh Delehanty. *Sacred Hoops: Spiritual Lessons of a Hardwood Warrior.*

Foreword by Senator Bill Bradley. Hyperion, 1995, 206pp. Middle School & Up.

- **SPORTS.** *African Americans; ethics; religion; sports (basketball); work.*
- **RELATED BOOKS:** *Rare Air: Michael on Michael* by Michael Jordan; *The Last Shot: City Streets, Basketball Dreams* by Darcy Frey.

 *You don't even have to be a sports lover to enjoy this one. However, give this to reluctant readers.*

Do you know me? I'm Phil Jackson, head coach of the Chicago Bulls basketball team, participant in the NBA World Championship five times, twice as a player and three times as a coach. But no one knows my name.

It doesn't matter. I have this crazy kind of belief in basketball. Basketball is the metaphor for life. A basketball team can prove that team effort can accomplish greater things than an individual. Michael Jordan is probably the greatest player of all time, but the 1991-1993 Chicago Bulls were even greater as a team. Michael Jordan's energy inspired his teammates to play their best to win three NBA championships. The Chicago Bulls were a solid, unbeatable unit, so good they made Michael Jordan play his best. As in life, the whole adds up to more than the sum of its parts. We plugged in the power of *Oneness* instead of the power of one man. It worked.

Do I sound like the Tom Cruise sports agent, Jerry Maguire? Well, I do have a philosophy about sports. You'll hear about it from time to time. Meanwhile, join me on the court for some *Sacred Hoops.*

# Jacques, Brian. *Redwall: Book One, The Wall.*

G. P. Putnam's Sons, 1986, 351pp. (Pbk.) Avon, 1990, 351pp. For all libraries. First in the **Redwall** series; **Mossflower, Prequel to Redwall; Mattimeo; Salamandastron; Mariel the Warrior; Mariel of Redwall; The Bellmaker; Outcast of Redwall; The Great Redwell Feast; Pearls of Lutra; The Long Patrol** follow. An Accelerated Reader selection.

- **FANTASY.** *Animals (mice); ethics; revenge; rivalry; rites of passage; survival.*

- **RELATED BOOKS:** *Mrs. Frisby and the Rats of NIMH* by Robert C. O'Brien; The *DiscWorld* series by Terry Pratchett.

*This series has already attained cult status. Think of it as a rodent **Star Wars,** with the battle between goodness and evil. The highly-developed characters might change from episode to episode, but it is all contained within the world of Redwall Abbey.*

Long ago and far away, in Mice Kingdom, was the Redwall Abbey. Redwall Abbey was occupied by mice dedicated to serving poor and sickly creatures. It was neutral territory to all bandits. None of the animal outlaws disturbed these mice because they knew these noble rodents might come to their aid one day.

Inside the Redwall Abbey lived the young mouse Matthias. Matthias was bored. Nothing exciting ever happened inside Redwall. He so longed for an exciting life like the legendary mouse, Martin the Warrior. Instead, Matthias was confined to Redwall, tending to the poor and sick, day after endless day.

Beware, Matthias, your wish is about to come true. The one-eyed sea rat Cluny and his cutthroats are on their way to change history forever!

**J**

## Jaffe, Nina and Steve Zeitlin. *The Cow of No Color: Riddle Stories and Justice Tales from Around the World.*

Pictures by Whitney Sherman. Henry Holt, 1998, 162pp. Elementary School & Up.

■ **FOLKLORE.** *Africa (Ghana, Nigeria); Asia (China, Vietnam, Laos, Korea); ethics; Middle East (India, Israel, Syria).*

■ **RELATED BOOKS:** *Go and Come Back* by Joan Abelove; *Juba That and Juba This* edited by Virginia Tashjian; *Making Up Megaboy* by Virginia Walter and Katrina Roeckelin.

 *A highly recommended read-aloud and discussion book for the young and the old.*

Once there was a king who was jealous of Nunyala, a wise woman who lived in an African village. He ordered her to bring him a cow of no color or she would face certain death. After thinking, the woman sent the king a message. This message saved her life. What was the message?

This book asks many questions having to do with justice and a sense of fair play. After the story is told, the authors leave it up to you to solve.

What's fair? What's the right thing to do? You decide.

## Jimenez, Francisco. *The Circuit: Stories from the Life of a Migrant Child.*

(Pbk.) University of Mexico, 1997, 134pp. Middle School & Up. Fiction Winner of the Boston Globe-Horn Book Awards; winner of the John and Patricia Beatty Award from the California Library Association; winner of the 1997 Americas Award.

■ **SHORT STORIES.** *Hispanic Americans; immigrants; work.*

■ **RELATED BOOKS:** *The House on Mango Street* by Sandra Cisneros; *Parrot in the Oven* by Victor Martinez.

 *These 12 short stories describe the dismal, struggling migrant life of young Panchito and his Hispanic family. The last story, "Moving Still," is particularly poignant as an immigration officer collects Panchito at his school. Unforgettable.*

"What's California like?" I asked my older brother Roberto. My family had traveled from Mexico for two days and nights on a train with little sleep. The wooden seats were hard, and the train rumbled on the tracks, making loud noises.

Roberto answered, assuredly, "I don't know, but Fito tells me that people sweep money off the streets. He said he saw it in a movie."

Papa laughed. "He's joking. But it's true life is better there."

Maybe our dreams will never meet our expectations. We expected high-paying jobs; instead, we worked as migrants, picking cotton. We expected to live in a fine *casa;* instead, we lived in a tent at a labor camp. We expected an excellent education; instead, we could barely understand English.

When will our dreams meet our expectations?

## Johnson, Angela. *Heaven.*

Simon and Schuster for Young Readers, 1998, 138pp. Middle School & Up. Winner of the Coretta Scott King Author Award.

■ **REALISTIC FICTION.** *Adoption; African Americans; secrets; self-identity.*

■ **RELATED BOOKS:** *Second Cousins* and *Plain City* by Virginia Hamilton; *Baby* by Patricia MacLachlan; *The Great Gilly Hopkins* by Katherine Paterson.

 *Note:* At 14, Marley discovers she has been adopted and that her Uncle Jack is her father. This award-winning book is recommended for reluctant readers, especially in the middle school.

Momma said it was destined we'd find Heaven. About 12 years ago Momma found a postcard on a park bench postmarked HEAVEN, OHIO. She said she'd been looking for Heaven all her life—so we moved: Momma, Pops, Butchy, and me.

Heaven had always been heaven. Then, one stormy afternoon, I discovered the truth. My parents are liars. My brother was a stranger, and Uncle Jack was part of the mystery of my past. Now I don't know who I am.

Do I have the perfect life, or is my life the perfect lie?

## Karr, Kathleen. *The Great Turkey Walk.*

Farrar Straus & Giroux, 1998, 208pp. Elementary School & Up. School Library Journal's Best Books selection.

■ **HISTORICAL FICTION.** *African Americans; animals (turkeys); Native Americans (Potawatomi); orphans; pioneer life; runaways.*

■ **RELATED BOOKS:** *The Great American Elephant Chase* by Gillian Cross; *Sunshine Rider: The First Vegetarian Western* by Ric Lynden Harden; *Tom Sawyer* by Mark Twain.

*Note:* This spirited, humorous book is in the **Tom Sawyer** tradition with some memorable characters: a drunken muleskinner, a fugitive slave, and a feisty girl. The main character, Simon Green, is academically slow, but has "horse sense." Recommended for reluctant readers who like humor and action.

Howdy, I'm Simon Green.

When my teacher Miss Rogers up and graduated me from the third grade, I was right honored. Folks snickered she graduated me to get rid of me. After all, I'm tall, 15, and failed the third grade four times!

Folks can snicker all they want. Miss Rogers turned out to be a friend. She even invested her life savings in my turkey business.

I got this here idea to take 1,000 turkeys from Missouri to Denver. Me and my partners plan to make $5 a head. 'Course this is 1860, and I gotta confront Indians, the U. S. calvary, and my scalawag of a father!

So, saddle up. Let's go on *The Great Turkey Walk*.

## Katz, Susan. *Snowdrops for Cousin Ruth.*

Simon and Schuster for Young Readers, 1998, 183pp. Elementary School & Up.

■ **REALISTIC FICTION.** *Death; family; rites of passage; trust.*

■ **RELATED BOOKS:** *The Barn* by Avi; *Toning the Sweep* by Angela Johnson; *Walk Two Moons* by Sharon Creech.

 *In her first novel, Katz presents a thoughtful yet unsentimental story about death, grieving, and healing. Nine-year-old Johanna also deals with a threatening bully.*

Eight months ago, my younger brother Johnny was hit by a car and killed. On that day, my sister stopped talking.

Susie sees a doctor, but I think I'm the crazy one. Johnny talks to me in my mind, and somehow I answer him back. I'm not permitted to speak Johnny's name aloud. My father has forbidden me. He says it makes Susie and my mother sad. I just don't want to forget my brother.

Cousin Ruth understands. "Sometimes," she said, "your heart knows more than your head. It's all right to talk about Johnny." Her wrinkled fingers touched her heart. "In here, a person never dies. In your heart, he lives forever. Don't forget that, Jo."

"I won't." I promised. "But what about my family? They don't know that Johnny still lives in their heart."

"Things will be better," Cousin Ruth assured me. "There's never been a winter without a spring. One day spring will come. One day they'll understand. Just give it time."

My mind whispered, "Hurry, Johnny. Bring the spring quickly and heal their aching hearts."

## Kerr, M. E. *Linger.*

HarperCollins, 1993, 213pp. Middle School & Up.

■ **ROMANCE.** *Ethics; love; problem parents; rites of passage; secrets; sex and sexuality; trust; war.*

■ **RELATED BOOKS:** *The Wind Blows Backward* by Mary Downing Hahn; *Forever* by Judy Blume; *Just a Summer Romance* by Ann M. Martin; *Perfect Strangers* by Jean Ferris.

 *Note: This coming-of-age novel splices Bobby's journal and letters with Gary's narrative, providing two viewpoints. Recommended for a reader who wants a thought-provoking, realistic look at the United States during the 1990s.*

Dear Lynn,

How would you feel about having a Desert Storm soldier for a pen pal?

Bobby Peel

*Dear Bobby,*

*About your pen pal, Lynn Dunlinger. Today I saw her coming from Lingering Pines with this guy in the snow. Something about the two of them was so different, it's hard to describe. If I were you, I wouldn't count on her.*

*Your brother,*

*Gary*

Sadly, Gary discovered a secret about Lynn at Linger, the restaurant owned by Lynn's father. His brother, Pvt. Robert Peel, is scheduled to return from the Persian Gulf around the Fourth of July. That will the perfect time for the real fireworks to begin. Should Gary tell his brother what he knows about Lynn and *Linger*?

## Kesey, Ken. *One Flew Over the Cuckoo's Nest.*

(Pbk.) Penguin, 1962, 272pp. High School & Up. An Accelerated Reader selection.

■ **REALISTIC FICTION.** *Mental illness; movie novels; rivalry.*

■ **RELATED BOOKS:** *I Never Promised You a Rose Garden* by Joanne Greenberg; *Catch 22* by Joseph Heller; *Catcher in the Rye* by J. D. Salinger.

 *This classic is a multifaceted work of art, in theme, plot construction, and character-ization. However, its subtle racism and sexism would not be politically correct today. Recommend this one to a mature reader who can ignore these deficiencies.*

When R. P. McMurphy arrived, things changed forever in the cuckoo's nest.

McMurphy was the first mental patient to take on Nurse Ratched by outsmarting her. He knew if he shouted at the Big Nurse, he would risk being sent to the Shock Shop. So all his requests, like watching a football game, were presented mild-ly and reasonably. For his protection, he also enlisted doctors or patients on his side.

Nurse Ratched had no fear of this upstart. For 30 years, she had brutally run this men-tal institution in a saccharine-sweet style that fooled no one. She had no intention of relin-quishing her power.

The war has begun. Who will be the victor of the Cuckoo's Nest?

## Kherdian, David, ed. *Beat Voices: An Anthology of Beat Poetry.*

Henry Holt, 1995, 144pp. High School & Up.

■ **POETRY.** *Class conflict; ethics; homosexuality; politics; sex and sexuality; substance abuse; war.*

■ **RELATED BOOKS:** *The Birth of the Beat Generation* by Steven Watson; *The Beat Book: Poems and Fiction of the Beat Generation*, edited by Anne Waldman; *The Portable Beat Reader*, edited by Ann Charters.

 *Depending on the readers, you might also mention that the Beat poets were the first to use profanity in their poetry. The poems are still as titillating and shocking as they must have been in the 1950s.*

The Beats were prophets of the future. The Beats introduced the Civil Rights movement, antiwar protests, drug use, and rap music. After the Beats, American conventions and customs were radically and forever changed.

Beat poetry began in San Francisco in 1955 when Allen Ginsberg gave a public reading of his poem *Howl*. From this prophetic and profane poem sprang coffee houses, poetry readings, paperback bookstores, and love-ins. Ginsberg's friend Jack Kerouac took the Beats one step further. He wrote *On the Road* based on his experiences with the Beats. For the first time, recreational drug use was endorsed. Through words alone, the Beats would inspire future generations.

The Beats heralded a cultural revolution that still reverberates today. See how similar Beat poetry is to rap music. Beat poetry is timeless because it speaks to hungry, angry minds. Especially today.

## Kilcher, Jewel. *A Night Without Armor: Poems.*

HarperCollins, 1998, 136pp. Middle School & Up. An ALA Best Book for Young Adults; Quick Pick for Reluctant Young Adult Readers.

■ **POETRY.** *Family; ethics; love; problem parents.*

■ **RELATED BOOK:** *A Lion's Hunger* by Ann Turner.

*You might read several of her poems, such as "You Tell Me," "We Talk," and "After the Divorce."*

Did you know the singer Jewel is also a poet?

Jewel has been writing poems since she was a young girl living with her family in Alaska. From Jewel's early years, her mother would gather Jewel and her brothers after school for "workshops" in music, visual art, and writing. Long before Jewel wrote songs, poetry filled her journals.

Some of these poems are about her childhood in Alaska and her relationships with her family and loved ones. She also movingly tells her of her journey on the road to fame.

Take this poetic journey with Jewel.

## King, Stephen. *Bag of Bones.*

Scribner, 1998, 529pp. High School & Up. Winner of the Bram Stoker Award for Horror.

■ **HORROR.** *Death; love; occult; single parents; work.*

■ **RELATED BOOKS:** *Rebecca* by Daphne Du Maurier; *Fear Nothing* and *Seize the Night* by Dean Koontz; The *Dark Tower* series by Stephen King.

*The master of suspense has paid homage to Daphne Du Maurier's* **Rebecca.** *Both books can be compared and analyzed by book groups.*

My dreams haunt me.

Last night, once again, I dreamed of Sara. Sara was not a female, but, just the same, she possessed my mind and spirit. *Sara Laughs* was the name of the house and property my deceased wife and I occupied. Joanna said it was my reward for being a best-seller horror writer. The property did have a sinister and macabre aura, with its low tree branches and its high, mossy logs on the main house.

In my dream, I drive closer and closer to the forbidden *Sara Laughs*. I see Jo's coffin. As I retreat from the car and walk towards the coffin, I notice it is open and that my wife is no longer in the coffin. My feet have turned to lead. Suddenly, the back door opens and this half-human runs shrieking towards me. In spite of the torn-away shroud that dances with the wind, I recognize this bag of bones. It must be Joanna.

I awake, trembling. Now I understand. She is alive. Sara is alive, even though my wife will not return. For four years, I have stayed away from my ghosts. It's time to return to my house, the root of my happiness and despair. Regardless of the outcome, I must confront this *Bag of Bones*.

# Kingsolver, Barbara. *Animal Dreams.*

HarperCollins, 1990, 342pp. High School & Up.

■ **REALISTIC FICTION.** *Caribbean and Latin America; death; family; Native Americans; pregnancy; secrets; sex and sexuality; war; work; women's issues.*

■ **RELATED BOOKS:** *The Bean Tree* and *The Poisonwood Bible* by Barbara Kingsolver; *A Yellow Boat in Blue Water* by Michael Dorris.

I'm the sister who didn't go to war.

That's how I'm described in my hometown. I haven't been back to Grace, Arizona, since high school, over 15 years ago. Now I've returned like a prodigal child hoping that I can be accepted. I lost a mother and an unborn daughter in Grace. I also lost myself.

My sister Hallie is the sister who went to war. She's helping the farmers raise their crops in Nicaragua. People in Grace are confused about South American countries so it's easier to say Hallie's gone to war. Ironically, they turn out to be right.

Hallie lived her dreams by going to Nicaragua. Me, I've always had strange dreams about a past I don't want to remember. My friend Loyd says, "If you want sweet dreams, you've got to live a sweet life."

My life isn't sweet, but I'm working on it.

# Kingsolver, Barbara. *The Bean Tree.*

(Pbk.) HarperPerennial, 1988, 232pp. High School & Up. **Pigs in Heaven** follows.

■ **REALISTIC FICTION.** *Adoption; immigrants; Native Americans; work.*

■ **RELATED BOOKS:** *Fried Green Tomatoes at the Whistle Stop Cafe* by Fannie Flagg; *Steel Magnolias* by Robert Harling; *In Country* by Bobbie Ann Mason.

 *Note:* This series is a favorite with readers who enjoy well-developed characters in a down-home style.

As I left Kentucky in my '55 Volkwagon bug, I made two promises to myself. One I kept, the other I did not.

I promised myself a new name. I am now Taylor Greer.

The second promise is that I would drive west until my car broke down. That's where I would stay. But when that happened in Oklahoma, I stayed only long enough to be given an abused, Native American baby. Then my baby Turtle and I were on our way.

We made it to *Jesus is Lord Used Tires* outside Tucson. Honest. That's the name of the place.

We also met Lou Ann and that's where our adventures began.

## Klier, John and Helen Mingay. *The Quest for Anastasia: Solving the Mystery of the Lost Romanovs.*

Secaucus, NJ: Carol, 1997, 246pp. Middle School & Up.

■ **NONFICTION.** *Death; family; Russia; politics; war.*

■ **RELATED BOOKS:** *Anastasia: The Lost Princess* by James Blair Lovell; *Anastasia: The Riddle of Anna Anderson* by Peter Kurth.

 *Interested readers will also want to read Peter Kurth's* **The Riddle of Anna Anderson.** *In spite of the DNA evidence, Kurth arrives at a different conclusion about Anna Anderson. Recommended also as a fascinating topic for a research paper.*

In 1994 a real-life mystery was solved. The DNA samples of a Russian princess and a Polish factory worker were compared. The factory worker, Anna Anderson, could not have been the youngest daughter of the last czar of Russia. Anastasia was not Anna Anderson.

Unfortunately, the real Anastasia was executed with her royal family on July 16, 1918. Her bones were recovered to prove it.

Why did Anna Anderson claim to be Anastasia? Why did so many experts believe her?

## Knowles, John. *A Separate Peace.*

(Pbk.) Bantam Books, 1959, 196pp. Part of a series: **Peace Breaks Out** follows. Middle School & Up. An Accelerated Reader selection.

■ **HISTORICAL FICTION.** *Death; physical disability; friendship; ethics; school; World War II.*

■ **RELATED BOOKS:** *Catcher in the Rye* by J. D. Salinger; *To Kill a Mockingbird* by Harper Lee.

 *This classic is still recommended in high schools. There is some mild profanity.*

I killed Finny, my best friend.

I don't think I meant to do it. It all started out as a stupid game that Finny invented. We were to climb a tree behind the woods of Devon School, walk out on the limb, and jump into the river. It was dangerous from that height, but we did it again and again. Finny told the headmaster we jumped for the war, but I think we did it out of boredom.

And then it happened. To this day I don't understand it. I did something that would change our world forever. My best friend would never recover, and neither would I. Now I have no desire to experience combat. I have met the enemy and that enemy was more dangerous than any Nazi. That enemy was myself.

## Koller, Jackie French. *The Falcon.*

Atheneum Books for Young Readers, 1998, 181pp. Middle School & Up. An ALA Best Book for Young Adults.

■ **REALISTIC FICTION.** *Diaries; physical disability; homosexuality; school; sex and sexuality; sports (wrestling); suicide.*

■ **RELATED BOOKS:** *Tangerine* by Edward Bloor; *Staying Fat for Sarah Byrnes* by Chris Crutcher; *Kissing Doorknobs* by Terry Spencer Hesser; *The Luckiest Girl in the World* by Steven Levenkron.

*Note:* The author uses a diary format with the clever device of a crossed-out text that hints of Luke's real feelings. For four years, Luke has lied to his parents about how he lost his eye. This lie leads to Luke's self-destructive behavior, resulting in another accident in which Luke injures his good eye. In the hospital, Luke's therapist gives Luke some insight into his masochistic behavior. An engrossing read.

Is this lame or what? At 17, I'm writing a journal. I'm only doing it because Mrs. Robinson, my English teacher, requires it. Now I'm addicted.

I find myself thinking a lot since I've started this journal. I'm not sure that's good. I've spent years not thinking about it, and now I'm thinking about it again. I thought climbing Top-o'-the-World would help me forget it. All climbing that mountain did was make me realize that I was taking stupid risks. I thought wrestling would make me forget, but all it did was make me terrified to face other heavyweights. I thought Megan could help, but she was too busy sitting on Tony Lieberman's lap during my wrestling match.

Now that I've landed in the hospital with another eye injury, I have to face the truth. My accidents aren't accidental. I just hope I have the courage to change.

## Krakauer, Jon. *Into Thin Air: A Personal Account of the Mount Everest Disaster.*

Villard, 1997, 293pp; (Pbk.) Anchor Doubleday, 1998, 293pp. Middle School & Up. An ALA Best Book for Young Adults; Quick Picks for Reluctant Young Adult Readers.

■ **NONFICTION.** *Asia; death; movie novels; sports (mountain climbing); survival.*

■ **RELATED BOOKS:** *Into the Wild* by Jon Krakauer; *Within Reach: My Everest Story* by Mark Pfetzer and Jack Galvin; *Alive: The Story of the Andres Survivors* by Piers Paul Read; *The Climb* by Anatoll Boukreev.

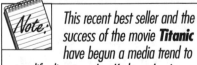

*Note:* This recent best seller and the success of the movie **Titanic** have begun a media trend to true-life disasters. Jon Krakauer's crisp, fast-paced style is in the Jack London tradition. Highly recommended read for groups or individuals.

On May 10, 1996, nine climbers died on a guided ascent to Mount Everest. Within the next months, three more climbers died. Why did veteran Himalayan guides and their inexperienced climbers keep ascending the mountain with a deadly storm brewing?

Nobody can speak for the leaders of the two guided groups because both men are dead. However, I, Jon Krakauer, was there as a writer and climber. I don't recall seeing threatening clouds. Of course, it is hard to be alert when your brain is depleted of oxygen.

Since I've returned, I've gone over the details repeatedly. The Everest climb rocked my life to its core. Some spent $65,000 apiece to be taken safely up Everest. Instead, multiple tragedies occurred.

What happened? I will take you through our climb step by step.

## Kurtz, Jane. *The Storyteller's Beads.*

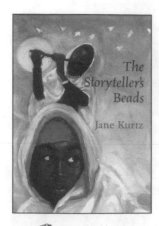

Harcourt Brace, 1998, 154pp. Elementary School & Up.

■ **REALISTIC FICTION.** *Africa (Ethiopia); physical disability; friendship; Jews; religion; religious prejudice.*

■ **RELATED BOOKS:** *Shadow Spinner* by Susan Fletcher; *Song of Be* by Lesley Beake.

 *There's an afterword describing the history of the ethnic groups in Ethiopia. Recommended as a multicultural read-aloud or discussion book.*

Grandmother handed Rahel the beads and said, "Here are storyteller's beads to take on your journey to Jerusalem. Before you go, I will tell you many stories. When you touch a bead, you will remember a story."

Rahel was blind, but she could hear and remember each story. She would escape Ethiopia and take these stories with her to her religious homeland, the *Beta-Israel*.

Sahay left Ethiopia because the rains didn't come, the food didn't grow, and the *Red Terror* had arrived in her village. She and her uncle ran away late at night, never to return.

When Sahay and Rahel met, they confronted two different worlds. Sahay was scornful of Rahel because Rahel was an Egyptian Jew (*Falasha*). Still, Sahay felt drawn to this blind girl who told such wonderful stories. Maybe together they could escape from this hostile country to a safer place.

Can these two girls overcome their prejudices and help each other escape? Can they survive if they don't?

## Lapierre, Dominque. *The City of Joy.*

Arrow Books, 1986, 517pp. Translated from the French by Kathryn Spink. High School & Up.

■ **REALISTIC FICTION.** *Death; ethics; homelessness; illness; India and Pakistan; movie novels; religion; religious prejudice; work.*

■ **RELATED BOOKS:** *A Passage to India* by E. M. Forester; *The God of Small Things* by Arundhati Roy; *Mother Teresa* by Navin Chawla.

 *Many high school book lists contain this one. The movie with Patrick Swayze is quite different. The book contains more messages of faith.*

Inside Calcutta, India, is a small space with more than 70,000 inhabitants, including Muslims, Hindus, Jains, Christians, and Buddhists. To our eyes, this area is a slum with its unemployment, starvation, and unsanitary living conditions. However, to the Christian priest Steven Kovalsky, Calcutta is truly a City of Joy. These inhabitants are the kindest and most spiritual of any human beings he has known.

Hasair Pal pulls a rickshaw to provide for his family. This backbreaking work turns humans into horses, but in the City of Joy this labor is worth the sacrifice. Sabia is a child dying of tuberculosis, and his agony is heard through the paper-thin walls, night after night. Yet the residents are more concerned about his suffering than their lack of sleep. Bondona is called *Angel in the City of Joy* because of her concern for all people of all religions.

Steven Kovalsky can never forget *The City of Joy*. Neither will you.

## Lasky, Kathryn. *Alice Rose and Sam.*

With afterword by author. Hyperion Books for Children, 1998, 252pp. Middle School & Up. Nominee for Edgar Allen Poe Award for Best Children's Mystery.

- ■ **HISTORICAL FICTION.** *Asian Americans; crime; death; pioneer life; racism; religion; women's issues.*
- ■ **RELATED BOOKS:** *The Ballad of Lucy Whipple* by Karen Cushman; *Oh, Those Harper Girls!* By Kathleen Karr; *Buffalo Women* by Bill Wallace; *The Celebrated Jumping Frog of Calaveras County and Other Sketches* by Mark Twain.

> *Note:* After the booktalk, ask students, "Who is Samuel Clemens?" The answer is, of course, Mark Twain. This book blends historical fiction and mystery for a satisfying read. Alice Rose is a plucky heroine; a Chinese immigrant, Hop Sing, adds to the western atmosphere. The afterword separates fact from fiction.

"Come quickly, Mr. Clemens." Alice Rose grabbed his hand and tugged him along. "I got a story for you."

"What story?"

"You know that gunslinger, the one hired to kill that judge in Carson City? He's probably with the Society of Seven, that secret religious group who murders people. That guy is hankering to kill a harmless drunk."

It was too late. The man lay in the dust, murdered in cold blood. "This is no run-of-the-mill murder, Mr. Clemens. For once, forget writing your outlandish tall tales about politicians. We need to investigate this."

The investigation began. Alice Rose and her friend, Samuel Clemens, planned to get to the bottom of this murder. They just hoped they lived long enough to tell the tale!

## Lawrence, Iain. *The Wreckers.*

Delacorte, 1998, 196pp. Middle School & Up. Nominee for the Edgar Allen Poe Award for Best Young Adult's Mystery; Quick Pick for Reluctant Young Adult Readers; School Library Journal's Best Books selection.

- ■ **ADVENTURE.** *Great Britain; Middle Ages; supernatural; survival.*
- ■ **RELATED BOOKS:** *Treasure Island* by Robert Lewis Stevenson; *Smugglers* by Iain Lawrence; *The Pirate's Son* by Geraldine McCaughrean.

> *Note:* The main character, John Spencer, tells a suspenseful tale of pirates, kidnapping, and ghosts. The author also includes an historical explanation of the practice of "wrecking." A sure-fire hit for reluctant readers.

My first time at sea ended in my first shipwreck.

In 1779, I was only 14 when my father's ship, the *Isle of Skye*, was tossed on the rocky shore somewhere in Great Britain. At first we were grateful for the cry, "Land ho! Land ho!" Afterwards, the waves pushed me overboard and I lost consciousness.

When I awoke, I saw three men coming in my direction. "This one's alive," said one, pointing his foot at a sailor I knew as Cridge. This man, our rescuer, raised his boot, set it on Cridge's head, and pushed him under the water.

Now I understood. These men weren't rescuers. They hadn't come to save us, but to plunder the ship and kill us. Will I be able to escape from *The Wreckers*?

## Lee, Marie G. *Necessary Roughness.*

(Pbk.) HarperTrophy, 1996, 228pp. Middle School & Up. An ALA Best Book for Young Readers.

■ **SPORTS.** *Abuse; Asian Americans; death; family; friendship; immigrants (Korea); interracial relations; love; problem parents; racism; school; sports (football).*

■ **RELATED BOOKS:** *Bull Catcher* by Alden Carter; *Bat 6* by Virginia Wolff; *Blue Star Rapture* by James W. Bennett.

 *The main character, Chan Kim, reflects on many issues besides sports: love, death, and Korean family traditions. Recommended especially for reluctant readers.*

Welcome to Minnesota, Land of Ten Thousand Hicks. My family and I have moved from Los Angeles and are staying at the Hell Motel. Actually, it's really the Hello Motel, but the O on the neon sign is almost out.

Let me give you a tour of my new high school. My twin sister Young and I are the only Asian Americans. It's a blond-haired, blue-eyed whiteout. Because I'm Asian, some idiots ask me if I'm a good kicker. I guess they think all Asians play soccer, but soccer is a lot different from football. Or so I found out.

My football coach believes in "necessary roughness." He's always chewing out the players in public, questioning their manhood, trying to get the large ones to flatten out the smaller ones. When some players blindfolded me, tied me up, and jammed me into a locker, I wonder if that's what the coach had in mind.

How much *Necessary Roughness* should I tolerate?

# Levenkron, Steven. *The Luckiest Girl in the World.*

(Pbk.) Penguin, 1997, 189pp. Middle School & Up. An ALA Best Book for Young Adults.

■ **REALISTIC FICTION.** *Abuse; mental illness; peer pressure; problem parents; responsibility; secrets; self-identity; sports (ice skating); trust.*

■ **RELATED BOOKS:** *The Best Little Girl in the World* by Steven Levenkron; *The Falcon* by Jackie Koller French; *Rats Saw God* by Rob Thomas; *Tangerine* by Edward Bloor.

 *Note:* *The author does a commendable job of sympathetically portraying Katie's stressful life that results in her self-mutilation, and how, through the help of a therapist, she overcomes it. Counselors should read and recommend this one.*

Everyone thought Katie was the luckiest girl in the world. She was pretty, smart, and on her way to be a champion figure skater.

What people didn't know was that Katie had many pressures, including an overbearing mother and an absent father. Whenever Katie was upset with herself, she would take her scissors and jab them into her arm. Her arm was covered with tiny scars as a result of her self-mutilation. Katie's secret was contained within one of the many compartments in her life. As long as she could hide this problem, she thought she could keep the walls from tumbling down.

One day, during a frustrating day at school, the floodgates opened. Katie's locker door didn't slam properly, and she banged it shut, again and again. In her fury, she began slamming her hand on the door, again and again. Students tried to restrain her, but she continued bashing her head against a wall, again and again.

Now *The Luckiest Girl in the World* has revealed her true self. Will she be lucky enough to find the help that she so desperately needs?

## Levin, Betty. *Look Back, Moss.*

Greenwillow, 1998, 152pp. With author's note. Elementary School & Up. Part of a series; **Away to Me, Moss** precedes.

■ **REALISTIC FICTION.** *Abuse; animals (dogs); ecology; ethics; politics; problem parents; responsibility; trust.*

■ **RELATED BOOKS:** *Sounder* by William Armstrong; *Shiloh* series by Phyllis Naylor; *The Trouble with Tuck* by Theodore Taylor; *The Summer of the Monkeys* by Wilson Rawls.

 *This book weaves a compelling story within a thoughtful depiction of both sides of the animal rights issue. Also includes basic knowledge of sheepdogs and their need to work. Recommended as a group book selection or as a read-aloud.*

Sometimes Jody was an accomplice to a crime. His job was to create a diversion so that his mom and Aunt Marie could rescue helpless animals. He didn't feel good about his family stealing animals. When he protested, they always reminded him to think of the animals he would save from suffering. As animal rights advocates, they were willing to go to any lengths to protect animals.

Lately, Jody was tired of the drama. When his mom botched an attempt to rescue sheep, she brought home an injured sheep-herding border collie. For the first time, Jody took an interest in an injured animal and named him Moss. Moss had traits Jody wished he had: dignity, bravery, and wisdom.

The problem was that Moss belonged to another family. Jody's mom had stolen Moss, excusing her actions by saying the dog needed to be saved from an abusive life. But was Moss abused or was Moss happiest herding sheep? That problem haunted Jody night after night.

In a flash, Jody saw a solution to his problem. It would take Moss's trust, but he might be able to pull it off. Jody reached down to hug Moss. "We're on our way, " he whispered to the dog. "We're on our way."

## Levitin, Sonia. *Silver Days.*

Simon and Schuster, 1989, 186pp. Elementary School & Up. Sequel to **Journey to America.**

■ **HISTORICAL FICTION.** *Class conflict; family; Jews; Holocaust; immigrants (German); religious prejudice.*

■ **RELATED BOOKS:** *Shadow of the Wall* by Christa Laird; *The All-of-a-Kind Family* series by Sydney Taylor.

 *A recommended book for a realistic portrayal of Jewish immigrants during the 1940s.*

After the horrors of Nazi Germany, the Platt family is finally united and safe in America, Land of the Free. Surely, they will have golden days for the rest of their lives. That dream fades with the nightmare of poverty and anti-Semitism.

At 13, Lisa feels shame and despair for her family. She longs to be American, but her clothes don't look right and her English is poor. Her parents have their own problems. Lisa's mother is consumed with finding her missing mother. Lisa's father has trouble finding a job. Only her six-year-old sister Annie seems to easily adjust to the new surroundings.

In spite of their struggles, the Platts have each other. Join them on their journey through their *Silver Days.*

## Lindbergh, Anne Morrow. *A Gift from the Sea.*

(Pbk.) Pantheon Books, 1985, 138pp. First published in 1955. High School & Up.

- ■ **SHORT STORIES AND ESSAYS.** *Ecology; ethics; family; hobbies; love; responsibility; work; women's issues.*
- ■ **RELATED BOOKS:** *Bring me a Unicorn* by Anne Morrow Lindbergh; *Return to the Sea: Reflections on Anne Morrow Lindbergh's Gift From the Sea* by Anne M. Johnson and Sara Steele.

*These essays are still relevant today. Recommended to language arts teachers and aspiring writers.*

The poet John Donne once wrote, "No man is an island." I disagree. I feel we are islands, all placed around a common sea.

I am Anne Morrow Lindbergh, married to Charles Lindbergh, the famous pilot. I have five children, many friends, many responsibilities. Yet, like an island, I am myself. Alone. I must find my personal peace within the axis of my mind.

Once I brought back a moon shell from my solitary vacation. It will remain on my desk to remind me of one thought: *solitude.* This shell will remind me that a woman must be as still as the axis of wheel in the midst of her many activities. Through solitude, she can save herself, her family, her friends, and perhaps even civilization. This moon shell will be *A Gift from the Sea.*

## Lindbergh, Reeve. *Under a Wing: A Memoir.*

Simon and Schuster, 1998, 223pp. Middle School & Up.

- ■ **BIOGRAPHY.** *Ethics; family; love; politics; World War II; work.*
- ■ **RELATED BOOKS:** *A Gift from the Sea* by Anne Morrow Lindbergh; *Charles A. Lindbergh: A Human Hero* by James Cross Giblin; *Lindbergh* by A. Scott Berg.

*This book and Anne Morrow Lindbergh's* **A Gift from the Sea** *are recommended as mother-daughter reads as well as for aspiring writers.*

"This is Reeve Lindbergh. She is Charles Lindbergh's daughter, you know."

"No, no, " A firm voice said. "You mean, she is Anne Morrow's daughter."

I am both, of course. I am the daughter of pilot Charles Lindbergh and writer Anne Morrow. How was it to grow up in a family of two legends? In their time they were as famous a couple as Franklin and Eleanor Roosevelt.

Actually, it was a highly functional and supportive family. My brother was kidnapped and killed before either I or my siblings were born. When I became an adult, I also lost my only child. My mother advised me to say goodbye to my dead child. I then realized my mother never had that opportunity with her own son's death.

Growing up, I heard the gossip that my father Charles Lindbergh was anti-Semitic. Once he visited Nazi Germany and publicly admired the government. Later he made a controversial speech that seemed to affirm it. I will try to explain my father's reasons why he might have said such despicable things.

Here is the human side to two legends that only a daughter can write.

## Lobel, Anita. *No Pretty Pictures: A Child of War.*

Greenwillow, 1998, 193pp. Middle School & Up. Top 10 Best Books for Young Adults; nominee for National Book Award for Young People.

■ **BIOGRAPHY.** *Europe (Poland); Holocaust; Jews; religious prejudice; World War II.*

■ **RELATED BOOKS:** *I Have Lived a Thousand Years* by Livia Bitton Jackson; *The Seamstress: A Memoir of Survival* by Sara Tuvel Bernstein; *The Diary of a Young Girl: The Definitive Edition* by Anne Frank.

 *A heart-wrenching book that lingers. Highly recommended.*

I was five when World War II began. The Germans marched into our Polish city with their shiny boots and bayonets. I was 12 when my brother and I were finally freed from the Nazi concentration camps. By a miracle, my younger brother and I survived.

It was hard for all my family. First, my father disappeared without warning. Then we heard the words *transported, concentration camp, liquidation.* My mother obtained illegal papers claiming she wasn't Jewish. With her help, my brother and I hid in a village with our Catholic nanny. My brother had to dress as a girl to protect himself. I had to pretend I wasn't Jewish.

Years later, after much success as a children's illustrator, I still occasionally felt the horror and losses of my childhood. It was difficult to write this autobiography. In my story, there are *No Pretty Pictures.*

## Lowry, Lois. *Anastasia Krupnik.*

Bantam, 1979. Middle School & Up. First in a series: **Anastasia Again; Anastasia at Your Service; Anastasia at this Address; Anastasia On Her Own; Anastasia, Ask Your Analyst; Anastasia Has the Answers; Anastasia Absolutely.** An Accelerated Reader selection.

■ **REALISTIC FICTION.** *Aging; death; diaries; family; illness (physical and mental); pregnancy; rites of passage; rivalry; school; women's issues.*

■ **RELATED BOOKS:** *Harriet the Spy* by Louise Fitzhugh; *A Girl Named Al* and the *Al* series by Constance Greene.

 *This book can be recommend for the mature elementary student. There is some profanity and mention of sex.*

Anastasia Krupnik keeps a green notebook of private information. Some of her list reads like this:

| THINGS I LIKE | THINGS I HATE |
|---|---|
| making lists | boys |
| my parents | babies |
| my grandmother | MY PARENTS! |
| Washburn Curry (maybe) | boys, except for Washburn |
| babies (especially Sam) | |

Join Anastasia as she takes you through each item on her list. She changes her mind (and list) constantly, but that's life for *Anastasia Krupnik!*

## Maclean, Norman. *A River Runs Through It and Other Stories.*

(Pbk.)  University of Chicago, 1976, 217pp. Middle School and Up. An Accelerated Reader selection.

- **SHORT STORIES.** *Death; family; ethics; hobbies; men's issues; substance abuse; work.*
- **RELATED BOOKS:** Books by Ernest Hemingway: *The Old Man and the Sea; The Nick Adams stories; Death in the Afternoon.*

*This novella is on many high school book lists because it is a favorite of reluctant readers and aspiring writers.*

My brother Paul was an artist. He could fly-cast better than any-body I've ever seen. He was a master with a fishing rod.

When we were growing up, my father would take us to the Blackfoot River near our home in Montana. That was our time to be together with each other, the river, and God. We took pride that we caught our own fish, sometimes disregarding helpful suggestions and advice.

Later, I would find myself standing and watching helplessly as my brother struggled to overcome his gambling addiction. As with his fly-fishing, I could not help him. Still, I remember him as an artist surrounded by water and laughter.

Travel with me through the river of Time, with only misty memories of an irretrievable past.

## Magorian, Michelle. *A Little Love Song.*

(Pbk.) Mammoth/Reed, 1993, 343pp. High School & Up.

- **ROMANCE.** *Diaries; Great Britain; mental illness; love; secrets; sex and sexuality; World War II.*
- **RELATED BOOKS:** *Pippa Passes* by Rumer Godden; *Snowfall* by K. M. Peyton; *Joy in the Morning* by Betty Smith.

*A romance for the mature reader.*

At 17, Rose became a woman. In 1943 she and her older sister Diana were sent to a sleepy seaside town away from London and the Nazi bombings. For the first time in their lives they were free of adult restriction. Rose learned how to dance the foxtrot, how to date, and, yes, even how to deliver a baby!

Maybe the secret about Mad Hilda had something to do with Rose's maturity. Mad Hilda owned their house and was considered mentally ill because she was locked in an asy-lum for eight years. When Rose discovered Hilda's carefully hidden diaries, she learned that people and situations aren't always what they seem.

Should Rose tell her friend Alec what she discovered about him?

## Mahon, K. L. *Just One Tear.*

(Pbk.) Lothrop, Lee and Shepherd, 1994, unpaged. Middle School & Up.

■ **REALISTIC FICTION.** *Crime; death; diaries; rites of passage; single parents; suicide; trust.*

■ **RELATED BOOKS:** *Mary Wolf* by Cynthia D. Grant; *Tigers Don't Cry* by Sharon Draper; *Making Up Megaboy* by Virginia Walter and Katrina Roeckelin.

*Note:* Written by a 14-year-old Australian girl, this book was written for a friend who had a similar experience. This short book may be useful for reluctant readers and creative writing instructors trying to encourage students to write about their emotions.

How can a 13-year-old boy deal with the murder of his father? How can he face the murderer during the trial? How will he have the courage to testify as an eyewitness?

The only way he can cope is by writing in his diary.

Here it is. Take a trip through hell and back.

## Maquire, Gregory. *Seven Spiders Spinning.*

Illustrated by Dirk Zimmer. (Pbk.) HarperTrophy, 1995, 132pp. Elementary school & Up.

■ **FANTASY.** *Ecology; responsibility; rivalry; school.*

■ **RELATED BOOKS:** *Of Two Minds* and the series by Carol Matas and Perry Nodelman; *Hob and the Goblins* and the *Hob* series by William Mayne.

*Note:* This fantasy alludes to many literary classics as well as popular culture. Some allusions may not be recognizable to younger students, but they will enjoy this lighthearted farce. Recommended as a read-aloud.

Thousands of years ago, during the Ice Age, seven deadly spiders were frozen solid in a glacier.

However, this story begins thousands of years later, during the Modern Age. Seven deadly Ice Age spiders thaw out and are on the move. While creeping through the Vermont woods, the spiders observe seven sixth-grade girls called the *Tattletales*. Each spider chooses a girl for its Mama. These spiders are devoted to protecting these girls at any cost.

The *Tattletales* do have rivals: the *Copycats*. These sixth-grade boys are plotting to achieve top status in school. Meanwhile, the spiders, growing bigger and deadlier, plan to disrupt the Halloween pageant. They plan to end the pageant by murder!

## Maynard, Joyce. *At Home in the World: A Memoir.*

St. Martin's, 1998, 347pp. High School & Up.

■ **BIOGRAPHY.** *Love; problem parents; rites of passage; secrets; sex and sexuality; substance abuse (alcohol).*

■ **RELATED BOOKS:** *In Search of Salinger* by Ian Hamilton; *Salinger: A Biography* by Paul Alexander; Joyce Maynard's other books: *To Die For; Baby Love; Domestic Affairs.*

 *Note:* Recommend this to those readers who admire Salinger's ***Catcher in the Rye.***

J. D. Salinger wrote *Catcher in the Rye* in 1951 to great acclaim. He shortly disappeared from the literary scene, becoming a recluse. He has not published anything in over 30 years. His personal life has been private. Until now.

In 1973, Joyce Maynard had a brief but intense relationship with Salinger. After their breakup, Maynard continued to write autobiographical pieces about her marriage and children, but never referred to Salinger. Until now.

Who is J. D. Salinger? What did he become? Why did he retreat from the world? What did the 39-year-old writer see in a girl of 18? Reportedly, Salinger is furious at the intrusion into his privacy. But, as Maynard protests, "This is my story, too."

For Joyce Maynard's story, read *At Home in the World.*

## Mayne, William. *Hob and the Goblins.*

Illustrated by Norman Messenger. DK, 1994, 140pp. Elementary School & Up.

■ **FANTASY.** *Great Britain; magic; responsibility; supernatural.*

■ **RELATED BOOKS:** *Harry Potter and the Sorcerers Stone* by J. K. Rowling; *The Borrowers* series by Mary Norton; *The Boggart* series by Susan Cooper.

 *Note:* A fantasy in the British tradition, Hob was the subject of several picture books published in Great Britain. The author, William Mayne, has brought the friendly household spirit to older readers. Especially recommended as a read-aloud.

"This little creature is talking," Meg Grimes said. She wrapped her fingers around the gnome to show her brother, Tom. "I heard words. In English."

"Go ahead," The gnome called Hob squeezed his tiny eyes. "Eat me quickly. Just a quick bite and a swallow."

Meg didn't want to eat Hob, thank goodness. In time, Meg's family accepts Hob as a friendly household spirit, usually invisible, with a job. Hob lives under the staircase. He likes his tea. He sweeps away quarrels and banishes trouble. He charms kettles into singing and stops milk souring. He also confronts dwarfs, witches, goblins, and gremlins who surround the Fairy Ring Cottage. The family's house stands over a crock of gold, and Hob must protect the family from the sorcerer Fluellen.

Hob was doing an excellent job of outsmarting the supernatural forces. Then the family made one major mistake. People are never to lend Hob clothes. That's when Hob becomes vain. He no longer does good deeds. He lets Mischief into the house and Worry come down the chimney.

When Hob dons the clothes, he leaves the house, job, and the Grimes family. "I wonder where I am, and I wonder when it is," he worries.

Will Hob be able to recover his memory? Can he return to his ongoing battle with the goblins and other threatening forces? Stay tuned to this hilarious fantasy about *Hob and the Goblins.*

# McCaffrey, Anne and Margaret Ball. Acorna: The Unicorn Girl.

(Pbk.) HarperPrism, 1998, 409pp. Second in a series; **Acorna's Quest** and **Acorna's People** follow. Middle School & Up.

■ **SCIENCE FICTION.** *Abuse; end of the world; ethics; love; magic; religion; women's issues.*

■ **RELATED BOOKS:** *Anne McCaffrey's The Unicorn Girl: An Illustrated Novel* by Micky Zucker Reichert, et al; other books by Anne McCaffrey, including *Freedom's Challenge; If Wishes Were Horses,* and her *Pern* dragon series; *Enchantress from the Stars* by Sylvia Louise Engdahl.

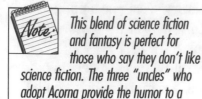 This blend of science fiction and fantasy is perfect for those who say they don't like science fiction. The three "uncles" who adopt Acorna provide the humor to a fast-paced space western.

"Acorna is not human. Whatever the doctors may believe, she is not deformed. Her race needs that horn in the middle of the forehead. We know she can use it to purify the air." Rafik leaned over the woman's desk, his eyes flashing with anger. "We will not allow you to operate on her. We found her in a survival pod floating in space. We may be three space prospectors, but Acorna is now our responsibility." Rafik's companions, Gif and Calum, murmured assent.

"I'm afraid, sir, Acorna is no longer your problem. As head of this department, I shall recommend psychological treatment for all of you. Meanwhile, Acorna's surgery is scheduled at 1330 hours."

"I'm afraid, madam, you better tell us how to get to Surgery. Now!" Calum perched his body on the corner of her desk. The lady closed her eyes, swayed, and fainted, dropping her head between her arms.

"I can help." A young woman had overhead the conversation and briskly stepped into the office. "Actually, my boss, Dr. Forelle, wants the surgery stopped, too. He believes she is a sapient alien. He wants to study Acorna. What do you want with her?"

"To take care of her," Gil said. "We've been taking care of her for over a year now."

"I believe you." The woman dropped her voice. "Don't let Dr. Forelle get her. He'll mine her brain for memories of language without caring what he does to the rest of her. It could be worse than surgery."

"Then we better hurry," Rafik said. "We must save Acorna!"

# McCaughrean, Geraldine. *The Pirate's Son.*

Scholastic, 1998, 294pp. Middle School & Up. An ALA Best Book for Young Adults.

■ **ADVENTURE.** *Africa (Madagascar); Great Britain; class conflict; crime; friendship; Middle Ages; supernatural; revenge; rivalry; rites of passage; survival.*

■ **RELATED BOOKS:** *The Princess Bride* by William Goldman; *The Shakespeare Stealer* by Gary L. Blackwood; *The True Confessions of Charlotte Doyle* by Avi.

*Note:* This swashbuckling yarn is an enjoyable romp that also provides a revealing look at Nathan's culture shock at native cultures and customs. Maud becomes a highly respected member, almost a sorceress, of the village clan. Especially recommended for reluctant readers who like action.

"Come with me to Madagascar," said the pirate's son. "I hate England and this pretentious school. I long to return to my clan village. My father met my mother on that African island. Now that you're an orphan, Nathan, you have nothing to keep you here."

Nathan Gull wanted to say no, but the word would not come from his lips. All his 14 years, he had read about pirates. He knew their ships, their ports-of-call, their homes, and their histories. Now Tamo White, a pirate's son, was asking him to sail to an exotic port-of-call. How could he say no to his only chance of a swashbuckling adventure?

"Yes, I'll go to Madagascar!" Nathan heard himself booming in an enthusiastic voice, but then he remembered. "I have a sister who's 13. What do I do about Maud?"

"Well, bring her along!" ordered Tamo.

Later, Nathan wondered if he had made the right decision to cast off with the pirate's son. By that time, it was too late to turn back to the safety of his books. One swashbuckling adventure followed another: pirate attacks, cyclones, lost ships, stolen treasures. As soon as one bloody swordfight ended, another gory brawl began.

Hop on board with *The Pirate's Son.*

## McGray, Carrie Allen. *Freedom's Child: The Life of a Confederate General's Black Daughter.*

Algonquin Books of Chapel Hill, 1998, 270pp. Middle School & Up.

■ **BIOGRAPHY.** *African Americans; interracial relations; racism; women's issues.*

■ **RELATED BOOKS:** *Slaves in the Family* by Edward Ball; *Having Their Say* by Elizabeth and Sara Delaney; *Cast Two Shadows: The American Revolution in the South* by Ann Rinaldi.

 *The author's loving tribute to her mother is written in an episodic, novelistic style that will be easily absorbed by reluctant readers. Mary Rice Hayes was a pioneer in civil rights and served as president of Virginia Seminary. Also recommended for curriculums discussing women's rights, slavery, the Reconstruction era, the Harlem Renaissance, and African-American history.*

In my mother's bedroom was a portrait of a Confederate general. Also, in that bedroom Mama gave birth to 10 children, all of them a mixture of two races, black and white. That picture of the white man in a Confederate uniform was my grandfather, General John Jones.

I never thought of him as my grandfather. Mama never talked about him. It took much searching for me to learn the fascinating story of my mother, Mary Rice Hayes Allen, born in 1876 to a slave and her master. That fact is not unusual in American history. What is unusual is that my grandfather publicly acknowledged his paternity, paid for his daughter's upkeep and education, and suffered social ostracism as a result.

The more I discovered about my mama's life, the more I wanted to know. Let me share her story with you.

## McGrath, Tom. *MTV: The Making of a Revolution.*

Running Press, 1996, 207pp. Middle School & Up.

■ **NONFICTION.** *Music; show business.*

■ **RELATED BOOKS:** *20 Years of Rolling Stone* edited by Jann S. Wenner; *The Rolling Stone Film Reader* edited by Peter Travers.

 *This entertaining book is also useful as a timely history of the 1980s.*

What do Madonna, Michael Jackson, Queen, and the Monkees have in common? These artists laid the foundation of MTV, the first cable station to play music videos continuously. MTV would forever change popular culture.

Before MTV, there were 30-minute programs with beginning, middle, and end. MTV ran videos continuously in no particular order. After MTV, singers released a video and a CD concurrently. MTV's "Unplugged" live concerts boosted the careers of many performers.

Participate in the celebration of the MTV Revolution.

## McKissack, Patricia C. and Fredrick L. McKissack. *Young, Black, and Determined: A Biography of Lorraine Hansberry.*

Holiday House, 1998, 152pp. Middle School & Up. An ALA Best Book for Young Adults.

■ **BIOGRAPHY.** *African Americans; illness; show business; self-identity.*

■ **RELATED BOOKS:** *A Raisin in the* Sun by Lorraine Hansberry and *To be Young, Gifted and Black: Lorraine Hansberry in her Own Words* edited by Robert Nemiroff.

 *Note: The text is skillfully integrated with pictures of Lorraine Hansberry's life. Patricia McKissack's **Great African Americans** series is also recommended, with biographies of Booker T. Washington, Frederick Douglass, George Washington Carver, Langston Hughes, Marian Anderson, and others.*

Lorraine Hansberry became famous when she was 28. In 1959 her play *A Raisin in the Sun* was acclaimed for its realistic portrayal of African Americans struggling to survive in an urban environment. She became as famous a playwright as Tennessee Williams and Arthur Miller.

However, Lorraine Hansberry was much more than a playwright. She was a civil rights activist, a brilliant essayist, and a friend to many, including writer James Baldwin, Malcolm X, and actor Paul Robeson. She was proud of her African heritage and tried to encourage other African Americans to feel pride, too.

Dead at 34, Lorraine Hansberry lived her short, fascinating life to the maximum. Talented, courageous, and opinionated, she inspired and continues to inspire others. Her early death was the only tragic thing about her.

## McMurtry, Larry. *Crazy Horse.*

Viking, 1999, 148pp. With bibliography. Middle School & Up. Part of the *Penguin Lives* series.

■ **BIOGRAPHY.** *Native Americans (Sioux); pioneer life; politics; war.*

■ **RELATED BOOKS:** *Crazy Horse: Sioux War Chief* by Peter Guttmacher; *Crazy Horse* by Mari Sandoz and Stephen B. Oates (Designer); *Crazy Horse and Custer* by Stephen E. Ambrose; *In a Sacred Manner I Live: Native American Wisdom,* edited by Neil Philip.

 *Note: This book is part of a biographical series, **Penguin Lives,** in which well-known authors detail the lives of Mozart, Saint Augustine, Charles Dickens, Jane Austen, and others. This novella will lure history, western, and Native Americans enthusiasts.*

We know him as Crazy Horse, but in life few knew him well. The Sioux called him Our Strange Man. Certainly the whites also helped to build his legend. However, we know more about his battles than we do about his thoughts. We know about his participation at the Battle of Little Bighorn and that he was assassinated at Fort Robinson on September 6, 1877. Those facts tell little about the man named Crazy Horse.

Still, his legend survives. What is the mystery behind Crazy Horse? What did he mean to the Sioux? What influence does Crazy Horse have on us today?

Join author Larry McMurtry to take a current look at a legend from the past: *Crazy Horse.*

## Meyer, Carolyn. *Voices of South Africa: Growing Up in a Troubled Land.*

Harcourt Brace Jovanovich, 1986, 244pp. Middle School & Up.

■ **NONFICTION.** *South Africa; apartheid; interracial relations; politics; racism.*

■ **RELATED BOOKS:** *Waiting for the Rain* by Sheila Gordon; *The Illustrated Long Walk to Freedom* by Nelson Mandela; *Kaffir Boy* by Mark Mathabane.

 *I also lived in South Africa from 1995 to 1998, during President Mandela's presidency. I found the book reflected many of my experiences with South Africans. They are a highly complex, diverse, and fascinating people. Highly recommended as a historical primary source.*

I cried when I left South Africa.

In 1985 I spent five weeks in a beautiful country that was diseased by apartheid. *Apartheid* was the Afrikaner word for *separateness*, a system of racial segregation. In 1985, the South African government had enforced apartheid for 38 years, to the world's displeasure. The United States had just boycotted trade with South Africa and requested the release of Nelson Mandela. During this time of turbulence and indecision, I chose to go to South Africa and talk to any South African who wanted to be heard.

I met a wide variety of people of all ages. They were *White, Black* and *Coloured*, terms that described the races within apartheid. In all my interviews, I used their words but not their real names. To reveal their identities would have endangered them.

I am not an expert on apartheid or South Africa. However, these voices of South Africa are experienced experts on living under the yoke of apartheid.

## Miklowitz, Gloria D. *Masada: The Last Fortress.*

Eerdmans Books for Younger Readers, 1998, 188pp. Middle School and Up.

■ **HISTORICAL FICTION.** *Diaries; death; Jews; love; Middle Ages; Middle East (Israel); religion; religious prejudice; suicide; war.*

■ **RELATED BOOKS:** *Masada by Neil Walderman.*

*Note:* Two diaries and two viewpoints are presented: one by a young Jewish man, Simon; the other by Flavius Silva, the Roman commander who has come to raze the Jews' last stand. There is a map and additional factual material on the battle on Masada in 70 CE. Recommended for book reports, group readings, and classes studying Roman, Jewish, or ancient history. Not recommended for readers under 10; the mass suicide may be too disturbing.

I, Simon, son of Eleazar ben Ya'ir, begin this journal in the Hebrew year 3833, here at Masada in the kingdom of Judea. We Jews have lived here for near three years, and still the Romans do not come.

We are lucky because we are armed and have supplies. Years ago, King Herod built this mound for protection from Anthony and Cleopatra. Now we are living here because the Romans have become greedy and intolerant of our religion. If necessary, we plan to die here.

I shall never forget that afternoon. John, Deborah, and I met as usual in the shade of Herod's great palace. We talked of our plans. I said I wanted to be a doctor one day.

Then I saw it, a distant dust cloud. I had no fear. Only vague awareness. After a time, the dust grew thicker. I thought it must be the *hamsin,* a hot, humid wind that blows for weeks. As the truth dawned, I gazed in astonishment at my friends, and our eyes locked with the unspoken, dreaded thought. Through the dust, we heard a distinct sound, the thud of thousands of feet marching, advancing on Masada.

We were being attacked!

## Miller, John E. *Becoming Laura Ingalls Wilder: The Woman Behind the Legend.*

University of Missouri, 1998, 306pp. High School & Up.

■ **BIOGRAPHY.** *Family; pioneer life; women's issues; work.*

■ **RELATED BOOKS:** *Laura's Album: A Remembrance Scrapbook of Laura Ingalls Wilder compiled by William Anderson; The Ghost in the House: A Life of Rose Lane Wilder by William Holitz.*

*Note:* Recommended for all Laura Ingalls Wilder fans.

Many of us know Laura Ingalls Wilder by the *Little House* TV series. Recently there has been controversy about the series. One scholar claims that Laura's daughter Rose wrote the books.

This author discusses that controversy. Certainly there was a complex relationship between Laura and her daughter, Rose Wilder Lane. Rose was a respected editor; Laura had written only a bimonthly column for a farm journal. As Laura wrote her *Little House* series, Rose assigned herself the task of editing and making suggestions to her mother. Their relationship was a confusing mixture of love, control, and guilt.

Forget what you've heard or read about Laura Ingalls Wilder. This book describes the woman behind the legend. Read how Mrs. A. J. Wilder, also known as Bessie Wilder, became Laura Ingalls Wilder.

## Morrison, Toni. *Sula.*

Alfred A. Knopf, 1973, 174pp. High School & Up.

- **REALISTIC FICTION.** *African Americans; death; friendship; rivalry; sex and sexuality.*
- **RELATED BOOKS:** *The Bluest Eye* by Toni Morrison; *My Eyes are Watching God* by Zeale Norton Thurston

*Note:* This is one incident from an intricately woven story about a lost and redeemed friendship. Toni Morrison's books are analyzed in many college English classes, so it's useful to recommend her books to college-bound mature readers.

Sula and Nel are both smart. They are also growing up black and poor in a small Ohio town. As young girls, they share an intense friendship that holds terrible secrets. One of their secrets involves a young boy and the river.

Sula and Nel were lying by the river, absently throwing in twigs and rocks. Chicken Little passed by and tried to climb a tree. Sula gave him a boost.

Chicken was elated. "I'm up high. I'm-a tell my brovver."

Sula and Nel mimicked him, "I'm-a tell my brovver; I'm-a tell my brovver."

Without thinking, Sula picked Chicken by his hands and swung him outward and around. He slipped from her hands and sailed over the water, still laughing. They expected him to reappear, but the water stayed peaceful and still.

Nel spoke first. "Someone saw."

A figure appeared on the shore. Was it Shadrack, the town's crazy who invented National Suicide Day? What would he do or say?

## Muller, Melissa. *Anne Frank: A Biography.*

With a note by Miep Gies. Translated by Rita and Robert Kimber. Henry Holt, 1998, 330pp. Middle School & Up.

- **BIOGRAPHY.** *Diaries; Europe (Holland); Jews; Holocaust; religious prejudice; World War II.*
- **RELATED BOOKS:** *Anne Frank: Beyond the Diary, A Photographic Remembrance* by Ruud Van Der Rol, et al.; *The Diary of a Young Girl: The Definitive Edition* by Anne Frank; *Anne Frank Remembered: The Story of the Woman Who Helped to Hide the Frank Family* by Miep Gies.

*Note:* Recommend this one as a follow-up to Anne Frank's diary. Muller tells the complete story in a compelling read.

Who was Anne Frank? Most of us know that she wrote a diary while hiding from the Nazis. However, Anne's diary covers only two years of her life, from ages 13 to 15.

This intensely researched biography covers all of her 15 years. The author, Melissa Muller, answers questions that millions of readers have asked: What kind of person was Anne's mother, whom Anne judged so severely? What were Anne's plans for the diary? Who betrayed the Franks' hiding place?

The answers will intrigue you.

## Myers, Walter Dean. *Monster.*

Illustrations by Christopher Myers. HarperCollins, 1999, 281pp. Middle School & Up.

■ **REALISTIC FICTION.** *African Americans; crime; death.*

■ **RELATED BOOKS:** *Making Up Megaboy* by Virginia Walter and Katrina Roeckelin; *The Taking of Room 113* by Mel Glenn; *Mary Wolf* by Cynthia D. Grant.

In my prison cell, I cry at night when the lights are out. I wait until someone is being beat up and crying for help. That way no one will hear and beat me up the following night.

I feel like I'm in a movie. Maybe I should write down this experience. The film will be the story of my life: Steve Harmon, 16 years old, on trial for murder.

I'll call my film what the prosecutor lady called me: MONSTER

*Note: With Myer's stylistic blend of Steve's journal entries and developing screenplay, the reader becomes both witness and juror. In view of recent school violence and juvenile crimes, this book addresses a timely topic. Also highly recommended for reluctant readers.*

*Jacket art copyright © 1999 by Christopher Myers. Used by permission of HarperCollins Publishers.*

## Napoli, Donna Jo. *For the Love of Venice.*

Delacorte, 1998, 245pp. Middle School & Up. An ALA Best Book for Young Adults.

■ **ROMANCE.** *Europe (Italy); love; politics.*

■ **RELATED BOOKS:** *Snowfall* by K. M. Peyton; *Pippa Passes* by Rumer Godden.

*An entertaining, multicultural, international romance for middle school students.*

Venice, Italy, is beautiful and mysterious. So is Graziella, the girl Percy meets in the ice cream shop.

Graziella shows Percy another Venice, one that tourists never see. He learns that the city of Venice is struggling to survive. Floods, foreign investments and local politics can change Venice forever unless someone takes action. Graziella and her comrades plan to protest Venice's hosting of Expo, an international world's fair.

Percy doesn't particularly care about politics. He just wants to take Graziella on a romantic boat ride through the canals.

Maybe somewhere they can find a spot to meet where their two worlds connect; maybe together they can be transformed *For the Love of Venice.*

## Napoli, Donna Jo. *Sirena.*

Scholastic, 1998, 210pp. Middle School & Up. An ALA Best Book for Young Adults.

■ **FOLKLORE.** *Love.*

■ **RELATED BOOKS:** *Beauty* by Robin McGinley; *Ella Enchanted* by Gail Carson Levine.

*Note:* *In Greek mythology, Philocretes was a friend of the hero Hercules, who bequeathed him his bow and poisoned arrows. On the way to the Trojan War, Philocretes was injured and left on the island Lemnos. Later, Philocretes would leave the island and use the poisoned arrows to kill the Trojan prince, Paris. This romance combines Greek mythology and mermaid folklore into an enchanting read. Recommended for students studying Greek mythology and all romance lovers.*

Like human beings, Sirena is mortal. She can gain immortality only through love with a human. That's why Sirena and her mermaid sisters sing to lure men from ships. So far, every man who has tried to follow the song has drowned.

Traumatized by the deaths, Sirena escapes to the isolated island Lemnos. To her surprise, she meets a Greek sailor, Philocretes, son of King Poeas.

Sirena knows that her song will cause death to the human. Yet how can she reject the love that can bring her immortality?

## Nasaw, Jonathan. *Shakedown Street.*

Delacorte, 1993. Middle School & Up.

■ **REALISTIC FICTION.** *Death; diaries; homelessness; illness; runaways; sex and sexuality; substance abuse.*

■ **RELATED BOOKS:** *The Beggar's Ride* by Theresa Nelson; *Slake's Limbo* by Felice Holman.

*Note:* *One of the better novels about the homeless.*

Shakedown Street. It's not a place. It's a state of mind.

On Shakedown Street, the mind is always focused on survival. Sometimes surviving involves panhandling, eating trash, and living in a gully under the freeway.

Cara writes a witty and cynical account of being homeless in a community of gypsies, tramps, and thieves. Her gypsy mother roams from one commune to another until a guru wipes her out financially. The tramp Wharf Rat knows all the ins and outs of begging. The thief Hoopa Joe promises to protect their possessions, but steals them instead.

Know what Arthur, a *Grateful Dead* follower, said? He said he never saw nobody get off Shakedown Street without a break, and he never saw nobody get a break. Give yourself a break. Treat yourself to Cara's journal of *Shakedown Street.*

## Nelson, Pam. *Cool Women: The Thinking Girl's Guide to the Hippest Women in History.*

Written by Dawn Chipman, Mari Florence, Naomi Wax. (Pbk.) Girl's Press, 1998, 104pp. For all libraries.

■ **BIOGRAPHY.** *African Americans; aging; class conflict; music; politics; responsibility; self-identity; show business; sports; women's issues; work.*

■ **RELATED BOOKS:** *Never Jam Today* by Carole Bolton; *Wild Women Run with the Wolves* by Clarissa Pinkola Estes; *Girl Power* by Hillary Carlip.

*Note:* The colorful Web site design adds to the appeal of the book, satisfying even younger students. Highly recommended for its brief biographical sketches of women in history. Unfortunately, an index is not included.

These cool women are not goddesses. They do not reside in the sky or stare down from lofty pedestals. These are real women who had the courage to face real life and win.

Women have always been an unsung part of history. This book celebrates their existence and contributions. These cool women range from baseball barnstormers to female spies, lady samurais, woman pirates, suffragists, and cowgirls.

Look into the eyes of the women in these photographs. Behind the eyes lie courage and a fearlessness of the unknown. You'll see why one woman said, "Well-behaved women rarely made history."

## Nelson, Theresa. *The Empress of Elsewhere.*

DK, 1998, 278pp. Elementary School & Up.

REALISTIC FICTION. *Animals (capuchin monkey); death; ecology; friendship; runaways; work.*

RELATED BOOKS: *Holes* by Louis Sachar; *The Children of Green Knowe series* by Lucy Boston.

*Note:* Recommended as an entertaining, humorous read-aloud.

Dear Danny,

I really miss you. How do you like Arizona?

Remember those creepy stories we heard about that rich lady, Miss Million Dillion? It's weirder than we ever dreamed. Turns out there's a monkey that lives at her haunted mansion. Me and Mary Al are supposed to go to that mansion every day to monkey-sit for three dollars an hour—apiece!

The old lady has her grandkid living with her. She's a brat. (Personally, I think that brat's initials stand for Juvenile Delinquent, not Joy Delores). J. D. always wears a wolf cap and snarls obscenities. That monkey, Empress, has better manners. Anyhow, J.D. gets this hare-brained scheme to put Empress on her grandmother's deserted island, so that the monkey is once again in her natural habitat.

This is where it gets like *Treasure Island*, except we have a monkey instead of a parrot. We steal a boat and get over to the jungle island. We find the magical place called *Elsewhere*. I'll keep you updated.

Your friend, James Henry

## Newman, Christopher. *The Devil's Own.*

(Pbk.) Bantam Doubleday Dell, 1997, 277pp. Middle School & Up.

REALISTIC FICTION. *Class conflict; ethics; Ireland; movie novels; politics; religious prejudice; revenge; trust; war.*

RELATED BOOKS: *Torn Away* by James Hennigan; *Hero* by Robert Cormier; *Making Up Megaboy* by Virginia Walter and Katrina Roeckelin.

> *Note:* One edition has the faces of Brad Pitt and Harrison Ford on the cover, which alone may sell the book, but this is actually a suspenseful, sympathetic portrayal of a terrorist. Recommended as a book report choice for young adult reluctant readers.

Frankie's father told him the Big Boy Rules: "You pick up a gun, you get a bullet."

When Frankie's father was gunned down before him, Frankie picked up a gun and became a terrorist. He joined the Irish Republic Army to avenge his dad's death. Soon Frankie McGuire became a wanted man all over the globe.

For survival, Frankie changed his name to Rory Devaney and escaped to Newark, New Jersey. The O'Meara family welcomed this handsome Irish lad into their house, not knowing Rory was a terrorist. Rory became attached to this openhearted family, especially the ethical Tom O'Meara. Rory was shocked to learn Tom was a policeman who had never killed.

When policeman and terrorist collide, they must play by the Big Boy Rules. Who will get the bullet?

## Nicholson, Joy. *The Tribes of Palos Verdes.*

St. Martin's, 1997, 218pp. High School & Up. An ALA Best Books for Young Adults selection.

REALISTIC FICTION. *Divorce; eating disorders; mental illness; peer pressure; problem parents; sex and sexuality; sports (surfing); suicide.*

RELATED BOOKS: *Rats Saw God* by Rob Thomas; *California Blue* by David Klass.

> *Note:* Through her character Medina, first-time novelist Nicholson describes the California lifestyle of the upper classes, exposing the dark side of affluence. This book contains profanity and sexual content. Recommended for the reluctant reader and, because of the content, the mature reader.

It was my Dad's idea to move to Palos Verdes. He says California reminds him of clean beaches, dolphins, and warm weather. My mother says California is full of divorced people, murderers, and earthquakes.

From those facts alone, it doesn't take a genius to figure out my parents don't get along. My Dad's a heart surgeon to the celebrities and spends his spare time staring at beach bimbos. My mother was a model until she expanded 10 dress sizes. Now she just wears a yellow bathrobe, stuffing her face with junk food. She relies on my twin brother, Jim, to protect her from the cold, cruel world. That leaves me out in the cold.

That's why I took up surfing. I forget all my problems when I'm riding a wave. Right now my dream is to surf with the Bay boys, to become their Gidget. After that, who knows? I'll just follow the surf and see where it takes me.

## Nicol, Barbara. *Beethoven Lives Upstairs: A Tale of Childhood and Genius.*

Illustrated by Scott Cameron. Orchard Books, 1993, unnumbered pages. Elementary School & Up.

HISTORICAL FICTION. *Europe (Austria); music; work.*

RELATED BOOKS: *Meet the Orchestra* by Ann Hayes, illustrated by Karmen Thompson; *Hallelujah Handel* by Susan Hammond; *Beethoven (Pocket Biography)* by Ates Orga.

*Note:* Explain to younger readers that these letters are fictional and provide a short, fascinating biographical sketch of Ludwig Beethoven.

7 September 1822, Vienna, Austria
Dear Uncle,

A man named Ludwig van Beethoven has moved upstairs into Father's old office. Uncle, I do believe this man is crazy.

Every morning at dawn Mr. Beethoven begins to make this dreadful noise on the piano upstairs. Not only does he pound the piano something fierce, but this dreadful howling occurs. Mother says I'm not to blame him. He's deaf and can't hear the noise.

One morning I opened the door to see my neighbors pointing and laughing at the upstairs window. There was this crazy Beethoven, staring at a sheet of music. Uncle, he had on no clothes!

I have heard he is working on a symphony. I hope he finishes it soon so we can have peace and quiet!

Christoph

P.S. Read *Beethoven Lives Upstairs* by Barbara Nicol if you want more details.

## Okimato, Jean Davies. *The Eclipse of Moonbeam Dawson.*

Tom Dawson, 1997, 187pp. Middle School & Up. IRA/CBC Young Adults' Choice Award.

REALISTIC FICTION. *Interracial relations; love; Native Americans; problem parents; stepparents.*

RELATED BOOKS: *The Window* and *A Yellow Raft in Blue Water* by Michael Dorris.

*Note:* A recommended middle school read, especially for newly enrolled students.

I'm Moonbeam Dawson. Wait, that's wrong. I'm *Reid* Dawson.

That's better. I'm terminating Moonbeam as a name. Sounds like a hippie living on a commune. Actually my mother was a hippie, I was her veggie-loving son, and we once lived on a commune. Those days are over.

Now I'm Reid Dawson, living off the coast of British Columbia in Canada. I've even met a girl I like, Gloria. I did tell her of my biracial identity: part white, part Haida Indian. That was cool with her. I'd better not plant too many surprises about my name and background. For once, let me seem like a normal guy of 15.

Goodbye, Moonbeam. I'm terminating you for another identity.

**P**

## Paris, Paula. *Titanic and the Making of James Cameron: The Inside Story of the Three-Year Adventure that Rewrote Motion Picture History.*

(Pbk.) Newmarket, 1998, 234pp. Middle School & Up.

NONFICTION. *Movie novels; show business; work.*

RELATED BOOKS: *James Cameron's Titanic* by Ed W. Marsh, photographs by Douglas Kirkland; *A Night to Remember* by Walter Lord.

The movie *Titanic* was the first to gross over $ 1 billion worldwide and to win 11 Academy Awards. The story behind the movie is just as fascinating.

At first, the director James Cameron took over three years to write and direct the film. He even went on dangerous underwater dives to the shipwrecked *Titanic*. The footage of the *Titanic* during the first minutes of the movie was taken during Cameron's expedition.

At first, the director wanted to cast an actor like Tom Cruise rather than Leonardo DiCapprio. Actress Kate Winslet wasn't Cameron's first choice either. After she auditioned, she told the director, "You don't have to choose me for Rose, but you've got to hire Leonardo." How right she was.

For more, book yourself an imaginary seat on the *Titanic*.

---

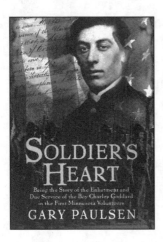

## Paulsen, Gary. *Soldier's Heart: Being the Story of the Enlistment and Due Service of the Boy Charley Goddard in the First Minnesota Volunteers.*

Delacorte, 1998, 106pp. A novel of the Civil War, with author's note, selected sources. Middle School & Up. Quick Pick for Reluctant Young Adult Readers.

HISTORICAL FICTION. *Civil War; death; mental illness; rites of passage; war.*

RELATED BOOKS: *With Every Drop of Blood* and *My Brother Sam is Dead* by James Lincoln and Christopher Collier; *Across Five Aprils* by Irene Hunt; *The Fighting Ground* by Avi; *The Red Badge of Courage* by Stephen Crane.

*Note:* Like the movie **Saving Private Ryan,** this novella is unsparing in its details of what actually happens on the battlefield: the noises and stench of dying men, the agony and fear, the diseases brought by unsanitary conditions. Paulsen bases Charley Goddard on a real-life Civil War enlistee who later suffers post-traumatic stress disorder and dies at 23, an old man with a soldier's heart. Highly recommended for group reads, especially social studies classes studying the Civil War.

*Make it stop now!* Charley realized he was screaming his thoughts on the battlefield: *Make these bullets stop now!*

Death was everywhere, nowhere. This is a mistake, Charley thought. I'm only 15. This will make me an old man with a Soldier's Heart.

Charley heard the bullets hitting the men around him and saw the men falling. Some screamed. Most hit the ground silently, dead on impact.

Charley started walking back, not running, as he prayed: *I'm not supposed to see this, God. No one should see this. How can You let this happen? How can You stop this? Whatever it takes, please stop it now!*

*Soldier's Heart by Gary Paulsen, copyright © 1998, Delacorte.*

## Pawlowski, Gareth L. *How They Became the Beatles: A Definitive History of the Early Years, 1960-1964.*

E. P. Dutton, 208 pp. Middle School & Up.

**NONFICTION.** *Great Britain; music; show business.*

RELATED BOOKS: *The Beatles* by Hunter Davies; *The Beatles: An Oral History* by David Pritchard, editor, and Alan Lysaght; *The Love You Make* by Peter Brown.

*Note:* Also useful for its photographs of life and times of the late 1950s and early 1960s.

During the 1960s two questions were asked by Baby Boomers: Where were you on November 22, 1963, when President Kennedy was assassinated? Did you see the Ed Sullivan Show when the Beatles appeared?

The Beatles were a phenomenon that were and are unsurpassed. They changed the look, attitude, music, and style of the 1960s. Without the Beatles, the 1960s would be very different, almost incomprehensible.

Like all success stories, the Beatles' saga had a beginning. They took time to develop their style and look. It was a steady progress that is luckily recorded through the author's extensive private collection of memorabilia. You'll see John Lennon, Paul McCartney, George Harrison, and Ringo Starr change from rockers to mods, from greasy hairstyles to mop tops, from Liverpool, England, to Hamburg, Germany. You'll see how this average band developed into the greatest and most successful rock band of all time.

Enjoy this blast from the past with the Beatles.

## Peck, Richard. *A Long Way from Chicago.*

Dial Books for Younger Readers, 1997, 148pp. A Newbery Honor Book; an ALA Best Book for Young Adults. Middle School & Up.

SHORT STORIES. *Abuse; class conflict; crime; ethics; family.*

RELATED BOOKS: *Harris and Me* by Gary Paulsen; *Soup* series by Robert Newton Peck; *Adventures of Tom Sawyer* by Mark Twain.

*Note:* In a whimsical style reminiscent of Mark Twain, Peck pays careful attention to midwestern life in America during the 1930s. The first story, "Shotgun Cheatham's First Night Above Ground," appeared in the anthology **Twelve Shots: Stories About Guns** edited by Harry Mazer. Highly recommended as a read-aloud and as a book report choice.

Many years back, during the Depression years, I was a city slicker from Chicago. You wouldn't think my sister and I would have to leave my hometown to see a corpse. Still, we traveled by train to Grandma Dowdel's to see our first stiff. Grandma was always showing us the strange side of life.

We visited Grandma each August for seven summers. Each summer became more outrageous. Like the time Grandma terrorized the Cowgill gang with a bottle of milk and a dead mouse. Another time she trespassed, poached fish, and caught the sheriff in his underwear—all in one day.

Are my memories true? Every word, and growing truer with each year.

## Peck, Robert Newton. *Cowboy Ghost.*

HarperCollins, 1999, 200pp. Middle School & Up.

Adventure. *Death; men's issues; pioneer life; responsibility.*

Related books: *Sunshine Rider: The First Vegetarian Western* by Ric Lynden Harden; *Looking After Lily* by Cindy Bonner; *Buffalo Woman* by Bill Wallace.

 **Note:** *Like the author's classic, **A Day No Pigs Would Die,** this one deals with the complexities of father-son issues, except this one is a pistol-waving adventure.*

"Titus, pay attention. A cattle drive is no Sunday social. It's a dung job for dust eaters. It's over 200 miles of trail grit, cold beans, and wet blankets. On top of that, there's cowdiggers."

"What's that?" I asked.

"Thieves. This cattle drive is a ripper of a ride."

I stared into my father's eyes, matching him in height, weight, and stature. I'm 16 and I'm ready. My father doesn't know I'm taking along my Cowboy Ghost. The Cowboy Ghost is my secret support and will tell me all I need to know. If that old Cowboy Ghost rides with me, he'll make me into a man that my father respects.

"Don't worry, Father. I'll handle the cattle drive. I won't let you down."

## Pfetzer, Mark and Jack Galvin. *Within Reach: My Everest Story.*

Dutton Books, 1998, 224pp. (Pbk.) Penguin, 1999, 208pp. Middle School & Up. Quick Pick for Reluctant Young Adult Readers.

NONFICTION ADVENTURE. *Asia; Caribbean and Latin America (Peru); death; diaries; hobbies and sports (mountain climbing); survival.*

RELATED BOOKS: *Into Thin Air* by Jon Krakauer; *The Climb* by Anatoll Boukreev; *Alive: The Story of the Andes Survivors* by Piers Paul Read; *Seven Years In Tibet* by Heinrich Harrer.

**Note:** *Mark Pfetzer is an inspiring role model for other teens. This page-turner also contains color photographs of the expeditions and is perfect for reluctant readers.*

All my dreams have been within reach. At nine, I became a fly-fishing champion. At 11, I had a karate black belt. At 15, I began my climb to the highest peak, Mount Everest. It's all in the decision.

Once I decide to do something, I set my goals and aim for the top. Just as in mountain climbing, I'll put one foot in front of the other and keep going. Always climbing, training, exploring new ways to challenge myself. Join me, Mark Pfetzer, on my climb past the ever-shifting Khumbu Icefall, over 300-foot crevasses, and high up in the Death Zone. Let's bring my Everest goal *Within Reach.*

## Pfitsch, Patricia Curtis. *Keeper of the Light.*

Simon and Schuster Books for Young Readers, 1997, 137pp. Elementary School & Up. An ALA Best Book for Young Adults.

HISTORICAL FICTION. *Death; class conflict; family; pioneer life; women's issues.*

RELATED BOOKS: *Birdie's Lighthouse* by Deborah Hopkinson; *Keep the Lights Burning, Abbie* by Peter and Connie Roop; *Caddie Woodlawn* by Carol Ryrie Brink.

Faith's mother began to read the letter. "It's dated August 1, 1872," she said. *"Dear Mrs. Sutton, We of the Lighthouse Board realize the hardship you've been under these past five months with the death of your husband. We have finally found a new keeper, a young man who will be able to keep the light burning.'"*

Faith interrupted impatiently. "We HAVE kept the light burning."

"Hush," said her mother. She went on reading, *"'On August 20th, a new keeper will be arriving at the lighthouse. We have procured a house in town that you may use after you vacate the lighthouse.'"*

Faith pounded her fist on the table. "I'm the keeper. Tell them we don't want to leave."

"No, Faith. I need to leave behind the tragedy of your father's death, and so do you. You need to go to school with girls your age. You need to learn what it is to become a grown woman, to become a real lady."

Faith shook her head, but held her tongue. She didn't want to be like the rest of the frivolous girls in town. She wanted to keep her promise to her father and to continue her duties as keeper of the light. Yet she knew that her father would wish her to obey her mother's wishes. "All right, Mother. I promise to forget my life as a keeper."

Faith kept her promise until the day of the disaster. A deadly storm arose, and Faith's mother was on a schooner bound for the rocks. Faith had to return to the lighthouse to make certain the light was burning bright for her mother's safe return. She just hoped she wasn't too late!

## Philip, Neil, ed. *In a Sacred Manner I Live: Native American Wisdom.*

Clarion Books, 1997, 93pp. For all libraries. An ALA Best Book for Young Adults.

NONFICTION. *Ecology; ethics; Native Americans; religion.*

RELATED BOOKS: *Earth Always Endures* edited by Neil Philip; *Crazy Horse in Stillness: Poems* by William Heyen; *Crazy Horse* by Larry McMurtry; *Black Elk Speaks* by John Neilhardt.

*Note:* *The booktalk could also include some of your favorite passages from this hauntingly beautiful book, which contains sepia-toned archival photographs. The editor, Neil Philip, covers almost four centuries of philosophical musings of Black Elk, Geronimo, Chief Seattle, Sitting Bull, and others. Highly recommended for all libraries.*

Native Americans have much to teach. Unfortunately, most whites were too occupied acquiring land to listen to the Native Americans' views on harmony and tradition. However, some of the Native American wisdom has survived. This anthology contains the words of Native American men and women who speak of peace, ecology, religion, and tradition. They lived their lives *In a Sacred Manner.*

## Pickover, Clifford A. *Strange Brains and Genius: The Secret Lives of Eccentric Scientists and Madmen.*

Plenum Trade, 1998, 332pp. High School & Up.

BIOGRAPHY. *Mental illness and disability; science.*

RELATED BOOKS: *Time: A Traveler's Guide* by Clifford A. Pickover; *A Brilliant Madness: Living with Manic-Depressive Illness* by Patty Duke and Gloria Hochman; *The Man Who Loved Only Numbers: The Story of Paul Erdos and the Search for Mathematical Truth* by Paul Hoffman; *Kissing Doorknobs* by Terry Spencer Hesser.

*Note: Pickover discusses mathematicians Oliver Heaviside and Paul Erdos, biographer Samuel Johnson, artist van Gogh, and others, stating that all these geniuses had obsessive-compulsive behavior. He also discusses manic-depression or bipolar disorder. The author, Clifford Pickover, has been described by his peers as a genius for his work as a high-tech inventor and researcher at IBM. This one is for the reader who enjoys an entertaining romp through scientific history.*

What is the connection between genius and madness?

There may be a thin line between genius and madness, between obsession and creativity. Many creative geniuses had curious deficiencies mixed with their obvious talents. For example, Tom Edison's assistant, Nikola Tesla, was obsessed with the number three and had a horror of pearl earrings. Did his neurotic behavior play some part in enhancing his creativity?

The author, Clifford Pickover, calls that example *Strange Brains.* Many great minds had odd compulsions. Perhaps the author's dedication says it best:

*This book is dedicated to the cracked, for they shall let in the light*

## Pike, Christopher. *Monster.*

(Pbk.) Archway/Pocket Books, 1992, 229pp. Middle School & Up.

HORROR. *Crime; death; peer pressure; revenge; school; secrets; survival.*

RELATED BOOKS: *Blood and Chocolate* by Annette Curtis Klause; *Companions of the Night* by Vivien Velde Vande.

*Except for the beginning, this horror novel has surprisingly little graphic violence.*

Mary Blanc walked into the party with a loaded shotgun and killed two people. Her best friend Angela Warner stopped her before she killed more. Mary's reason for the deaths? "Because they were no longer human."

Angela thinks Mary is crazy. At first. Until she becomes one of them, one of the monsters that crave human flesh so they can eat humans alive, turning them into ghouls or zombies.

These monsters will stop at nothing and nothing will stop these monsters!

## Pinkwater, Daniel. *The Education of Robert Nifkin.*

Farrar, Straus & Giroux, 1998, 168pp. High School & Up.

HUMOR. *School.*

RELATED BOOKS: *Catcher in the Rye* by J. D. Salinger; *Getting Lincoln's Goat* by E. M. Goldman; *The Toilet Paper Tigers* by Gordon Korman.

 *Note:* Because of the profanity, this off-the-wall, irreverent book should be given to mature readers.

My parents believe in the principle "What doesn't kill you makes you stronger—or kills you." So, writing this essay for college will either get me admitted—or won't.

In this essay, I'm supposed to write about my high school experiences. Remember, you asked for this.

Riverview High School smells. The odor is a pungent mixture of food, chlorine, exhaust fumes, cheap perfume, acne cream, and stale cigarettes.

The teachers hate any form of Communism, especially any Russian-sounding name like mine, Robert Nifkin. So to prove I was a flag-waving patriot, I joined ROTC. Big mistake. It was like the Bad Posture Club with slouches and slumps of all varieties. We had trouble with left-face and right-face because we kept confusing our left and our right.

For more of my insane high school experiences, read my college admittance essay in *The Education of Robert Nifkin.*

## Plimpton, George. *Truman Capote: In Which Various Friends, Enemies, Acquaintances, and Detractors Recall His Turbulent Career.*

Doubleday, 1997, 498pp. High School & Up.

BIOGRAPHY. *Homosexuality; show business; sex and sexuality; substance abuse (alcohol & others); work.*

RELATED BOOKS: *Conversations with Capote* by Lawrence Grobbel; *In Cold Blood* by Truman Capote.

 *Note:* See page 36 for the booktalk on Truman Capote's ***In Cold Blood.*** The author's interview style would be of interest to writing classes or as a primary source.

Who was Truman Capote?

He was the real-life character Dill in *To Kill a Mockingbird.* He was the writer of *In Cold Blood*, a true-life drama of two men who were hanged in Kansas for murder. He also wrote *Breakfast at Tiffany's* which was later made into a movie with Audrey Hepburn. He was a jet-setter who hobnobbed with the rich and famous. He was a regular at *Studio 54*, the disco haven of the Seventies. He was the first celebrity openly to declare himself gay. Certifying his eccentric appeal, artist Andy Warhol idolized Truman Capote.

His life was a series of dramas with the earth as his stage. Everyone from Jackie O to Greta Garbo, Candice Bergen, Frank Sinatra, and Mia Farrow expresses an opinion about *Truman Capote.* You'll be highly entertained.

**P**

## Pope, Nick. *The Uninvited: An Expose of the Alien Abduction Phenomenon.*

Overlook, 1998, 316pp. With index and appendices. Middle School & Up.

NONFICTION. *Abuse; crime; politics; survival.*

RELATED BOOKS: *Abduction, Human Encounters with Aliens* by John E. Mack; *Alone in the Universe? Aliens, the X-Files and God* by David Wilkinson; *The Unofficial X-Files Companion* by Ngaire Genge.

 This book's subject will interest many reluctant readers.

Nick Pope is the real-life version of Agent Fox Mulder in *The X-Files.* He investigates UFO sightings for the British Government's Ministry of Defense. Now he's gone one step further. He's taking you on a spaceship to view the UFO phenomenon, supported by hard data.

Literally thousands have claimed to be abducted by aliens. They are ridiculed by the media, scientists, and governments. Regardless, these people won't deny their experiences with aliens. Perhaps there is more to this than meets the eye.

Nick Pope was a cynic when he began. Now he is a believer. You, too, could change your attitude on aliens.

## Pournelle, Jerry. *Starswarm: A Jupiter Novel.*

Tom Doherty, 1998, 349pp. Middle School & Up. Fifth in the **Jupiter** series; **The Orlando Sentinel; Beowulf's Children; Footfall; Higher Education** precede.

SCIENCE FICTION. *End of the world; computers; science.*

RELATED BOOKS: Books by Robert Heinlein: *Stranger from a Strange Land; The Star Beast; Citizen of the Galaxy; Time for the Stars.*

 This compelling sci fi thriller does not require reading the previous books in the Jupiter series. Lead **Star Wars** fans to this and you may win science fiction fans for life.

Kip always remembered hearing the Voice in his head. The Voice would answer Kip's thoughts and always told Kip not to tell anyone about the Voice. Kip told Uncle Mike almost everything, but he never mentioned the Voice.

The Voice always said the same thing about Kip's parents. "YOU WILL BE TOLD ABOUT YOUR PARENTS WHEN YOU ARE OLD ENOUGH. I MAY NOT TELL YOU NOW."

After hearing this continuously, Kip finally asked Uncle Mike, "How did my parents die? Is that why we're stuck on the planet Purgatory at the Starswarm Station?"

"Can't tell you that, Kip. All I can say is that your parents weren't really related to me. I worked for your father and promised to raise you. When you're old enough, I'll work for you. They had important work to do, and so will you."

If anything, Kip had more questions, but the Voice and Uncle Mike refused to answer. What was the Voice? Why will Uncle Mike work for Kip? What important mission must Kip complete?

Try *Starswarm.* It's out of this world!

## Pratt, Jane. *Beyond Beauty: Girls Speak Out on Looks, Style and Stereotypes.*

Edited by Alexandra Arrowsmith and Antoinette White. Designed by Jennifer Wagner. (Pbk.) Clarkson Potter, 1997, 158pp. Middle School & Up. Top 10 Quick Picks for Young Adults; Quick Picks for Reluctant Young Adult Readers.

NONFICTION. *Self-identity; women's issues.*

RELATED BOOKS: *Young Beauty* by Jane Pratt; *Real Girl, Real World: Tools for Finding Your True Self* by Heather M. Gray and Samantha Phillips; *Brave New Girls: Creative Ideas to Help Girls Be Confident, Healthy and Happy* by Jeanette Gadeberg.

I'm Jane Pratt, editor of *Sassy* and *Jane* magazines. Since I was young, I wanted to expand the definition of what's beautiful for young women. Beautiful is confidence, beautiful is smart, beautiful is quirky, fat, thin, tall, short. Beautiful is unusual rather than same same same.

> *Note:* This oversized book will be a favorite with many young women who are searching for their own beauty and identity. All races and many cultures are included.

The girls profiled here have a variety of different looks. Natalie Portman, Christina Ricca, and Monica are well known, but other profiles include girls who are varied in personality and interests. The idea with all of these girls is not to hold yourself up to them for comparison, but to find your beauty just as they did. Perhaps you'll discover that your inner self is *Beyond Beauty.*

# Pullman, Philip. *Clockwork: Or All Wound Up.*

With illustrations by Leonid Gore. Arthur A. Levine, 1996, 112pp. (Pbk.) Arthur A. Levine Books, 1998, 128pp. Middle School & Up. An ALA Best Book for Young Adults; Quick Pick for Reluctant Young Adult Readers; School Library Journal Best Books selection.

HORROR. *Ethics; Europe (Germany); Middle Ages; supernatural.*

RELATED BOOKS: *The House with a Clock in its Walls* by John Bellairs; *The Boxes* by William Sleator; The *Sally Lockhart Trilogy* by Philip Pullman: *The Ruby in the Smoke; Shadow of the North; The Tiger in the Well.*

> *Note:* Pulman draws from classic literature, interweaving elements from ***Frankenstein, Pinocchio,*** and ***Faust*** into a suspenseful fantasy. Great for reluctant readers and as a read-aloud.

"I'm a failure," Karl murmured. The boy took a slow, steady drink of brandy. "Tomorrow I'm expected to present a figure for the famous clock of Glockenheim. Visitors from all over Germany will come to see this masterpiece. And I have nothing to show."

A mysterious stranger, dressed in black, moved slowly down the bar, closer to Karl. "You know, dear boy, I can help you. You're a clockmaker. You know how to regulate a watch and repair a church clock, but our lives are clockwork, too."

"I don't understand," Karl said.

"We can control the future, my boy, like we wind up the mechanism in a clock. Say to yourself: I will have a figure by tomorrow, and, like a clock, you will wind up your future. The world has no choice but to obey." The man pointed to the sledge behind him. "Under this canvas is the figure that will bring you glory."

Karl uncovered the most perfect sculpture he had ever seen: a knight in armor, holding a sharp sword. When Karl touched the sword, he drew back his hand, flinching at the blood. "It's like a razor. I'm a little afraid of him."

"Afraid of a little tin man? I think he is a better bargain than the shame you will experience tomorrow without him. Do you want him?"

"Yes. No. I don't know. Yes!"

"Then he is yours. You have wound up the future, my boy. It has already begun to tick." Before Karl could change his mind, the mysterious stranger swept his black cloak around him and vanished into the night.

# Quindlen, Anna. *How Reading Changed My Life.*

(Pbk.) Ballantine, 1998, 94pp. Middle School & Up.

NONFICTION. *Hobbies (reading); self-identity.*

RELATED BOOKS: *How to Read A Book* by Mortimer Adler and Charles Van Doren; *Bookworms: Great Writers and Readers Celebrate Reading* edited by Laura Furman and Elinore Standard.

>
> *Note:* This is recommended for book groups or as a gift for your favorite bookworm.

When I read, I enter into a parallel universe. I'm on an untraveled path, and yet I don't feel a stranger. All readers must be restless spirits, for why would we leave our familiar world for an unconquered one?

I'm Anna Quindlen, author of *One True Thing.* I'm much more than a writer. I'm a reader. Why does reading send me on a time warp through my mind? Why do I return forever changed?

Let's take the reading flight together to explore this territory.

## Quindlen, Anna. *One True Thing.*

(Pbk.) Bantam Doubelday Dell, 1997, 298pp. High School & Up.

REALISTIC FICTION. *Death; family; illness; women's issues; work.*

RELATED BOOKS: *Ellen Foster* by Kaye Gibbons; *Here on Earth* by Alice Hoffman; *The Divine Secrets of the Ya-Ya Sisterhood* by Rebecca Wells.

*A recommended read for groups, especially mother-daughter.*

I know what the police, the newspapers, the lawyers, and my family are saying. They are wrong. I did not kill my mother. I just wish I had.

I guess they all feel I betrayed them. I left my hometown for fame and glory as a journalist. I returned only to help my mother cope with her death sentence of cancer. I never dreamed that I was helping to end my own life.

So I guess I did kill someone. I killed that heartless and superficial part of myself that longed to be everything my mother wasn't. My mother represented the one true thing that mattered. That *One True Thing* was love.

## Rapp, Adam. *Missing the Piano.*

Viking, 1994, 198pp. Middle School & Up. An ALA Best Book for Young Adults.

REALISTIC FICTION. *Abuse; ethics; men's issues; peer pressure; school; self-identity.*

RELATED BOOKS: *Slot Machine* by Chris Lynch; *Rats Saw God* by Rob Thomas.

*Recommend this one to older students who are new to a school or community.*

I've just had the rug pulled out from under me. Just to get rid of me, my dad and stepmother have enrolled me in a military academy. My real mom and sister are touring with the company of *Les Miserables.*

Well, I'm on my own tour of being miserable. First, they shaved off all my hair. I look either like an acorn or like I've had chemotherapy! Take your choice. Next, the school assigns me to the Delta Company, a group that values sadistic inspections. I don't recall enlisting in the Green Berets, but that must be where I am.

How am I supposed to enjoy my life when I'm busy being GI Joe?

## Read, Piers Paul. *Alive: The Story of the Andes Survivors.*

J. P. Lippincott, 1974, 352pp. High School and Up.

NONFICTION. *Death; ethics; movie novels; survival; Caribbean & Latin America.*

RELATED BOOKS: *Into Thin Air* and *Into the Wild* by Jon Krakauer; *Within Reach: My Everest Story* by Mark Pfetzer and Jack Galvin; *Seven Years in Tibet* by Heinrich Harrer.

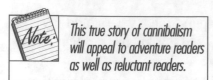 *This true story of cannibalism will appeal to adventure readers as well as reluctant readers.*

On October 12, 1972 an Uruguayan airplane crashed in the Andes Mountains in South America. The plan carried five crewmen and 40 passengers. Some were killed instantly.

Those who survived formed an ordered society. They distributed tasks according to ability. It took will and determination to survive a plane crash with temperatures and wind chill well below freezing. It also took food.

"Do you know what Nando said to me?" Carlitos said to Tito. "He said if he wasn't rescued, he'd eat one of the dead pilots. I guess he's gone crazy."

"I don't know," said Tito. "It might be the only way to survive."

---

## Reise, Kathryn. *PaperQuake: A Puzzle.*

Harcourt Brace, 1998, 264pp. Middle School & Up. An ALA Best Book for Young Adults; nominee for Edgar Allen Poe award for Best Young Adult Mystery.

MYSTERIES, THRILLERS. *Physical disability; rivalry; self-identity; supernatural.*

RELATED BOOKS: *Dream Spinner* by Joanne Hoppe; *SOS Titanic* by Eve Bunting; *Flash Fire* by Caroline B. Cooney.

Two earthquakes in two days. Two mysterious letters in two days. Very strange.

Violet was terrified of earthquakes. Those cryptic messages on aging yellow-stained paper didn't help her fears. Who was Hal, the writer of the letters? Were they meant for her or someone else who lived almost 100 years ago?

There appeared to be a haunting connection between the letters and Violet's own life. Those letters warned "V" of her turbulent relationship as a triplet with her twin sisters. Could these messages have been sent to her from the past as warnings of her untimely death?

## Remnick, David. *King of the World: Muhammad Ali and the Rise of an American Hero.*

Random House, 1998, 326pp. High School & Up.

SPORTS BIOGRAPHY. *African Americans; physical disability; men's issues; politics; religion; sports (boxing).*

RELATED BOOKS: *The Muhammad Ali Reader* edited by Gerald Lyn Early; *Michael Jordan: Playing for Keeps* by David Halberstam; *Malcolm X* by Bruce Perry.

 *The author weaves Ali's heroic life with the civil rights movement and boxing, also providing fascinating biographies of boxers Floyd Paterson and Sonny Liston. The insightful and entertaining style makes this one a winner with all readers, especially reluctant readers who love sports.*

"This guy must be done/ I'll stop him in one," the boxer Cassius Clay bragged to reporters. During the 1960s, Cassius Clay seemed to be an amusing sideshow, a rapper before rap was born. Most reporters were uncertain of his boxing talent, unaware if he could "float like a butterfly, sting like a bee." Time would prove those reporters wrong.

By 1970, Cassius Clay was Muhammed Ali, the heavy-weight champion of the world. He had joined the Nation of Islam, changed his name, and refused to fight in Vietnam. "I ain't got no quarrel with them Vietcong," Ali said. That infamous line summed up the feeling of many anti-war protesters. That decision cost Ali everything: his title, his popularity, and millions of dollars. In time, his star would rise again. Muhammad Ali would change the world of sports and go on to change the world.

Find out how Muhammad Ali became *King of the World*.

## Rice, Anne. *Interview with the Vampire: The First Book in the Vampire Chronicles.*

Alfred G. Knopf, 1992, 274pp. High School & Up. *The Vampire Chronicles* continues with The Vampire Lestat; Queen of the Damned; Tale of the Body Thief; Memnoch the Devil; The Vampire Armand; Vittorio the Vampire.

HORROR. *Ethics; sex and sexuality; supernatural; homosexuality.*

RELATED BOOKS: *Companions of the Night* by Vivien Velde Vande; *Blood and Chocolate* by Annette Curtis Klause.

Louis tells his horrifying story to a young male reporter:

"In 1991, at the age of 25, I became a vampire.

"Until then, I was living with my family on a plantation in New Orleans. This vampire Lestat wanted the plantation for his own. Thus, Lestat turned me into a vampire and into his slave. I roamed at night, never seeing the sun, drinking blood for nourishment.

"After hundreds of years, I'm ready to tell my complete story. I'll even confess to our raising a young vampire girl named Claudia. I'll tell our three stories: Lestat's craving for human killings, Claudia's urge to leave Lestat, and my desperate desire never to kill humans.

"What a strange mixture of vampires are we!"

**R**

## Richburg, Keith B. *Out of America: A Black Man Confronts Africa.*

HarperCollins, 1997, 257pp. High School & Up.

BIOGRAPHY. *Africa; African Americans; racism; war; work.*

RELATED BOOKS: *Out of Africa* by Isaak Dinesen; *The Mind of South Africa* by Allister Sparks.

*Note:* This book is currently very controversial in some African countries and provokes some heated discussions.

I watched the dead float down a river in Tanzania.

I am an African-American journalist. What I saw and felt may shock you. I certainly intend to shock you. I felt that emotion as well as rage, sorrow, and bewilderment. These sentiments began nagging me when I first set foot in Africa.

I am also embarrassed because I was also thinking: *There but for the grace of God go I.* My ancestors were from Africa but were kidnapped and brought to America in chains. Because of my ancestors I was born and raised in Detroit. And for that I am glad. Yes, glad!

I never intended to feel that way. My opinions of Africa were formed over many years of traveling through Kenya, Somalia, Tanzania, and South Africa.

Yes, my opinions are controversial. I intend that as well.

Take this trip to Africa with me as a black man *Out of America.*

## Rinaldi, Ann. *Cast Two Shadows: The American Revolution in the South.*

Harcourt Brace, 1998, 281pp. With author's note and bibliography. Middle School & Up. An ALA Best Book for Young Adults.

HISTORICAL FICTION. *African Americans; American Revolutionary War; interracial relations; racism; women's issues.*

RELATED BOOKS: *A Stitch in Time (The Quilt Trilogy); Wolf by the Ears; Time Enough for Drums* by Ann Rinaldi; *Johnny Tremain* by Esther Forbes.

*Note:* This fictional account involves Caroline Whitaker's defiant stand against the British. She is biracial, an African American and white, and lives on a South Carolina plantation. Many issues of American colonial history are discussed in this page-turner.

It was late morning in 1780 when they hanged my best friend, Kit Gales. I sat on my horse, watching helplessly while the British soldiers hanged my friend. Then they insisted that Kit hang for three weeks with a placard forbidding his burial.

Next, the English soldiers hauled my daddy to prison. I hear the English plan to send him to Bermuda.

Then Johnny, my almost-brother, needed my help in escaping from the British army.

At one time I thought being a woman kept me out of politics. Now I know everyone has a different breaking point. For some, it had been the stamps. For others, it was the tea in Boston.

I've reached my breaking point. I will no longer tolerate these British. Give me liberty or give me death!

## Rinaldi, Ann. *In My Father's House.*

Scholastic, 1993, 321pp. Middle School & Up.

HISTORICAL FICTION. *Civil War; ethics; family; politics; revenge; rivalry; secrets; stepparents.*

RELATED BOOKS: *The Last Silk Dress* and *Wolf by the Ears* by Ann Rinaldi; *Across Five Aprils* by Irene Hunt.

*Note:* Rinaldi's notes tell of the authenticity of the site during the beginning and end of the War Between the States.

The American Civil War is a house divided, a nation torn apart.

The McLean family is involved in the war from the beginning to the end. In the beginning, the Battle of Bull Run was fought on the McLean property. At the end, Generals Lee and Grant signed the surrender in the McLeans' drawing room.

Meet the McLeans. The father is a proud and stubborn abolitionist, although he buys and sells slaves. Oscie, Will's stepdaughter, is also proud and stubborn, but a defender of the Old South and slavery. Maria is a Southern belle who falls for a Yankee prisoner of war. Mary Ann is a slave Oscie believes is a witch.

*In My Father's House* is based on real people and places. It reveals the struggles of the Southern people. In order to change, the Old South must die so that equality is available for every person, both in the McLean house and in the nation.

## Roberts, Willo Davis. *Pawns.*

Atheneum Books for Young Readers, 1998, 154pp. Elementary School & Up.

MYSTERY, THRILLERS. *Crime; death; orphans; pregnancy; rivalry; suicide.*

RELATED BOOKS: *Walk Two Moons* by Sharon Creech; *The Dollhouse Murders* by Betty Ren Wright; *Scared Stiff* by Willo Davis Roberts.

*Note:* An engrossing, if predictable, mystery for book reports and group readings.

"Hello, I'm Dora, Ricky's wife."

Teddi drew in a sharp breath. *Ricky's wife?* Ricky was dead, recently killed in a plane crash. Teddi didn't even know Ricky was married. Neither did Ricky's mother. Teddi had been living with Mamie Thane since her parents died, and she knew that Mamie had no knowledge of her son's marriage.

Because Mamie was excited about meeting her dead son's wife, she didn't appear to notice Dora's odd behavior. Teddi noticed. She noticed how Dora assumed she could live in the house, even taking Teddi's bedroom. She noticed that Dora said she was pregnant with Rick's child, but Dora had no pictures, identification, or stories about their life together. She also noticed that, just before boarding the plane, Rick had taken a $250,000 life insurance policy. Rick listed his mother as beneficiary. Why would Rick list his mother instead of his pregnant wife?

Was Dora who she said she was? If not, how could Teddi prove it?

## Rowling, J. K. Harry Potter and Sorcerer's Stone.

Illustrations by Mary Grandpre. Arthur A. Levine Books/Scholastic, 1997, 309pp. British title: *Harry Potter and the Philosopher's Stone.* Elementary School & Up. An ALA Best Book for Young Adults; British National Book Award for Best Children's Book of the Year; Top 10 Best Books for Young Adults; School Library Journal's Best Books selection; Smarties Prize, ABBY award. First in a series: **Harry Potter and the Chamber of Secrets; Harry Potter and the Prisoner of Azkaban** follow; future episodes planned.

FANTASY. *Magic; supernatural; rivalry.*

RELATED BOOKS: *The Secret of Platform 13* by Eva Ibbotson; *The Lion, The Witch and the Wardrobe* series by C. S. Lewis; *A Wrinkle in Time* series by Madeleine L'Engle; *Redwall* series by Brian Jacques; books by Diana Wynne Jones: *Dogsbody; Charmed Life; Howl's Moving Castle.*

*Note:* This acclaimed book was an instant children's classic. Rowling plans to write a seven-volume series. For booktalk presentations, you could place the acceptance letter on appropriate stationary and read it aloud. Or you could skip the letter and go into the rest of the booktalk. Elementary teachers or parents can use this book as an entertaining read-aloud.

Dear Harry Potter,

*We are pleased to announce your acceptance into the Hogwarts School of Witchcraft and Wizardry. Term begins September 1. We await your owl.*

*Minerva McGonagall*

*P. S. PARENTS ARE REMINDED THAT FIRSTS ARE NOT ALLOWED THEIR OWN BROOMSTICKS.*

Harry Potter hadn't even applied to the Hogwarts School of Witchcraft and Wizardry. The Underground did it for him. In the supernatural world, Harry was famous. He was the only known surviving victim of You-Know-Who. His parents were killed by You-Know-Who. (Voldemort was so evil that no sorcerer said his name aloud.) From this terrifying experience, Harry had a scar on his forehead in the shape of lightning. This lightning scar proved to the Underground that he had magical powers. Maybe Harry could develop his sorcerer skills and terminate You-Know-Who.

Does Harry Stone defeat You-Know-Who? Will the Underground be free of this treacherous villain? Only this enchanting series can reveal the answers.

# Roy, Arundhati. *The God of Small Things.*

Random House, 1997, 321pp.; (Pbk.) HarperCollins, 1998, 336pp. High School & Up. An Oprah Winfrey Book Selection.

REALISTIC FICTION. *Abuse; death; India and Pakistan; sex and sexuality; sexual abuse; single parents.*

RELATED BOOKS: *The City of Joy* by Dominque Lapierre; *A Passage to India* by E. M. Forester.

 *Note:* This little-known author was brought to center stage when Oprah Winfrey selected this title as her book choice. Recommended for groups or for the mature reader.

It all began when Sophie Mol came to Ayemenem, a town in southern India. Sometimes a few dozen hours can affect a lifetime. When this happens, these few dozen hours must be examined like an aging photograph. Accounted for.

Sophie Mol visited Ayemenem for only a week. She left Ayemenem in a coffin.  She left her family behind in grief and bewilderment.

The twins Estha and Rahel had grown to love their cousin within that week. Sophie Mol understood their desire to be unconditionally loved by their mother Ammu. Sophie Mol ran away with them that fateful day to demonstrate her support for their actions. That support led Sophie Mol to a watery grave.

On the other hand, perhaps the story begins during a Marxist demonstration when Sophie Mol's aunt saw the Untouchable Velutha.

Perhaps the story begins thousands of years ago. The Love Laws told their ancestors who were the Touchable People and the Untouchables.

Maybe it doesn't matter where or when the story begins, but how it ends and who delivers it. Therefore, this story is brought to you by *The God of Small Things*.

# Rubinstein, Gillian. *Under the Cat's Eye: A Tale of Morph and Mystery.*

Simon and Schuster for Young Readers, 1998, 204pp. Originally published in Australia. Elementary School & Up.

FANTASY. *Animals (cats); computers; supernatural.*

RELATED BOOKS: *The Changeover* by Margaret Mahy; *To Visit the Queen* by Diane Duane; *Shape-Changer* by Bill Brittain; *The Dark Side of Nowhere* by Neil Shusterman; *Harry Potter* series by J. K. Rowling.

*Note:* This Australian author has written a compelling, sometimes confusing, story with an agreeable, if unusual, main character, Jai. Jai's parents are from India and are protective and loving. See how **Star Wars** and **Harry Potter** fans like this one.

When Jai peered through the keyhole, he jumped away from the door. Two green globes, like the eyes of an animal, stared back at him!

The door opened with a loud creak. "Ah, welcome to our school. I'm Mr. Drake. You must be Mr. and Mrs. Kala. Say goodbye to your parents, Jai. You'll see them soon."

With a sinking heart, Jai watched his parents leave. Something was eerie about this boarding school. First, there were the mysterious boy and girl who leaped in front his father's car, almost getting killed. They left behind a ring with a half-animal face. Then Jai met Kitty, an alien, shape-changer cat who warned Jai of the evil headmaster. Mr. Drake would try to steal Jai's soul.

Can Jai escape the dark side of the force?

**R**

## Ryan, Pam Munoz. *Riding Freedom.*

Drawings by Brian Selznick. With author's notes. Scholastic, 1998, 138pp. Elementary School & Up.

HISTORICAL FICTION. *Animals (horses); physical disability; orphans; pioneer life; runaways; secrets; women's issues.*

RELATED BOOKS: *Cool Women: The Thinking Girl's Guide to the Hippest Women in History* edited by Pam Nelson; *Caddie Woodlawn* by Carol Ryrie Brink; *Buffalo Woman* by Bill Wallace; *The True Confessions of Charlotte Doyle* by Avi.

 *Note:* Ryan bases this historical novel on the true story of Charlotte Darkey Parkhurst, who, in the nineteenth century, disguised herself as a boy and made a living as a stable hand, then as an expert coach-driver, even voting in 1868 as a male. Entertaining read-aloud and group read for younger readers.

"I'm running away and I'm going tomorrow. I'm not staying in this orphanage, especially now that you're getting adopted." Charlotte looked at her friend. She already missed him, and he hadn't even gone yet. It wasn't fair. A young boy like Hayward could travel around without questions. As she considered this, a plan began to weave inside her mind. "I'm going to need some of your clothes, Hay."

"Sure, Charlotte, but be careful. You can't afford to get caught."

"Don't worry, Hay, I won't. And one day I'll find you. We're gonna have a ranch, remember? Right now I'm gonna need some scissors and some money for the stagecoach that comes tomorrow. I'll ask Vern if he can help."

The next morning Charlotte, with cropped hair and dressed in denim overalls, began her long walk to the stagecoach. She didn't have much time before Mrs. Boyle would be fussing about Charlotte not showing up for her daily breakfast chores.

That thought caused Charlotte to run. She couldn't miss that stagecoach. She was on a journey to a new life. She was now a young boy.

## Rylant, Cynthia. *I Had Seen Castles.*

Harcourt, Brace, 1993, 97pp. High School & Up. An Accelerated Reader selection.

HISTORICAL FICTION. *Aging; love; responsibility; sex and sexuality; World War II.*

RELATED BOOKS: *A Separate Peace* by John Knowles; *Marjorie Morningstar* by Herman Woulk; *Solider's Heart* by Gary Paulsen; *A Farewell to Arms* by Ernest Hemingway.

 *Note:* Be aware that this contains some discreet sexual scenes. Recommended for older reluctant readers.

"You will be an old man one day, John. I'm sure of it. You will be an old man." So says my beloved Ginny.

I turned 18 on August 7, 1942. The next day I enlisted in the United States Army. When I enlisted, I had never experienced much of life. The only adult experience I had known was loving Ginny.

Ginny is against the war. Any war. She wants me to register as a conscientious objector. But I would rather die in battle than be judged a coward.

Fifty years later I am still haunted by this memory. Maybe writing down my

## Sachar, Louis. **Holes.**

Farrar, Straus and Giroux, 1998, 233pp. For all libraries. Newbery Award winner; National Book Award for Young People; ALA Best Book for Young Adults; Top 10 Best Books for Young Adults; Quick Pick for Reluctant Young Adult Readers; School Library Journal's Best Books selection; winner of the Christopher Award.

REALISTIC FICTION. *Abuse; class conflict; crime; disability (mental); ethics; family; friendship; interracial relations; men's issues; peer pressure; responsibility; runaways; survival.*

RELATED BOOKS: *There's a Boy in the Girl's Bathroom* by Louis Sachar; *The Great Gilly Hopkins* by Katherine Paterson; *Harriet the Spy* by Louise Fitzhugh.

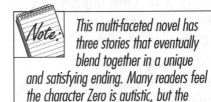 *This multi-faceted novel has three stories that eventually blend together in a unique and satisfying ending. Many readers feel the character Zero is autistic, but the author never labels Zero. A must-read.*

My family has the worst luck. It was all because of my no-good-dirty-rotten-pig-stealing-great-great-grandfather. (That's a family joke. We say that because my family carries a curse by a one-legged gypsy.)

I'm Stanley Yelnats IV. (Yelnats is Stanley spelled backwards. That's another family joke.) I have the worst luck. I'm always in the wrong place at the wrong time. Like that time those sneakers fell from the sky. I took them. How did I know those sneakers were stolen?

That's why I ended up at Camp Green Lake. When the judge said to choose between jail or a juvenile detention camp, I chose camp. Some camp. Every day I have to dig a hole, five feet down, five feet wide. Each day it gets harder because of the blisters and sore muscles.

While I'm digging holes, I'm digging up my past. Why did the first Stanley Yelnats lose his money to Kissin' Kate Barlow? Why can't my dad recycle sneakers? Why am I constantly blamed for things I didn't do? What can I do to break the family curse?

Come dig these *Holes* with me. I'm digging for the truth.

---

## Salisbury, Graham. **Under the Blood-Red Sun.**

Delacorte, 1994, 244pp. Elementary School & Up.

Historical fiction. *Asian Americans; death; friendship; immigrants; interracial relations; racism; World War II.*

Related books: *Journey to Topaz* and *Journey Home* by Yoshiko Uchida.

 *This book does an excellent job of portraying the horror of the war from all viewpoints. There are no villains here, only innocent people destroyed by war.*

On December 7, 1942 in Honolulu, Hawaii, there was an explosion under the blood-red sun. The Japanese bombed Pearl Harbor, and the United States declared war on Japan. Tomikazu Nakaji's world was forever changed.

Tomi's family was Japanese American. His grandfather liked hoisting the Japanese flag and polishing his samurai sword. After the Japanese attack, the neighbors resented this pride in their heritage. Tomi's father and grandfather were sent to a Japanese concentration camp and his mother lost her job. At 12, Tomi had to become the man in the family. He didn't know if he had the strength or courage. He felt so alone.

What of Tomi's best friend, Billy, a *haole* or white boy? Will Tomi lose his friends as well as his family? What will happen to his life?

## Scieszka, Jon and Lane Smith, illustrator. *Math Curse.*

Viking Children's Books, 1995, unnumbered pages. Elementary School & Up.

HUMOR. *School.*

RELATED BOOKS: Books by Jon Scieszka and Lane Smith: *The Stinky Cheese Man and Other Fairly Stupid Tales; The Frog Prince, Continued; The True Story of the Three Little Pigs.*

 *Note:* The book introduces higher math concepts in a humorous, entertaining style. Lane Smith's bold illustrations add to the fun. Some observant readers discovered a mistake on the page of prime numbers. See if you can spot it.

You have the curse.

It starts on Monday at school. A teacher says, "You can think of almost anything as a math problem."

That's when it begins. You think of everything as a math problem and it's driving you crazy.

Like, you have 10 things to do in only 30 minutes' time. Can you do it without missing the bus? Why can't you keep 10 cookies without someone taking three away? Does tunafish + tunafish = fournafish?

That's the math curse. Find out if the math curse is "catching."

## Scieszka, Jon and Lane Smith. *Squids Will be Squids: Fresh Morals, Beastly Fables.*

Designed by Molly Leach. Viking, 1998, unnumbered pages. Elementary School & Up. Quick Pick for Reluctant Young Adult Readers.

HUMOR. *Animals; ethics.*

RELATED BOOKS: *The Stinky Cheese Man and Other Fairly Stupid Tales* and *The True Story of the Three Little Pigs* by Jon Scieszka and Lane Smith; *Garfield* series by Jim Davis.

 *Note:* Booktalkers should select and read one of these 18 fables, then have enough copies available for reluctant readers and goofballs of all ages. Elementary teachers could introduce or read an Aesop fable; middle and high school teachers could use this to encourage students to write a modern fable.

Ever heard of *Aesop's Fables*? Aesop was this Greek guy who told fables. Fables are these stories that use animals as the main characters. These animals, like Lion or Mouse, act like people, sometimes being greedy, stupid, or careless. There's always a moral at the end to tell you how not to be greedy, stupid, or careless.

Aesop isn't alive today. If he were, he might tell these modern fables. These fables have modern morals, like "He who smelt it, dealt it." Or, as the author, Jon Scieszka, moralizes, "If you are planning to write fables, don't forget to change the people into animals and avoid places with high cliffs."

## Senna, Danzy. *Caucasia.*

Penguin Putnam, 1998, 353pp. High School & Up. Alex Award; School Library Journal's Best Books selection.

REALISTIC FICTION. *African Americans; homosexuality; interracial relations; problem parents; racism; rites of passage; runaways; single parents; secrets; sex and sexuality; women's issues.*

RELATED BOOKS: *The Color of Water* by James McBride; *Freedom's Child: The Life of a Confederate General's Black Daughter* by Carrie Allen McCray; *A Yellow Raft in Blue Water* by Michael Dorris.

 *Note:* This debut novel is a well-crafted coming-of-age story that explores the complex issues of racism in America. Recommended for mature readers and book groups.

Some time ago I disappeared. I disappeared into America, the easiest place to get lost. Dropped off, without a name, without a record. Now I only have memories of something lost.

This is what I remember. Back in 1970, I used to be Birdie Lee, living with a black father and white mother. Before I saw myself, I saw my sister, Cole, three years older than me. We even spoke our own language, *Elemeno.*

Cole was dark, so, of course, I assumed I was dark. My lightness would cause me a different set of problems than Cole endured. When Cole left with our father, and my mother ran away with me, I was blindly unaware I was saying goodbye to Cole, a sister I had known for only eight short years. I became Jesse Goldman, a white Jewish girl. Boston was far behind us. New Hampshire was my life.

For years I played the game, as if I were a separate person, watching the drama unfold. One day I left my lies behind. I killed Jesse Goldman so that Birdie Lee could live. In order for Birdie to live again, I had to find my sister.

## Service, Pamela F. *Stinker from Space.*

Charles Scribner's Sons, 1988, 83pp. Elementary School & Up.

SCIENCE FICTION. *Animals (skunks); friendship; science.*

RELATED BOOKS: *Shape-Changer* by Bill Brittain; *Alien for Rent* by Betsy Duffey; *A Wrinkle in Time* series by Madeleine L'Engle.

 *Note:* Booktalkers can write Tsynq Yr on a card to demonstrate the delightful word play; Phonetically, Tsynq Yr is, of course, Stinker. Recommended also for group reads or as a read-aloud.

"You're—you're a skunk." Karen backed up slowly, as she stared at the animal. "Skunks can't talk."

"Obviously, then, I am not a skunk." The skunk continued talking, but was hungrily eyeing the food in Karen's hand. "Let me define my problem. I'm in the Space Corp of Sylon Confederacy. Somehow my spaceship was damaged, and I landed in this sector. I borrowed this so-called skunk body from a passerby. My earlier body was fatally wounded in the crash."

"Wow," Karen breathed. She offered a cookie to the skunk.

The skunk eagerly consumed the cookie and asked, "Could you direct me to the nearest space-port? I have to return to my planet with valuable military information. Also, can you direct me to the nearest place where I could obtain more of this delicious nourishment?"

"Oh, that," Karen laughed. "That's a peanut butter cookie. Sure. I'll take you home and we'll get you back to space somehow. What's your name?"

"I am called Tsynq Yr."

"Stinker?" Karen whooped with laughter. "Your name is Stinker? That's perfect. I'll call you *Stinker from Space.*"

## Shoroto, Russell. *Gospel Truth: The New Image of Jesus Emerging from Science and History, and Why It Matters.*

Riverhead Books, 1997, 305pp. With notes, bibliography, and index. High School & Up.

NONFICTION. *Religion; religious prejudice.*

RELATED BOOKS: *The Historical Jesus* by John Dominic Crossan and *The Historical Evidence for Jesus* by G. A. Wells.

Who was the real Jesus? Unfortunately, we have little tangible evidence about the life and death of Jesus, only the Gospels and the Dead Sea Scrolls. It would take a detective to separate the myth from the reality.

Fortunately, there are detectives to help solve the mystery of Jesus. The Jesus Seminar was founded in 1985 and consists of leading biblical scholars. This ongoing seminar is in search of the historical Jesus. The scholars attempt to separate the truth from the fiction.

What were the circumstances of Jesus' birth? Did he produce miracles? How did he die? Did he overcome death? All these questions, and more, are pondered and studied.

Join these scholars on their quest for the truth, the *Gospel Truth.*

## Shusterman, Neal. *The Dark Side of Nowhere.*

Little Brown, 1997, 185pp. Elementary School & Up. An ALA Best Book for Young Adults; Quick Pick for Reluctant Young Adult Readers.

SCIENCE FICTION. *End of the world; secrets; self-identity.*

RELATED BOOKS: *Black Suits from Outer Space* by Gene DeWeese; *The Shape-Changer* by Bill Brittain; *Alien for Rent* by Betsy Duffey; *Stinker from Space* by Pamela Service.

*Note.* Reluctant teenage readers and older elementary students will enjoy this quick-paced plot written from a teenager's point of view. The plot is reminiscent of the movie **Invasion of the Body Snatchers,** without the sinister elements.

America the Bland. That's what life was like in all my 14 years in Billington. That's before I found out my parents were aliens.

After that, I wondered how I could be so blind. I thought about my lifetime of monthly shots. I remembered the message carved in the deserted house: *God Help Us.* I recalled how the school janitor gave me a mysterious glove that could shoot BB pellets from each finger. At last the pieces began to fit into a weird pattern. America the Bland has now turned into America the Weird.

If my parents are aliens, who am I? Where am I? On *The Dark Side of Nowhere.*

## Singer, Marilyn, editor. *Stay True: Short Stories for Strong Girls.*

Scholastic, 1998, 204pp. Middle School & Up. An ALA Best Book for Young Adults.

SHORT STORIES. *African Americans; Hispanic Americans; love; peer pressure; problem parents; rites of passage; self-identity; single parents; stepparents; women's issues.*

RELATED BOOKS: *Cool Women: The Thinking Girl's Guide to the Hippest Women in History* edited by Pam Nelson, written by Dawn Chipman, Mari Florence, and Naomi Wax; *Girl Power* by Hillary Carlip; *Beyond Beauty* by Jane Pratt.

*Note:* The authors include respected young adult writers such as M. E. Kerr, Norma Fox Mazer, and Rita Williams-Garcia. Peni R. Griffin's "The Truth in the Case of Eliza Mary Muller, by Herself" is a haunting drama of a sexually abused teenager killing her stepfather. Other stories are excellent, discussion-promoting read-alouds.

The title says it all. *Stay True: Short Stories for Strong Girls.* These 11 short stories are about girl power with a "you go girl" attitude.

Cindy works behind the refreshment stand at a dance, dreaming of love, until she meets her fairy god-mother, who turns her dream into a nightmare. Marguerite dances to her own music until she takes the lead with the shy Roland. Monica poses as the Statute of Liberty, protesting her sexist duties at home.

All these girls stay true. As Molly-be-Gone says, "We females must make a pact to ourselves. We must *Stay True.*"

---

## Skurzynski, Gloria. *Cyberstorm: A Novel with a Virtual Reality Twist.*

Macmillan Books for Young Readers, 1995, 137pp. Elementary School & Up. An ALA Best Book for Young Adults.

SCIENCE FICTION. *Aging; computers; family; friendship; time travel.*

RELATED BOOKS: *Virtual War* by Gloria Skurzynski; *Virtual World* by Gillian Cross; *Starswarm: A Jupiter Novel* by Jerry Pournelle.

*Note:* The author gives an **Alice in Wonderland** and **Wizard of Oz** spin on virtual reality. Give this one to those computer lovers who think they dislike reading.

We interrupt our video vision program with this flash from cyberspace:

*Today, July 2, 2015, a most unusual phenomenon occurred. Twelve-year-old Darcy Kane and her dog Chip are trapped in a virtual reality game called Rent-A-Memory. They accidentally entered this game and began reliving the memories of Mrs. Evelyn Galloway, 85, when the computer malfunctioned.*

*More news follows, live, as it happens.*

Erik is stunned. His best friend is trapped inside a computer! Luckily, he has an idea that might work. It is risky, though. To get to Mrs. Galloway's house, he has to risk being throttled by Jay Hawking, but Erik is willing to fight the bully to rescue Darcy.

Meanwhile, inside cyberspace, another disaster occurs. Jealous of Darcy reliving *her* memories, Mrs. Galloway jumps into the virtual reality game. Now two human beings and a dog are locked in cyberspace. These three have arrived in Oklahoma in 1959 while a terrible tornado rages. The debris flying around feels real enough, striking them with a forceful, stinging impact.

Trapped in cyberspace, will these three escape the reality of a *Cyberstorm*?

## Skurzynski, Gloria and Alane Ferguson. *Wolf Stalker.*

National Geographic Society, 1997, 147pp. With afterword and color photographs. First in the *National Parks Mystery* series. Elementary School & Up.

ADVENTURE. *Animals (wolves); ecology; single parents; survival; African Americans.*

RELATED BOOKS: *The Maze* by Will Hobbs; *Hatchet* series by Gary Paulsen; *Deathwatch* by Robb White.

*The afterword, maps, and color photographs of Yellowstone Park elevate this predictable plot to an educational adventure.*

Crack!

"Get down! That was a gunshot!" Troy pushed Jack and Ashley to the ground. Troy was familiar with gunfire from his inner-city environment, but he certainly didn't expect to hear that sound at Yellowstone National Park. He didn't even know his foster family that well, but his protective nature took over.

"That man in the bushes shot the wolf!" Ashley shrieked. "Jack, quick, take his picture."

As Jack fumbled with his camera lens, he didn't see Troy climbing down the bank. "Hey, where do you think you're going?" Jack hollered. "Get back here. You'll get lost."

Not even turning around, Troy answered, "The wolf's hurt. I'm gonna find it."

Meanwhile, unknown to Troy, the wolf stalker placed his rife over his shoulder. "Don't care how long it takes," the hunter murmured to his prey. "You're mine."

## Sleator, William. *The Boxes.*

Dutton Children's Books, 1998, 196pp. Middle School & Up. Top 10 Best Books for Young Adults; Top 10 Quick Picks for Reluctant Young Adult Readers.

SCIENCE FICTION. *Supernatural; time travel.*

RELATED BOOKS: *The Dark Side of Nowhere* by Neal Shusterman; other books by William Sleator: *The Beasties; The Night the Heads Came; Singularity.*

*This intricately plotted sci-fi thriller leaves an open ending, possibly for a sequel.*

"Don't even think about opening these two boxes," Uncle Marco said. "I'm leaving them with you because you're the only one I can trust. You can't tell anyone about the boxes."

"What's in them?" I asked.

"They're not my boxes, Annie. They don't belong to anyone, but they must be guarded and protected. Of course, they can't be in the same place; they can't be anywhere near each other. One can go in your room; the other, in the basement. Just make certain your Aunt Ruth doesn't find out." Uncle Marco looked at his watch. "Let's hurry. It's five o'clock. She'll be home soon."

As time passed, I couldn't think of anything but those boxes. Would it hurt to just peek inside one of those tempting, exotic boxes? So, like Pandora, I opened the box in the basement. Suddenly I was filled with dread. What had I done?

## Smith, Janice Lee. *Serious Science: An Adam Joshua Story.*

Drawings by Dick Gackenbach. HarperCollins, 1993, 73pp. Elementary School. Tenth book in the **Adam Joshua Capers**. Series also includes titles **The Monster in the Third Dress Drawer; There's a Ghost in the Coatroom; Nelson in Love; It's Not Easy Being George; The Turkeys' Side of It; The Show-and-Tell War; Turkey Trouble; Superkid; The Kid Next Door and Other Headaches; The Baby Blues; The Christmas Ghost.**

HUMOR. *Science; rivalry; school.*

RELATED BOOKS: *Aldo* series by Johanna Hurwitz; *Fudge* series by Judy Blume.

Does a fish have ESP? Can mold grow on dirty socks? Can a solar system be eaten by hungry humans? Is this the future of the universe?

No, it's the Science Fair! For the first time, the younger students can submit science projects for their Science Fair. As a guideline, Mr. D invented the Frankly Fantastic Fully Foolproof Fine Fish Food Fancy Fish Feeder.

Mr. D's project was an inspiration for Adam Joshua. He planned to make a spectacular model of the solar system, but everything kept going wrong. First, his little sister and dog ate his model. Then, the class bully, Elliot Banks, stole his idea!

The night before the Science Fair, Adam Joshua came up with another idea. It was a really amazing, absolutely terrific, stunningly spectacular idea. "I'll show Elliot Banks what happens to people who steal ideas," he grinned. "If there is ever an invention that would save the world and keep snoopy pests away, this is definitely it. Look out, world. I'm ready for some *Serious Science*!"

## Smith, Robert Kimmel. *Bobby Baseball.*

Illustrated by Alan Tiegreen. Delacorte, 1989, 165pp. Elementary School & Up.

SPORTS. *Problem parents; responsibility; rivalry; sports (baseball).*

RELATED BOOKS: *Baseball Fever* by Johanna Hurwitz; *The Trading Game* by Alfred Slote; *Bull Catcher* by Alden Carter.

*Note:* This book is sometimes used as a group read because it combines baseball with the complexities of father-son relationships. Also recommended for younger reluctant readers.

One day I'll be known as Bobby *"Baseball"* Ellis. The biggest thing in my life is baseball. Dad says I have baseball in my blood.

My Dad's name is Charles *"Chuck"* Ellis. I have his baseball card from the Arkansas Travelers. He now sells insurance and coaches my baseball team.

Dad says he's the boss on the baseball field. He insists I'm better on second base. I think I'm a better pitcher. He thinks he has the right to yell at me. I hate him when he does that.

When Dad benched me, I lost my temper and quit the team. Now it looks like my dream of Bobby Baseball will stay a dream. Am I right? Is it more important to be a team player or to be *Bobby Baseball*?

## Smith, Roland. **Sasquatch.**

Hyperion Books for Children, 1998, 188pp. Elementary School & Up. Top 10 Quick Picks for Reluctant Young Adult Readers.

ADVENTURE. *Ecology; science; supernatural; survival.*

RELATED BOOKS: *The Psychic Sasquatch and their UFO Connection* by Jack Lapseritis; *Reef of Death* and *Loch* by Paul Zindel.

 *The author, a research biologist, provides fascinating information about cryptids, legendary animals that are believed to exist, but can't be proven, and about volcanoes, especially Mount St. Helens in Washington. A page-turner for all readers.*

"The following photographs were taken 10 days ago. I'm not gong to tell you where I took them for obvious reasons." The crowd got very quiet, as one photograph after another flashed on the screen. They gave a collective gasp as they viewed the monstrous creature. "Any questions from the crowd?"

"Did you follow him?"

"Yes, I did, but by the time I got to the top, the Sasquatch was gone."

In the audience, Dylan turned to stare at his dad. Sasquatch? Bigfoot? Somehow this was all connecting to his dad's hunting trip last week, when he came back with torn clothes and a scratched face.

After the meeting, Dylan got his dad alone. "What's this about, Dad? Do you think you saw Bigfoot?"

"I prefer the Native American name, Sasquatch. Yes, son, I did see something. Now I know what I saw. And I know exactly where Clyde took those pictures. I'm going back to that spot on Mount St. Helens."

Dylan gulped. "Okay, Dad, but I'm going with you. Together, we'll find the *Sasquatch.*"

## Snyder, Zilpha Keatley. **The Runaways.**

Delacorte, 1999, 245pp. Elementary School & Up. *School Library Journal* starred review.

REALISTIC FICTION. *Abuse; friendship; problem parents; runaways; secrets.*

RELATED BOOKS: *While No One Was Watching* by Jane Leslie Conly; *The Empress of Elsewhere* by Theresa Nelson.

 *Although the 1950s setting seems irrelevant to the plot, the characters are well developed for an entertaining read.*

It must have been standing in the town's graveyard and seeing her name on the tombstone. Dani O'Donnell had carved the name herself, but realized that she could easily die in this town if she didn't take action. So, a few months before her 13th birthday, Dani O'Donnell decided to run away. She had thought of running away from Rattler Springs, Nevada, for at least four years, but this time she made definite plans.

The problem was that Dani had two friends who wanted to join her: Stormy, a nine-year-old kid with a bad temper; and Pixie, an imaginative new girl seeking adventure. They had a way of thwarting Dani's plans. Stormy kept getting caught up in Pixie's fantasies. For instance, are Pixie's parents really like Frankenstein, making monsters from dead bodies?

Puh-leeze, thought Dani, I'm not worried about Pixie's nonsense. I've got more important worries, like, when will we finally get our chance to become *The Runaways*?

# Soto, Gary. *Buried Onions.*

Harcourt Brace, 1997, 149pp. Middle School & Up. An ALA Best Book for Young Adults.

REALISTIC FICTION. *Crime; death; Hispanic Americans; men's issues; self-identity; substance abuse.*

RELATED BOOKS: *Parrot in the Oven: My Vida* by Victor Martinez; *The House on Mango Street* by Sandra Cisneros.

*Note:* Soto writes in a wryly observant style that lightens the somber plot. All of Gary Soto's books are well-written excursions into Hispanic America.

For me, living in Fresno, there was nothing to do except eat, sleep, and watch for drive-by shootings. I had dropped out of City College, studying air-conditioning. I quit after my cousin, *mi primo* Jesus, got killed. He made the mistake of talking to a guy in a rest room This guy pushed a dirty blade in *mi primo's* clean heart.

My *tia* Dolores, Jesus' mother, wants me to settle matters. I'm supposed to find the murderer and ice him. She doesn't know I've become a dinosaur. Too old to run with gangs and too messed up to get good jobs.

What's to become of my life?

# Sparks, Christine. *The Elephant Man.*

Macdonald Futura, 1980, 272pp. High School & Up. An Accelerated Reader selection.

HORROR. *Disability; friendship; science; self-identity.*

RELATED BOOKS: *The Autobiography of a Face* by Lucy Grealy; *The Heart is a Lonely Hunter* by Carson McCullers.

Dr. Fredrick Treves had never seen such a freak of nature as the Elephant Man. Most circus exhibits, such as the Bearded Lady, were phonies. However, he couldn't believe those two horribly deformed feet, knotted with veins and covered with scaly skin. Whoever or whatever was behind that curtain was genuinely monstrous.

John Merrick was the Elephant Man's name, an ordinary name for such a hideous creature. His face was enormous and distorted with a bone protruding from the forehead like an elephant's trunk.

Where did John Merrick come from? What could scientists learn from this genetic mutation?

Dr. Treves had to discover the truth about this mysterious monster called *The Elephant Man.*

## Sparks, Nicholas. *Message in a Bottle.*

Warner Books, 1998, 322pp. (Pbk.) Mass Market Paperback, 1999, 370pp. High School & Up.

ROMANCE. *Death; divorce; movie novels; love; sex and sexuality; single parents.*

RELATED BOOKS: *The Notebook* by Nicholas Spark; *The Bridges of Madison County* by Robert James Waller; *Summer Sisters* by Judy Blume.

After 26 days and 738 miles, the message in a bottle ended its journey at Theresa Osborne's feet. She was walking the beach in Cape Cod and discovered the bottle. Inside the bottle was a peculiar message. The message contained a letter from someone named Garrett who expressed his heartbreak at losing the love of his life, Catherine.

The message in the bottle intrigued Theresa. Who were Garrett and Catherine? Where are they now? What was their story?

Read how a message in a bottle, tossed into the sea, transformed two people forever.

## Springer, Nancy. *I am Mordred: A Tale from Camelot.*

Philomel Books, 1998, 184pp. Middle School & Up. An ALA Best Book for Young Adults; Quick Picks for Reluctant Young Adult Readers.

FOLKLORE. *Great Britain; magic; Middle Ages; rivalry; revenge; war.*

RELATED BOOKS: *The Winter Prince* by Elizabeth Wein; *Mary Stewart's Merlin Trilogy: The Crystal Cave; The Hollow Hills; The Last Enchantment* by Mary Stewart; *The Lost Years of Merlin* by T. A. Barron; *Passager* and *Hobby*, part of the *Young Merlin trilogy* by Jane Yolen.

*Note:* The legend of King Arthur never dies. English and language arts teachers can use all the books about King Arthur for a takeoff into fantasy and folklore.

When I was a baby, my father tried to kill me.

I am Mordred. I am the only son of King Arthur of Camelot.

When I was young and helpless, my father placed me on a frail boat and cast me adrift on the sea. Luckily, a fisherman and his wife discovered me.

One fateful day, many years later, a lady in green arrived, riding her dapple gray horse. This sorceress called Nyneve bought me for a purse of gold. Later she informed me that I was the son of King Arthur and his sister! King Arthur was both a father and an uncle to me!

Many years before, the great wizard Merlin predicted that, because of this incestuous relationship, King Arthur would die at his only son's hands. That is why my father tried to kill me.

I am bewildered and humiliated by these events far beyond my control. How can I prevent myself from fulfilling Merlin's prophecy? Or, instead, am I destined to murder my father?

## Stanley, Thomas J. and William D. Danko. *The Millionaire Next Door: The Surprising Secrets of America's Wealth.*

Longstreet, 1996, 258pp. High School & Up.

NONFICTION. *Class conflict; responsibility.*

RELATED BOOKS: *The Courage to Be Rich* and *The Nine Steps to Financial Freedom* by Suze Orman; *You Have More than You Think* by David Gardner and Tom Gardner.

 *This readable, brief book can be used in a variety of subjects, especially classes in sociology, psychology, and economics.*

Do you think you can spot a millionaire?

Take a look around your neighborhood. You might know a millionaire. The family might even live next door! Many of America's millionaires live simple lives in middle-class neighborhoods. Yet they are wealthy beyond our dreams.

Who are the rich in America? What do they do? How did they become rich? More important, how can you join these millionaires?

Get the answers in the informative *The Millionaire Next Door.*

---

## Steel, Danielle. *This Bright Light: The Story of Nick Traina.*

Delacorte, 1998, 291pp. High School & Up.

BIOGRAPHY. *Death; mental illness; suicide.*

RELATED BOOKS: *Darkness Visible: A Memoir of Madness* by William Styron; *Living with Manic-Depressive Illness* by Patty Duke and Gloria Hochman.

 *This heart-wrenching book about an adolescent diagnosed as a manic-depressive who eventually commits suicide details the traumas Nick and his family endured during his long struggle with mental illness. Recommended especially for school counselors and psychology classes.*

I wish I knew about Nick then. Maybe the ending would be different.

I'm Danielle Steele, author of many best sellers like *The Gift* and *Mixed Blessings.* Nick Traina was my son. When Nick was only 19, I lost him forever.

He was always a strange one. For example, as a teen, he dyed his hair from green to blue to sapphire to jet black. Hair color, like music, became his obsession. His hair color must have reflected his constantly changing emotions.

Always popular and well-liked, he showed another side of himself in his journals: *"I wish I'd die and it would all be over. I love life and everyone but me."*

How I wish we had read his journals before it was too late.

**S**

## Steinbeck, John. *Of Mice and Men.*

(Pbk.) Penguin USA, 1993, 107pp. First published in 1937. High School & Up. An Accelerated Reader selection.

REALISTIC FICTION. *Disability (mental); death; ethics; friendship; racism; responsibility.*

RELATED BOOKS: *Cannery Row* and *The Grapes of Wrath* by John Steinbeck; *To Kill a Mockingbird* by Harper Lee; *One Flew Over the Cuckoo's Nest* by Ken Kesey.

 *Note:* This tragic novella is about the complex bond between two migrant workers, one being mentally disabled. Be aware that the word "nigger" is used frequently, a harsh reflection of American life in the 1930s.

"Lennie, you remember where we're going now?"

Lennie looked startled, and then embarrassed. He was a huge man and walked heavily, dragging his feet. "I forgot."

George tilted up his head to look sharply at Lennie. "You think I ain't got nothing to do, but spen' my time tellin' you things, and then you forget 'em, and I tell you again. Now, look—we're gonna work on a ranch like the one we come from up north. This time you ain't gonna do no bad things like you done in Weed, neither."

Lennie looked puzzled. "Like I done in Weed?"

"So ya forgot that too, did ya? Well, I ain't gonna remind ya, fear ya do it again. Jus' stay away from people and let me do all the talkin'. Got that?"

Lennie squinted his eyes and then exclaimed, "They run us out of Weed!"

"No, you fool, "George said with disgust. "We run. They was lookin' for us, but we run. Me, I could live so easy without you. I don't know why I keep you hangin' 'round me. All right, Lennie, let's go. We're ready to forget the past and start a new life."

## Stewart, Mary. *The Moon-Spinners.*

(Pbk.) Ballantine Books, 1962, 223pp. Middle School & Up.

MYSTERY/THRILLERS. *Crime; death; love; Middle East (Crete); movie novels; survival.*

RELATED BOOKS: *The Ivy Tree, This Rough Magic,* and *My Brother Michael* by Mary Stewart.

 *Note:* Although Mary Stewart's mysteries are out-of-print, many libraries have them. As a teenager, I read these mysteries and was swept away by the independent spirit of the heroines visiting exotic locations. Also, Stewart cleverly blends literary allusions into her romantic thrillers.

I arrived in Crete one day earlier than my scheduled arrival, prepared to meet my aunt for an exotic vacation. It was considered unusual for a young woman to travel alone, but I enjoyed my independence. I spoke adequate Greek, and, being British, I felt I could handle any problems that might occur.

I was wrong. While wandering on a little-used path in the foreboding White Mountains, I met a young man in hiding. Mark warned me not to get involved with the murder he and his brother had witnessed. I tried to obey, but, like The Moon-spinners spinning moonlight, I was intertwined into this sinister affair. When I arrived at the inn, I met the very people responsible for the murder!

## Strasser, Todd. *How I Spent My Last Night On Earth.*

Simon & Schuster Books for Young Readers, 1998, 169pp. High School & Up. Top 10 Best Books for Young Adults. Part of the **Time Zone High** series: **How I Changed My Life; Girl Gives Birth to Own Prom Date; How I Created My Perfect Prom Date** precede.

Humor. *Computers; end of the world; love; science; school; sex and sexuality.*

Related books: *Thwonk* and *Squashed* by Joan Bauer; books by Ellen Conford: *A Royal Pain; Crush; If This Is Love, I'll Take Spaghetti.*

 *Note:* This series is narrated by teen Allegra "Legs" Hanover in quick-witted dialogue. Can also be recommended to mature middle school readers.

What would you do if you were told you had only 24 hours before an asteroid obliterated Earth?

You'd do what I'm doing, what everyone at Time Zone High is doing. You'd seize the day and make the most of your short life.

That's what I'm doing. I plan to date the Totally Inappropriate Guy, Andros Bliss.

I don't plan to die alone, having never experienced love. Or passion. Or Bliss.

So, I'll dump my platonic boyfriend, Derman, and follow my Bliss. Stick around so I can tell you *How I Spent My Last Night on Earth.*

## Summers, Anthony. *Goddess: The Secret Lives of Marilyn Monroe.*

Sphere, 1986, 620pp. High School & Up.

BIOGRAPHY. *Mental illness; orphans; self-identity; sex and sexuality; show business; substance abuse (alcohol and drugs); women's issues.*

RELATED BOOKS: *Marilyn Monroe* by Barbara Leaming; *Marilyn* by Norman Mailer; *Dorothy Dandridge* by Donald Bogel.

 *Note:* The book is long, but even a reluctant reader will be engrossed in this real-life drama that involves the Kennedys, Joe Dimaggio, Arthur Miller, Frank Sinatra, the Mafia, and the FBI.

Don't judge a book by its cover.

Have you heard that cliché? In this case, don't judge Marilyn Monroe by her cover.

On the outside, Marilyn Monroe was beautiful, talented, and famous. On the inside, Marilyn Monroe was Norma Jeane Baker with many insecurities.

Norma Jeane Baker was born in 1926 as an illegitimate child to a mentally unstable mother. During her youth Norma Jeane moved from various foster homes to an orphanage.

Eventually Norman Jeane transformed herself into Marilyn Monroe. She partied with the rich and the famous, including President Kennedy. She married baseball legend Joe Dimaggio and playwright Arthur Miller.

However, Marilyn could never totally banish Norma Jeane from her psyche. Her insecurities eventually led to her mysterious death in 1962.

Marilyn had many secret lives. Which was the real person?

## Sweeney, Joyce. *The Spirit Window.*

Delacorte, 1998, 243pp. Middle School & Up. An ALA Best Book for Young Adults.

REALISTIC FICTION. *Aging; death; ecology; ethics; family; love; Native Americans (Cherokee); problem parents; substance abuse (alcohol); stepparents; supernatural.*

RELATED BOOKS: *A Yellow Raft on Blue Water* by Michael Dorris; *Tangerine* by Edward Bloor; *The Maze* by Will Hobbs; *Shadow* by Joyce Sweeney.

 *Note:* Sweeney skillfully blends mystery and romance in a narrative of ecological awareness.

Well, Toto, looks like we're not in Kansas any more. We're in Florida visiting my grandmother Lila in her enchanted Oz. Her wildlife sanctuary is a paradise, a perfect place for a 15-year-old photographer like me. Like the movie, I'm changing my film from black-and-white to color.

The colors, sounds, and physical beauty of Turtle Island are beyond belief for this city girl. That's where I meet Adam, Lila's 18-year-old gardener, part Cherokee, and a definite candidate for the coveted Golden Babe award. Like Lila, Adam is a fierce protector of the untamed beauty of Turtle Island.

Everything turns topsy-turvy when my grandmother dies. Dad and his drinking buddy Skip want to turn Turtle Island into a shopping mall. Even I find that hard to swallow. How can Adam and I make Dad see that Turtle Island is an ecological paradise, an Oz beyond our dreams?

## Sykes, Shelley. *For Mike.*

Delacorte, 1998, 197pp. Middle School & Up. Nominee of the Edgar Allan Poe Mystery Award for Young Adults; Honor Book in 14th Annual Delacorte Press Prize.

MYSTERIES, THRILLERS. *Supernatural; secrets.*

RELATED BOOKS: *Zero to the Bone* by Michael Cadnum; *The Killer's Cousin* by Nancy Werlin; *Acquainted with the Night* by Sollace Hotze; *Rebecca* by Daphne du Maurier.

 *Note:* This suspenseful mystery, narrated by Mike's best friend Jeff, has plenty of twists and turns to entice a reluctant reader or mystery lover.

In my dream, I hear Mike calling my name.

In my dream, I answer, "Mike, where are you?"

Mike says, "Help me out. Get Kirby, then come get me."

I wake up, shivering. I've dreamed this for two straight nights. Mike has been gone for three weeks. I didn't know then I would be one of the last people to see him. What does that weirdo Kirby have to do with Mike's disappearance?

My friend Berry tells me the dream could be prophetic, a prediction of the future. Together we begin our search for Mike, following the clues he leaves in my dreams.

Wherever you are, Mike, I'm coming to find you.

## Thoreau, Henry David. **Walden.**

With essays by E. B. White and Max Lerner. Running Press, 1990, 207pp. First published in 1845. Middle School & Up. An Accelerated Reader selection.

SHORT STORIES, ESSAYS. *Animals; ecology; ethics; men's issues; pioneer life; politics; responsibility.*

RELATED BOOKS: *Into the Wild* by Jon Krakauer; *The Old Man and the Sea* by Ernest Hemingway.

*Note:* E. B. White claims that all graduating seniors should be given a copy of this book for it advances a good argument for traveling light and trying new adventures.

In the summer of 1845, I began two years of living alone, in the woods, in a house I built myself, near Walden Pond, in Concord, Massachusetts. I have returned to civilized life a much wiser man.

I went to the woods because I wished to live life deliberately, and to see if I could learn what it had to teach. I wanted to live Spartan-like, to reduce life to its minimal terms. In our man-made society, we live meanly, like ants, with our lives frittered away by possessions. I say, simplicity, simplicity, simplicity!

Join me on my quest for truth in the beatific simplicity of *Walden*.

## Tillage, Leon Walter. **Leon's Story.**

Collage art by Susan L. Roth. Farrar Straus Giroux, 1997, 107pp. For all libraries. Nonfiction winner of the Boston Globe-Horn Book Awards.

BIOGRAPHY. *Abuse; African Americans; death; family; racism.*

RELATED BOOKS: *Malcolm X Talks to Young People* by Malcolm X; *Coming of Age in Mississippi* by Anne Moody; *Roll of Thunder, Hear My Cry* by Mildred Taylor.

*Note:* Tillage's matter-of-fact story is transcribed from a taped oral testimony. Recommended as a read-aloud to elementary classes, so the teacher can provide vital background information and encourage discussions about ethics, morality, history, social change, and civil rights.

I'm Leon Walter Tillage. This is my story.

I was born on January 19, 1936, and was raised in a small town in North Carolina. I used to curse my color, my blackness. That's because, in those days, everything was separated by color. That's why my father stayed poor as a sharecropper, and the Johnsons, who owned our property, stayed rich.

My family lived in a broken-down house, wore hand-me-down clothes, and walked to school four miles away. Whenever we walked home from school, we would run whenever we saw a school bus. The white students on the bus would call us names. Sometimes the bus driver would stop the bus so they could chase us and throw stones.

From school, we learned we had certain rights: freedom of speech, freedom of religion. We learned about the Constitution of the United States. When our parents said, "Don't go on those civil rights marches. You'll get killed or beaten," we said, "What's the difference? We're getting killed and beaten anyway, so let us be beaten to change things."

This is my story, how it was back then and how things gradually changed.

# Tsukiyama, Gail. *Women of the Silk.*

St. Martin's Press, 1991, 270pp. High School & Up.

HISTORICAL FICTION. *Abuse; China; death; friendship; trust; work; women's issues.*

RELATED BOOKS: *The Good Earth* by Pearl Buck; *Bound Feet and Western Dress* by Pang-Mei Natasha Chang; *Daughter of the River* by Hong Ying.

*Book lovers like to recommend this multicultural gem to other book lovers.*

We are sisters of the silk. We are Chinese women living in rural China in 1926. Most of us were sold by our parents to earn money working in the silk factory. Most of us will never see our parents again. Out of loneliness we become like sisters, sharing our hopes and dreams.

I am Pei, tall and strange-looking because my father is a *Hakka*, the guest people who migrated from the North. My best friend is Lin, beautiful and educated. Our friend Me-li is in love with a university boy so she refuses to marry the boy her parents have selected for her. How often we have wished we could have foreseen the disaster that would befall Me-li.

All of us have different hope and dreams, but we are all suffering under the oppression of the owner of the silk factory. Our sister Chen Ling organizes us to protest the long hours and low wages. We participate in an event the village has never seen—a strike!

# Turner, Ann.  *A Lion's Hunger: Poems of First Love.*

Illustrated by Maria Jimenz. Marshall Cavendish, 1998, 47pp.  Middle School & Up. An ALA Best Book for Young Adults; Quick Pick for Reluctant Young Adult Readers.

POETRY. *Diaries; love; women's issues.*

RELATED BOOKS: *A Night Without Armor* by Jewel; poetry by Emily Dickinson and Walt Whitman.

*This diary of poems, illustrated with subtle and warm watercolors, is narrated by a nameless young girl who relates the agonies and ecstasies of love. This book can inspire others to write poetry.*

Last Autumn
—Purple, orange, flaming red—
I saw you
—Lean, long, liquid—
You filled a need
—a toothless space—
A lion's hunger
to be fed.

Now buried mementos
—Photograph, ring,  bracelet—
With an invisible you
—Anxiety, agony, acceptance—
A lion's hunger
finally satisfied.

# Tyler, Anne. *The Accidental Tourist.*

Alfred A. Knopf, 1985, 342pp. High School & Up.

REALISTIC FICTION. *Love; men's issues; movie novels; single parents; trust; work.*

RELATED BOOKS: *Breathing Lessons* and *A Patchwork Planet* by Anne Tyler.

**Note:** During a booktalking presentation, when saying the title, point to the book cover with the armchair logo.

*Accidental Tourist in France. Accidental Tourist in Germany. Accidental Tourist in America.*
All these travel books are by Macon Leary. All the book covers have no author's name, just a logo: an armchair on the cover.

Truthfully, Macon hates to travel. He also hates his life since his son has been senselessly murdered and his wife of 20 years has left him.

Then Macon meets an eccentric dog obedience trainer named Muriel Pritchett. She takes this Accidental Tourist on an exciting journey to a place where he has never traveled: *Accidental Tourist in Love.*

# Tyler, Anne. *Dinner at the Homesick Restaurant.*

Fawcett Columbine, 1982, 303pp. High School & Up.

REALISTIC FICTION. *Abuse; death; eating disorders; family; revenge; rivalry; single parents; work.*

RELATED BOOKS: *Prince of Tides* by Pat Conroy; *Fried Green Tomatoes at the Whistle Stop Cafe* by Fannie Flagg.

**Note:** Recommend Anne Tyler's books to readers who love a compelling story with unforgettable characters.

After her husband left her, Pearl Tull had been an angry mother. Her children, Cody, Jenny, and Ezra, seemed to remember only poverty, loneliness, and blows for bad behavior. Where had Pearl gone wrong?

Strangely, enough, the Tulls probably had spent more time with each other than happy families did. It was as if what they couldn't get right, they had to replay. Now that they were grown, they regularly met at Ezra's restaurant, the Homesick Restaurant. But not once had the family ever finished one of Ezra's dinners. Someone would become offended by another's words or actions and stomp off in a rage.

When would this family get it right so their agony would end? Must Pearl die to set things right?

## Van Draanen, Wendelin. *Sammy Keyes and the Hotel Thief.*

(Pbk.) Alfred A. Knopf, 1998, 163pp. Elementary School & Up. Winner of the Edgar Allen Poe Award for best children's mystery. Part of a series: **Sammy Keyes and the Skeleton Man** precedes; **Sammy Keyes and the Runaway Elf** and **Sammy Keyes and the Sisters of Mercy** follow.

MYSTERIES, THRILLERS. *Crime; peer pressure; school.*

RELATED BOOKS: The Herculeah Jones mystery series by Betsy Byars: *The Dark Stairs; Tarot Says Beware; Dead Letter; Death's Door; Disappearing Acts.*

 *Note:* *This entertaining series is perfect for young mystery lovers and reluctant readers, with a live-wire sleuth who copes with a bully, a hostile police officer, and a nosy neighbor. Middle school students will enjoy the series, too.*

Gram told me one day my binoculars were going to get me into trouble. One day I saw a man stealing money from a hotel room across the street. Trouble was, he saw me too. I even waved at him! Gram is right. I'm in trouble!

I'm Samantha Keyes. Call me Sammy. I'm always in some kind of fix, but no one can talk me out of this. I don't care what Officer Borsch thinks. I'm going to capture that hotel thief!

## Walker, Paul Robert. *Bigfoot and Other Legendary Creatures.*

Illustrated by William Noonan. With annotated bibliography. Harcourt Brace, 1992, 56pp. (Pbk.) Harcourt Brace, 1997, 64pp. Elementary School & Up.

NONFICTION. *Ecology; science.*

RELATED BOOKS: *Sasquatch* by Roland Smith; *Loch* and *Reef of Death* by Paul Zindel; *Sasquatch: The Apes Among Us* by Rupert T. Gould.

 *Note:* *Walker discusses seven "monsters": Bigfoot, Yeti, Mongolia Almas; Nessie, the giant octopus Lusca; the dinosaurian Mokele-Mbembe; and the huge winged Kongamato, the latter two from tropical Africa. Each chapter begins with a fictional account, telling a compelling horror story, and then follows with a brief explanation of the legend with any solid evidence of the existence of the creature. Great for reluctant readers.*

Did you know that over 2,000 people have reported seeing Bigfoot? That over 4,000 people claim to have seen the Loch Ness monster? Yet there is no scientific evidence of these creatures' existence. Are these monsters fact or fiction?

Bigfoot tracks have been found in California, Oregon, Washington, and British Columbia. From those tracks, experts estimate that Bigfoot would be over seven feet tall and weigh up to 800 pounds. Some researchers believe Bigfoot may be the descendant of a prehistoric ape called Gigantopithecus.

The Loch Ness monster lives in one of the lakes in the Scottish highlands. Blurry photographs show a dark creature 20 to 40 feet long, with at least one hump, thin neck, and small head. Researchers think it could be an aquatic reptile thought to be extinct.

Find out more intriguing facts about *Bigfoot and Other Legendary Creatures.*

## Walsch, Neal Donald. *Conversations with God: An Uncommon Dialogue, Book Three.*

Hampton Roads, 1998, 392pp. High School & Up. Third part of a series: **Conversations with God, Book One;**
**Conversations with God, Book Two** precede.

Nonfiction. *Ethics; religion; responsibility.*

Related books: Books by Wayne Dyer, Marianne Williamson, Joel Goldsmith.

*Note:* *A good discussion book for older readers.*

Is it hard to believe that I would have a conversation with God? Believe me, no one is more surprised than I.

I'm the author, Neal Donald Walsch. This conversation between God and me began in 1992. I was angry at God, so I wrote him an angry letter filled with questions about life, death, and all in-between. To my surprise, I got an answer. My hands began automatically moving on my keyboard, as if I were operating a Ouija board. I was amazed at the answers. When I published this book, quite frankly, I was scared what the readers would think.

To my surprise, the readers wanted more dialogue. They thought the words rang true and were filled with helpful advice. God discusses everything from how to make a relationship work to the cosmology of the universe.

Maybe you will get the same peace of mind that God gave me through our conversations.

## Walter, Virginia and Katrina Roeckelin. *Making Up Megaboy.*

DK Graphics, 1998, 62pp. Middle School & Up. An ALA Best Book for Young Adults.

REALISTIC FICTION. *Crime; death; ethics; men's issues; problem parents.*

RELATED BOOKS: *Monster* by Walter Dean Myers; *Mary Wolf* by Cynthia D. Grant; *The Killer's Cousin* by Nancy Werlin; *The Facts Speak for Themselves* by Brock Cole.

*Note:* *This graphically interactive book presents questions about teenage crime without answering any of them. The reader's job is to answer these provocative questions. Highly recommended for guidance counselors, sociology classes, and discussion groups.*

Why would Robbie Jones shoot someone on his 13th birthday?

Robbie isn't talking, except to admit that he did it. Everyone else— from the media to his classmates to his best friend Ruben—has opinions. They all try to answer this question: How could a quiet, ordinary seventh-grade boy just take out a gun and shoot someone whom he didn't even know?

## Wells, Rebecca. *Divine Secrets of the Ya-Ya Sisterhood.*

(Pbk.) HarperPerennial, 1997, 356pp. High School & Up. Winner of the ABBY Award.

REALISTIC FICTION. *Abuse; friendship; problem parents; women's issues.*

RELATED BOOKS: *Women Who Run with the Wolves* by Clarissa Pinkola Estes; *The Group* by Mary McCarthy.

 An enthusiastic "you go, girl" book for the young at heart. Recommended as a mother-daughter group read.

Sidda received a thick package from her estranged mother. Inside were a letter and a brown leather scrapbook, stuffed with letters and photographs. Sidda gingerly opened the scrapbook, truly honored that her mother would share this treasure. The yellowed pages exposed a 50-year friendship among four women who called themselves the Ya-Yas.

The Ya-Yas had opinions about everything. Something great was "Ya-Ya." Like the time the four went skinny-dipping in the town's water tank at midnight, Ya-Ya. When they were arrested and booked for a night in jail, Ya-Ya-No!

Maybe the scrapbook can help Sidda recover from her mid-life depression. Your spirits will definitely soar at these outrageous women who run with the wolves.

Ya-Ya!

## Welter, John. *I Want to Buy a Vowel: A Novel of Illegal Alienation.*

(Pbk.) Berkley Books, 1997, 231pp. Middle School & Up.

HUMOR. *Class conflict; crime; Hispanic Americans; immigrants (Guatemalan); politics.*

RELATED BOOKS: *Begin to Exit Here: A Novel of the Wayward Press* by John Welter; books by humorists Dave Barry and Lewis Grizzard.

 This satire pokes fun at immigration laws in an amusing, entertaining style.

Alfred Santayana illegally crossed the Mexican border into Texas. He said the only American expression he knew, a phrase he had heard on TV in Guatemala in South America. Of course, he hadn't a clue to its meaning: "I want to buy a vowel."

"Jackass," retorted the lady. She continued walking down the street.

Wonderful, thought Alfred. A new word to learn. America is filled with wonderful words, interesting jobs, and fancy places to live. How wonderful is this America.

Many residents in the town aren't so sure about Alfred. Some strange, devilish things are going on that have a Satanic twist. Is Alfred the Satan figure who puts chicken giblets and Vienna sausages on sacred bones? There's something devilish about a man who says, " My broker is E. F. Hutton. The best part of waking up is Folgers in your cup. For sinus, think Sinex."

Did Alfred end up buying a vowel? Was he the giblets guy? Find out in this wickedly funny novel on illegal alienation: *I Want to Buy a Vowel.*

# Werlin, Nancy. *The Killer's Cousin.*

Delacorte, 1998, 229pp. Middle School & Up. Winner of the Edgar Allen Poe award for Best Young Adult Mystery; Top 10 Quick Picks for Reluctant Young Adult Readers.

Mysteries, thrillers. *Crime; death; secrets; suicide; supernatural.*

Related books: *Are You Alone on Purpose?* by Nancy Werlin; *For Mike* by Shelley Sykes; *Jumping the Nail* by Eve Bunting; books by Mary Higgins Clark.

 *This award-winning, expertly paced psychological thriller builds to a suspenseful climax. David, as narrator, withholds the details of his girlfriend's murder until the end, adding to the suspense. A must-read for older mystery lovers.*

My name is David Bernard Yaffe. Sound familiar? You might not remember my name, but surely you've seen the newspapers and tabloids. There's a famous photograph of my father and mother outside the courthouse in Baltimore. My father is a criminal lawyer. Some of the tabloids said that was the reason the jury voted not guilty.

To escape the press, I went to Massachusetts to live with my Uncle Vic and Aunt Julie. Bad idea. They have their own drama. Since their daughter Kathy died, they haven't spoken to each other. They use my 11-year-old cousin, Lily, to communicate. That's weird.

Lily's just as weird. She even had the gall to ask me, "When you killed her, did you feel powerful ? Were you glad? Even for a minute?" Great. I have to live with my conscience, and now I have a hostile cousin who thinks I'm a killer. She spies on me, destroys my computer files, and glues my CDs in their cases. I also hear Kathy's ghost, a humming shadow, whispering, *Help Lily.*

Who's the crazy one: me, the killer, or Lily, *The Killer's Cousin*?

# Williams, Michael. *The Genuine Half-Moon Kid.*

Lodestar Books, 1994, 199pp. Middle School & Up. An Accelerated Reader selection.

REALISTIC FICTION. *Abuse; Africa (South Africa); death; interracial relations; orphans; problem parents; sex and sexuality.*

RELATED BOOKS: *Video Dreams* by Jenny Hobbs; *Boikie, You Better Believe It* by Dianne Hofmeyr.

 *A book that is multicultural and entertaining, as the reader travels on Jay's odyssey looking for his grandfather's box. In the box are items that will forecast Jay's future as a writer.*

Go figure this one, Jay-o. You're bound on some crazy journey all through South Africa to find some box your grandfather left you. *Ja*, going through a township and orphanage, meeting all kinds of weird and wonderful people like May, Carol, Levi, and Klasie. *Ja*, finding out all kinds of fascinating stuff about me grandfather and, well, about myself actually.

So just what's in this bloody box, anyway? It ought to be worth it, hey?

## Willis, Connie. *To Say Nothing of the Dog or How We Found the Bishop's Bird Stump at Last.*

Bantam, 1997, 434pp. Middle School & Up. An ALA Best Book for Young Adults; Alex Award.

SCIENCE FICTION. *Great Britain; supernatural; time travel.*

RELATED BOOKS: *To Visit the Queen* by Diane Duane; *Howl's Moving Castle* by Diane Regan Jones; *A Wrinkle in Time* by Madeleine L'Engle; *Harry Potter* series by J. K. Rowling.

Ned Henry has jet lag. He's badly in need of rest. He's been shuttling back and forth between the 21st century and the 1940s looking for something called the bishop's bird stump. Lady Schrapnell always gets what she wants, and she wants the bishop's bird stump.

However, this vacation has turned into a nightmare. Ned is sent back to Victorian England in the summer of 1888 for what he thinks is some down time. Instead, he meets fellow historian Verity Kindle, who has inadvertently brought something from the past forward in time. That something is a cat, Princess Arjumand.

Of course, bringing something from the past can alter history forever. Ned and Verity must correct the mistake and make things right in the universe. When they return to Victorian England, they meet some hilarious characters: table-rapping spiritualists, eccentric Oxford dons, and an exceedingly spoiled lady.

Can these two time-travelers correct the error and bring the universe back to its usual chaotic state?

## Wolff, Virginia Euwer. *Bat 6.*

Scholastic, 1998, 230pp. With author's note. Elementary School & Up. School Library Journal's Best Books selection.

HISTORICAL FICTION. *Asian Americans (Japanese); interracial relations; racism; rivalry; sports (baseball); women's issues; World War II.*

RELATED BOOKS: *A League of their Own* by Sara Gilbert; *Journey to Topaz* and *The Journey Home* by Yoshika Uchida; *Under the Blood-Red Sun* by Graham Salisbury.

*From the photographs on the cover, the book appears to be nonfiction, but is a fictional account of a girl's baseball team in rural Oregon in the 1940s. Told in 21 different first-person voices, the story gives each member of the two girls' softball teams one or more turns at bat as narrator. Along with women's softball, the author raises questions about war and race.*

We were so tired of hearing about the war. War this, war that. World War II was over and done. It was 1949. Hubba hubba ding ding.

Instead of war, we girls talked about team practice for Bat 6. For 49 years, local sixth-grade girls had played a baseball game called *Bat 6*. People were already calling us 50-year girls. Both teams, all 21 of us, were geared up and ready to go, go, go. Forget the war. Focus on Bat 6. Hubba hubba ding ding.

We didn't understand that, during that time, we carried the war with us. Aki had just returned from a Japanese concentration camp. Shazam claimed that she wouldn't play baseball with anyone Japanese. Since Lorelei's father refused to enlist and Daisy's father went into combat, they refused to speak to each other. No one dreamed that all these buried feelings would explode into a tragedy.

We didn't understand that, just like our parents, we were reliving our own little war. Who will win this war, this war of *Bat 6*?

# Woodson, Jacqueline. *If You Come Softly.*

G. P. Putnam's Sons, 1998, 181pp. High School & Up. Top 10 Best Books for Young Adults.

ROMANCE. *African Americans; death; homosexuality; interracial relations; love; racism; single parents.*

RELATED BOOKS: *A White Romance* by Virginia Hamilton; *The Broken Bridge* by Philip Pullman; *Half and Half: Writers on Growing Up Biracial and Bicultural* edited by Claudine C. O'Hearn.

 *Note:* In alternating chapters, Woodson tells about the dysfunctional home life of Ellie and Miah. Their interracial romance confronts prejudice head-on. Ellie's sister, Anne, is a lesbian who disapproves of the romance.

"Elisha," Marion called. "Come, tell me about your first day at Percy."

*I met a boy,* Elisha wanted to scream. *His name is Jeremiah and he's black. How about that? Will this piece of news send you out again, abandoning me like last time?*

Across town, Jeremiah's mother had the same interest. "Tell me about your first day at Percy, Miah."

"It's okay. It's whiter. Much whiter. I don't think they know I'm the son of a famous actor. That's okay with me."

*Not only that, but I met a fly white girl,* Miah thought. *Tomorrow, if I see her again, I'm going to ask her name. After that, who know where it will lead? Wherever it goes, I'm ready to follow.*

# Wrede, Patricia C. *Star Wars, Episode 1: The Phantom Menace.*

Based on the screenplay and story by George Lucas. (Pbk.) Scholastic, 1999, 178pp. Elementary School & Up.

SCIENCE FICTION. *End of the world; movie novels; supernatural; survival.*

RELATED BOOKS: *Star Wars, Episode 1: Incredible Cross-Sections* by David West Reynolds, et al; books by John Christopher: *When the Tripods Came; The White Mountains; The City of Gold and Lead; The Pool of Fire.*

 *Note:* The enormous success of **Star Wars** is the perfect opportunity to lead readers to science fiction and fantasy. Have students try other fantasy books by Patricia C. Wrede, who has written the hilarious twisted fairy tale series, **Dealing With Dragons.** Other recommended writers are John Christopher, Terry Brooks (who has written a more complex version of the movie), Sylvia Louise Engdahl, Stephen Hawking, Isaac Asimov, and others listed in the genre index.

*A long time ago in a galaxy far, far away ...*

Most of you recognize that phrase as the beginning of the *Star Wars* saga. Now, enjoy the story of *The Phantom Menace,* based on the screenplay, with more details than the movie.

Relive Darth Vader's journey as a young boy named Anakin Skywalker. Experience the adventure of two Jedi knights, Obi wan Kenobi and Qui Gon Jin, who rescue a Queen and her people from an Imperial invasion. Experience the battle between the Dark Side and the Force.

Throughout this imperial battle, may the Force be with you.

**W**

## Wright, Betty Ren. *Too Many Secrets.*

Scholastic, 1997, 116pp. Elementary School & Up. Part of a series; **The Ghost Comes Calling** precedes.

MYSTERIES, THRILLERS. *Animals (dog and parrot); crime; friendship; problem parents; secrets.*

RELATED BOOKS: *The Dollhouse Murders* by Betty Ren Wright; *The Dark Stairs* by Betsy Byars; *The Egypt Game* by Zilpha Keatly Snyder; *The Pink Motel* by Carol Ryrie Brink; the Sammy Keyes series by Wendelin Van Draanen.

*This mystery is perfect for younger readers—suspenseful but not too violent.*

Jeannie gasped as she opened Miss Beane's sewing kit. "Look at this. There's money tucked in the ripped lining of this box. I'll bet the burglar was trying to find this when we scared him off."

Chad hated the idea of a burglar searching through Miss Beane's things while she lay helpless in the hospital. "We better call the sheriff."

"Oh, right." Jeannie said sarcastically. "Our big chance to solve a crime and you don't even want to try. We could be a team—Nichols and Weldon, Detectives. We might even get a reward. Unless you can't keep a secret."

Chad stared at her. *Secret.* His dad had a secret. It wasn't fair. His dad had a girlfriend, and everyone knew but Chad. In fact, his neighbor Jeannie knew it first and told Chad.

"Okay," Chad said slowly. "That's fine with me. We'll solve the crime. In the meantime, we'll keep this investigation our little secret."

**X**

## X, Malcolm as told to Alex Haley. *The Autobiography of Malcolm X.*

Ballantine Books, 1964, 460pp. Middle School & Up.

BIOGRAPHY. *African Americans; ethics; interracial relations; racism; religion; responsibility; single parents; substance abuse (alcohol and drugs).*

RELATED BOOKS: *Malcolm X* by Bruce Perry; *The Fire Next Time* by James Baldwin; *Little X: Growing Up in the Nation of Islam* by Sonsyrea Tate.

*Alex Haley (before **Roots**) tells the haunting story of Malcolm X, in Malcolm's own words. This masterpiece changes lives.*

I'm Malcom X.

Look, forget all that you think you know about me. I want to tell you the truth about me, not those lies that you may have heard.

Certainly my story is not pretty. I have been a hustler, drug user and dealer, thief, and convict. I overcame all of that when I joined the Nation of Islam to become one of the leaders of the civil rights movement. I was assassinated in 1965, three years before Martin Luther King was gunned down. Done in by violence, just as I predicted.

Read my story in my words and then decide for yourself. Am I really the person you thought I would be?

## Ying, Hong. *Daughter of the River.*

Translated by Howard Goldblatt. Grove, 1997, 278pp. High School & Up.

BIOGRAPHY. *Abuse; China; class conflict; family; secrets; self-identity; sex and sexuality; suicide; women's issues.*

RELATED BOOKS: *Red Scarf Girl: A Memoir of the Cultural Revolution* by Ji Li Jiang; *Bound Feet and Western Dress* by Pang-Mei Natasha Chang; *Children in China* by Michael Karhausen; *Women of the Silk* by Gail Tsukiyama.

 *Note:* Hong Ying's frank, sometimes brutal memoir tells the story of her awakening, and also of China's awakening after the Cultural Revolution. Because of its graphic realism, give this to a mature reader who enjoys a multicultural biography, to an adult reading group, or to students studying China during and after the Cultural Revolution.

No one remembered my birthday for 18 years.

I was born in China in 1962 during the three-year famine. My family of eight were struggling to survive in a two-room house on stilts above the southern bank of the Yangtze. Decades of coolie labor left my mother physically and emotionally exhausted. My father ignored me, as did my brothers and sisters. The only person who was interested in my views was my married history teacher. I held back with everyone but him. With him, I was free from harsh judgments and hurtful blows.

On my 18th birthday, my mother confessed something that turned my life into a lie. She told me more than my ears wanted to hear. She shattered me into a million broken dreams.

Now my life of embarrassed shame makes sense. In my family, I had felt a real, unexplained hostility that haunted me. Now, the confirmation of that hatred freed me. I would take this yearning, this longing, and force myself out of my poverty-stricken world. Somehow this *Daughter of the River* would succeed.

## Yolen, Jane and Coville, Bruce. *Armageddon Summer.*

Harcourt Brace, 1998, 266pp. Middle School & Up. An ALA Best Book for Young Adults; Quick Pick for Reluctant Young Adult Readers.

REALISTIC FICTION. *End of the world; love; religion.*

RELATED BOOKS: *Phoenix Rising* by Karen Hesse; *The Dark Side of Nowhere* by Neil Shusterman; *How I Spent My Last Night on Earth* by Todd Strasser.

 *Note:* This blend of romance and end-of-the-world horror is written in first person. Jane Yolen wrote Marina's viewpoint; Bruce Coville wrote Jeb's. Good for writing classes studying point of view.

On Thursday, July 27, 2000, the world will end.

That's what Reverend Beelson has told his congregation of Believers.

Jed's dad believes. So does Marina's mom. Both families escape to Mount Weeupcut. According to Reverend Beelson, only 144 people will survive. The Believers, a religious cult, will be the only survivors on Earth.

Jeb and Marina have a hard time accepting that their parents are loony tunes. When they find each other on Mount Weeupcut, they can finally share their feelings with each other.

Will love be part of this *Armageddon Summer*?

## Yolen, Jane and Martin H. Greenberg, editors. Vampires: A Collection of Original Stories.

(Pbk.) HarperTrophy, 1991, 228pp. Middle School & Up.

HORROR. *Supernatural.*

RELATED BOOKS: *Ma and Pa Dracula* by Ann M. Martin; *Companions of the Night* by Vivien Velde Vande; *Look for Me by Moonlight* by Mary Downing Hahn.

I have in my hand 13 stories about vampires. Each story is suited for every taste—as long as the taste is blood!

There's all kinds of vampires: mall-rat vampires, squeamish vampires, and shaman vampires. People just like you and me confront these vampires. Clarisse has a cousin Jasper who keeps the curtains and shutters crossed until nightfall. Janine discovers something strange about this hunk who asks her for a date. Lily meddles with a young boy's grave and pays the consequences.

Enjoy these stories, but beware. The next neck at risk could be your own!

## Zindel, Paul. Reef of Death.

HarperCollins, 1998, 177pp. Middle School & Up. An ALA Best Book for Young Adults; Quick Pick for Reluctant Young Adult Readers.

Horror. *Australia; ecology; supernatural.*

Related books: *Sasquatch* by Roland Smith; *Loch* by Paul Zindel; *Monster* by Christopher Pike.

**EEEEEEEEEEEEEE**

Two people heard the eerie sound off the Great Barrier Reef in Australia. Arnhem, an Aborigine boy, was diving underwater for sunken treasure. His sister Muruul was watching above the water in a kayak. Both heard the piercing scream.

*Note:* This book has graphic violence.

The creature heard the sound, too. It swished its huge tail and propelled its powerful fins to capture its prey. It spotted the young frantic boy kicking to get back to the surface. Within seconds, its tremendous jaws snapped Arnhem's torso in two.

Later, they found Muruul shivering in the kayak. She was still screaming.

Who or what is this monster from this reef of death?

*Cover copyright © 1998 by Wayne McLoughlin. Jacket design by Alison Donalty. Jacket © 1998 by HarperCollins Publishers. Used by permission of HarperCollins Publishers*

# Author Index

# Title Index

# Age-Level Index

Sometimes this index lists the same book at various age levels since the book can be appreciated at different reading stages. For instance, *Holes* by Louis Sachar and *Stephen Hawking's Universe* can be appreciated at any age, and are contained in the Elementary, Middle and High School titles.

## HIGH SCHOOL TITLES (Ages 15 & Up)

# Genre Index

# Subject Index

## MIDDLE AGES

## MIDDLE EAST

## MOVIE NOVELS

## MUSIC

## NATIVE AMERICANS

## NEW ZEALAND

## OCCULT

see Supernatural

## ORPHANS

## PEER PRESSURE

## PIONEER LIFE

## POLITICS

## WOMEN'S ISSUES

## WORK

## WORLD WAR I

## WORLD WAR II

# Genre and Subjects for Booktalks

## GENRE

Adventure
Biography
Classics
Fantasy
Folklore
Historical fiction
Horror
Humor
Mysteries, thrillers
Nonfiction
Poetry
Realistic fiction
Romance
Science fiction
Short stories
Sports

## SUBJECTS

Abuse
Aging
Adoption
Africa
African Americans
American Revolutionary War
Animals
Asia
Asian Americans
Australia
Caribbean and Latin America
China
Class conflict
Civil War, 1860-1865
Computers
Crime
Death
Diaries
Disability
Divorce
Eating disorders
Ecology
End of the world
Ethics
Europe
Family
Friendship
Great Britain
Hispanic Americans
Hobbies
Holocaust
Homeless
Homosexuality
Illness
Immigrants
India
Interracial relations
Ireland
Jews
Love
Magic
Men's issues
Middle Ages
Middle East
Movie novels
Music

Native Americans
Orphans
Peer pressure
Pioneer
Pioneer life
Politics
Pregnancy
Problem parents
Racism
Religion
Religious prejudice
Responsibility
Revenge
Rites of passage
Rivalry
Runaways
School
Science
Secrets
Self-identity
Sex and Sexuality
Sexual abuse
Show business
Single parents
Sports
Stepparents
Substance abuse
Suicide
Supernatural
Survival
Time travel
Trust
Vietnam War
War
World War I
World War II
Women's issues
Work